Sacred War

Nationalism and Revolution in a Divided Vietnam

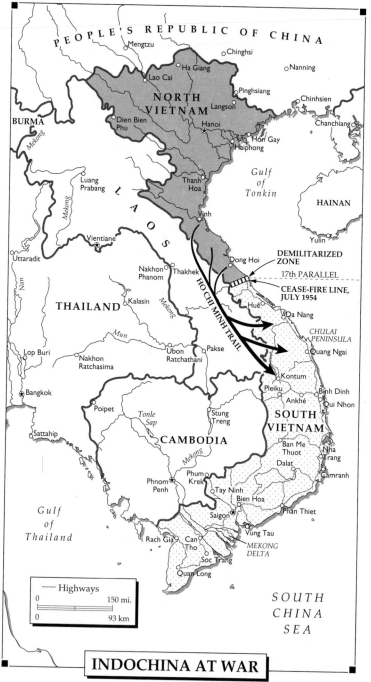

PEOPLE'S REPUBLIC OF CHINA

Mengtzu
Chinghsi
Nanning

Ha Giang
Lao Cai
Pinghsiang
Chinhsien

NORTH
VIETNAM
Langson
Chanchiang

BURMA
Dien Bien
Phu
Hanoi

Hon Gay
Haiphong

Thanh
Hoa

Gulf
of
Tonkin

HAINAN

Luang
Prabang
Vinh

Yulin

Vientiane

Uttaradit

Dong Hoi
**DEMILITARIZED
ZONE**

Nakhon
Phanom
Thakhek
17th PARALLEL

**CEASE-FIRE LINE,
JULY 1954**

THAILAND
Huế

Kalasin
Da Nang

HO CHI MINH TRAIL

*CHULAI
PENINSULA*

Mun

Lop Buri
Nakhon
Ratchasima
Ubon
Ratchathani
Pakse
Quang Ngai

Kontum
Binh Dinh

Bangkok
Pleiku
Ankhé
Qui Nhon

Poipet
*Tonle
Sap*
Stung
Treng
**SOUTH
VIETNAM**

Sattahip
Ban Me
Thuot
Nha
Trang

CAMBODIA
Dalat

Mekong
Camranh

Phum
Krek
Tay Ninh
Bien Hoa

Phnom
Penh
Phan Thiet

Saigon

*Gulf
of
Thailand*
Vung Tau

Rach Gia
Can
Tho
*MEKONG
DELTA*

Soc Trang

Quan Long

*SOUTH
CHINA
SEA*

----- Highways

0 _____ 150 mi.

0 _____ 93 km

INDOCHINA AT WAR

Sacred War

Nationalism and Revolution in a Divided Vietnam

William J. Duiker
The Pennsylvania State University

Boston, Massachusetts   Burr Ridge, Illinois
Dubuque, Iowa   Madison, Wisconsin   New York, New York
San Francisco, California   St. Louis, Missouri

This book was set in Palatino by Ruttle, Shaw & Wetherill, Inc.
The editors were Peter Labella and Larry Goldberg;
the production supervisor was Richard A. Ausburn.
The cover was designed by Carla Bauer.

McGraw-Hill

A Division of The McGraw-Hill Companies

SACRED WAR
Nationalism and Revolution in a Divided Vietnam

9   BKM BKM   0 9 8 7 6 5 4 3 2 1

ISBN 0-07-018030-X

Library of Congress Cataloging-in-Publication Data

Duiker, William J., (date).
    Sacred war: nationalism and revolution in a divided Vietnam /
William J. Duiker
        p.   cm.
    ISBN 0-07-018030-X
    1. Vietnamese Conflict, 1961–1975—History.   2. Indochinese War,
1946–1954.   I. Title.
DS557.7.D84   1995
959.704'3—dc20
                                                            94-14473

About the Author

WILLIAM J. DUIKER is Liberal Arts Professor of East Asian Studies at The Pennsylvania State University. A former foreign service officer with posts in Taiwan and South Vietnam, he received his doctorate in Far Eastern History at Georgetown University in 1968. He has written widely on topics connected with modern China and Vietnam and is the author of, among others, *The Communist Road to Power in Vietnam* (Westview, 1981) and *China and Vietnam: The Roots of Conflict* (Berkeley, 1987). His monograph entitled *U.S. Containment Policy and the Conflict in Indochina* will be published in late 1994.

To Laura and Claire,
in the hope that they may live in a better world

Contents

List of Maps and Illustrations

Maps

Illustrations

Preface

During the height of the Vietnam War, students on college campuses throughout the United States took part in protest marches, waving Viet Cong flags and chanting Ho-Ho-Ho Chi Minh. Actress Jane Fonda, writer Mary McCarthy, journalist Harrison Salisbury, and other prominent personalities visited Hanoi and returned with favorable accounts of the United States' adversary in North Vietnam. Such incidents were graphic evidence that the conflict in Vietnam was no ordinary war.

Not all Americans, of course, were so smitten with Ho Chi Minh and his beleaguered regime in far-off Indochina. For every young American who marched against the war, perhaps ten others went off to war in the firm belief that they were saving the world from communism. For them and for millions of their compatriots, Ho Chi Minh was not the kindly Uncle Ho portrayed in the North Vietnamese media but a totalitarian leader in the same league as Fidel Castro, Nikita Khrushchev, and Mao Zedong.

In reality, neither of these portraits of Ho Chi Minh and the movement he led were especially accurate, for the American people knew virtually nothing about North Vietnam or the black pyjama–clad underground fighters in the South, perceptively called "the faceless Viet Cong" by one writer. Outside of Ho Chi Minh and his fabled but equally mysterious military strategist Vo Nguyen Giap, other leading figures of the Hanoi regime were almost totally unknown, not only to the American public but also to U.S. government officials and intelligence analysts, for whom the nature of the enemy was the subject of endless speculation but little informed knowledge. There were a few scholarly studies of the Communist movement by Vietnam watchers in the academic community, but Vietnam specialists were as much a rarity in American educational institutions as they were in the halls of the State Department. Put simply, after two decades of involvement in the bitter conflict in Indochina, the U.S. government, like the American people as a whole, knew almost nothing about Vietnam.

Today, two decades after the fall of Saigon, information about the Vietnam War has become a veritable growth industry in the United States. Novels, memoirs, television documentaries, and feature films paint a vivid picture of the war and its impact on a generation of Americans deeply divided about their nation's role in that tortured land. The release of U.S. government documents relating to the war has triggered a new effort by scholars to expose the conflict to intensive historical analysis, while memoirs by the major participants in the policy-making process have provided additional insight into the reasons for American involvement.

By contrast, there is little information available in English on the Vietnamese side of the war. Documentary materials and official histories of the war have been published in Hanoi, and personal accounts written by Vietnamese military commanders or émigrés who once served in the ranks of the resistance movement have shed some light on the nature of the revolutionary movement and the objectives of its leadership. But a clear picture of the war from Hanoi's point of view is still elusive, because the materials have not yet been translated or are not widely available in the United States. What were the origins of the war in Vietnam? What factors made individual Vietnamese decide to give their allegiance to Ho Chi Minh and his revolutionary movement instead of to his nationalist rivals? What was life like in North Vietnam during the bombing or in the Viet Cong tunnels at Cu Chi, less than 30 miles from Saigon? These are questions that are vital to our understanding of the war but have not yet received comprehensive treatment in the English language.

With this book I have tried, at least partially, to fill that gap. As an American who served with the U.S. State Department in South Vietnam during the war, I can hardly hope to see the war from a Vietnamese perspective. But over a period of two decades of research and writing, I have explored the rise of the Vietnamese nationalist movement and the strategy followed by Ho Chi Minh and his colleagues to bring about a Communist victory in the conflict, as well as the consequences of the war inside Vietnam and in the region as a whole. Other scholars have written perceptively about the early years of the Communist Party, the character of the North Vietnamese regime and society, and the inner workings of the Viet Cong movement in the South. In order to make the book as up-to-date as possible, I have made use of recently published sources in several languages, as well as captured documents and hard-to-locate materials published in the Vietnamese language. I have also had extensive conversations with a number of scholars in Vietnam about various aspects of the Vietnamese revolution. For reasons of discretion, I have chosen not to mention them by name here.

It is my purpose to present a balanced and judicious analysis of the Vietnam side of the war in the belief that a clear understanding of the Vietnamese perspective on the conflict is in very short supply in the United States. Of the textual materials and readings assigned to students in college courses on the war, very few appear to present the Vietnamese point of view or explain the relationship between the war and modern Vietnamese history. I have sought to adopt a dispassionate approach to the topic, although I am fully aware that it is virtually impossible to avoid subjective judgments on the war, especially for those of us whose lives were so directly affected by it over a period of many years. In choosing *Sacred War* as the title for this book, I do not mean to imply that the struggle carried on by Ho Chi Minh and his followers was necessarily the morally superior one (although that is the title of a party history of the war against the French), but rather that, ideology apart, the concept of national independence and unity was a sacred issue to virtually all Vietnamese.

It would be impossible for me to thank all those who have contributed in various ways to this study, since in a sense it is the product of three decades of exposure to the history of modern Vietnam. I am grateful to the College Fund for Research in the College of Liberal Arts, as well as the Institute for the Arts and Humanistic Studies at The Pennsylvania State University, for financial support on various occasions to undertake research on the topic in France and Vietnam. The Social Science Research Council, through its Indochina Scholarly Exchange Program, kindly awarded me a grant in 1990 to conduct research in Hanoi on a biography of Ho Chi Minh. A recent trip to Vietnam sponsored by the Ford Foundation provided me with new insight into various aspects of the war. Invitations from the Institute for International Relations, the Institute of History, and the Institute of Marxism-Leninism in Hanoi gave me the opportunity to share views and information with Vietnamese scholars. Finally, grants from the Harry S. Truman and Lyndon Johnson libraries enabled me to obtain materials on two of the key presidential eras dealt with in this book.

Among the multitude of individuals who have given me assistance in the course of this study, I would like to single out a few whose help has been especially useful. Georges Boudarel, George Herring, Stanley Karnow, David Marr, Al Patti, Douglas Pike, Keith Taylor, Bui Tinh, and Bill Turley all provided me with useful materials or counsel in the course of carrying out the research. To Christopher Rogers of McGraw-Hill, I owe my thanks for suggesting the project, and to American history editor Peter Labella my gratitude for helping to carry it through. I would also like to express my thanks to the following reviewers, whose suggestions were unusually helpful in improving the quality of the manuscript in an earlier version: David D. Buck, University of Wisconsin at Milwaukee; Laura L. Davis, Pasadena City College; and Michael Schaller, University of Arizona. None of the above, of course, bear any responsibility for the final product.

The historical photographs used in this book have been obtained from the following sources: *Suc Manh Dan Quan Tu Ve Viet Nam* (Cuc Dan Quan Tu Ve–Bo Tong Tham Muu, 1987); *The Failure of Special War, 1961–65* (Hanoi: Xunhasaba, n.d.); *Quan Doi Nhan Dan Viet Nam, 1944–1979* (Hanoi: Quan Doi Nhan Dan, 1979); *Ho Chu Tich Song Mai Trong Su Nghiep Chung Ta* (Hanoi: Viet Nam Thong Tan Xa, 1970); Hai Thu, *North Viet Nam against U.S. Air Force* (Hanoi: Foreign Languages Press, 1967); *The Indochinese Peoples Will Win* (Hanoi: Foreign Languages Press, 1970); and *Bac Ho Voi Luc Luong Vu Trang Nhan Dan* (Hanoi: Quan Doi Nhan Dan, 1976).

I have thanked my wife Yvonne on previous occasions for her help in bringing publications to fruition, but I would like to do so again. She knows why.

William J. Duiker

List of Abbreviations

In Text

ARVN	Army of the Republic of South Vietnam
ASV	Associated State of Vietnam
CCP	Chinese Communist Party
COSVN	Central Office of South Vietnam
CPSU	Communist Party of the Soviet Union
DMZ	Demilitarized Zone
DRV	Democratic Republic of Vietnam
FEF	French Expeditionary Forces
FUNK	National United Front of Kampuchea
ICC	International Control Commission
ICP	Indochinese Communist Party
JCS	Joint Chiefs of Staff
KCP	Kampuchean Communist Party
KPRP	Khmer People's Revolutionary Party
MACV	Military Assistance Command, Vietnam
NATO	North Atlantic Treaty Organization
NCRC	National Council for Reconciliation and Concord
NEP	New Economic Policy
NIE	National Intelligence Estimate
NLF	National Liberation Front
NSC	National Security Council
OSS	Office of Strategic Services

PAVN   People's Army of Vietnam
PCF   French Communist Party
PLA   People's Liberation Army
PLAF   People's Liberation Armed Forces
POW   Prisoner of War
PRG   Provisional Revolutionary Government
PRP   People's Revolutionary Party
PSF   French Socialist Party
RVN   Republic of Vietnam
RYL   Revolutionary Youth League
SEATO Southeast Asia Treaty Organization
SRV   Socialist Republic of Vietnam
VC   Vietnamese Communists, or Viet Cong
VCP   Vietnamese Communist Party
VNA   Vietnamese National Army
VNQDD Vietnamese Nationalist Party, or Viet Nam Quoc Dan Dang
VRL   Vietnamese Revolutionary League
VWP   Vietnam Workers' Party

In Footnotes

CKC   *Cuoc Khang Chien Chong My Cuu Nuoc, 1954–1975*
DDRS   Declassified Documents Reference Service
FRUS   *Foreign Relations of the United States*
JPRS   Joint Publications Research Service
LSQD   *Lich Su Quan Doi Nhan Dan Viet Nam*
NCLS   *Nghien Cuu Lich Su*
USVN   *United States-Viet-Nam Relations, 1945–1967*
VDRN   *Vietnam Documents and Research Notes*
VNA   *Vietnam News Agency*

Sacred War

Nationalism and Revolution in a Divided Vietnam

Introduction

The vast majority of the historical accounts, novels, and films about the Vietnam War that have appeared in the English language during the past few years have dealt with the American side of the war. With a few notable exceptions, the Vietnamese people and the leaders of their governments in Hanoi and Saigon have been faceless and indistinct.

This tendency in the United States to view the war as an American experience is understandable. For a decade or more, Vietnam was a constant reality that brought sorrow to thousands of families across the country, undermined the spirit and self-confidence of the American people, and soured a generation of young Americans on the political system and institutions under which they had been raised.

But this perception of the war as an *American* tragedy has had some unfortunate consequences. It ignores the real hardship that the war inflicted on the Vietnamese people, who suffered more than 1 million casualties in dead and wounded throughout the northern and southern parts of the country. On a more practical plane, it also perpetuates the questionable assumption that there was an easy American solution to the problem. Americans often ask, for example, why the United States "lost" the war. Why, with its vaunted military power and technological superiority, was the United States unable to defeat a relatively small nation with a ragtag army of guerrillas and regular troops in a conflict that lasted nearly a decade? The usual answer is that the United States failed to apply its military force effectively and thus fought the war without a clear-cut strategy for victory. That argument was presented most recently by President George Bush, when he promised the American people that the Persian Gulf conflict would "not be another Vietnam." American troops, he said, "will have the best possible support in the entire world, and they will not be asked to fight with one hand tied behind their back."

I do not mean to imply that the United States could not have totally destroyed North Vietnam if it so chose. But from a historical perspective, the most striking fact about the Vietnam War is probably not why the United States lost, but why the Communists won. After all, Vietnam was only one of several countries in Southeast Asia that won its independence from colonial rule after World War II. In all other instances, the political parties which took power at the moment of independence were noncommunist in their political orientation. But in Vietnam, it was the Indochinese Communist Party (ICP), under the guidance of the revolutionary leader Ho Chi Minh, that seized power in Hanoi from surrendering Japanese forces in August 1945. Then, having created an independent Democratic Republic of Vietnam (DRV) later in the fall, the Communists were soon compelled to defend the fruits of their victory against the French, who sought to restore their authority in their former colonial empire of Indochina. After nearly a decade of war, during which time the United States assisted the French in the hope of stemming the advance of communism in Southeast Asia, a settlement was reached at Geneva in 1954 which divided Vietnam into two parts: the DRV, with its capital at Hanoi in the north, and a noncommunist regime, with its capital at Saigon in the south.

In the late 1950s, the struggle in Vietnam resumed, as Communist-led forces in the south attempted to overthrow the Saigon regime and bring about the reunification of the country under the DRV. Once again, the United States intervened, this time directly. Eventually, the size of the U.S. military presence reached a level of over 500,000 uniformed men and women, while U.S. planes dropped more than 15 million tons of explosives—equivalent to the power of 400 Hiroshima-sized atomic bombs—in an abortive effort to avert a Communist victory. Yet despite this massive commitment by the greatest military power in the history of the world, the Communists were able to bring about the withdrawal of U.S. troops and then, with the conquest of Saigon in the spring of 1975, complete their triumph and unify the entire country under communist rule. By any standard of measurement, it was a stunning achievement.

To understand the full implications of the war in Vietnam, then, we must go beyond decisions made in Washington and ask ourselves what it was about the Communist movement in Vietnam and its frail leader with the wispy beard that enabled it to hold the greatest military power in the world to a standoff and eventually force its withdrawal in 1973. In the first place, why did the Indochinese Communist Party manage to best its rivals and achieve the dominant position in the regional anticolonial movement? How did party leaders organize and motivate their followers to wage a bloody and protracted thirty-year struggle against vastly superior odds? How did a handful of hard-bitten leaders in Hanoi outsmart the "best and the brightest" (to cite the famous phrase of author David Halberstam) in the American foreign policy establishment and compel them to accept a stunning defeat, with worldwide reverberations?

Our primary task in this book will be to answer these questions. To see more clearly the perspective from Hanoi, it is important to understand that the so-called American phase of the war was only a relatively brief if bitter interlude in a longer struggle of the Vietnamese people to free their homeland from foreign invaders and unify their country under a single independent government. That struggle began in the late nineteenth century, when the French conquest not only deprived the Vietnamese of their national independence but also threatened to undermine their traditional culture, a culture which had endured for more than 2000 years but which was now unable to withstand the shattering impact of modern Western values and institutions.

By the turn of the century a number of divergent political, socioeconomic, and intellectual currents had begun to eddy and swirl inside Vietnamese society. The most dominant was what might loosely be called a capitalist democratic current, influenced above all by the glittering achievements of the modern West. Further to the left was the ICP, influenced in the abstract by the views of radical European philosophers like Karl Marx, and more concretely by the results of the 1917 October Revolution in Russia. In the highly turbulent years following World War I, advocates of both approaches competed to fill the cultural vacuum left by the collapse of the traditional order while simultaneously seeking to mobilize their forces to evict the French and restore national independence.

This process was by no means unique to Vietnam. It was taking place in colonial societies throughout Asia, as well as in countries only partially under colonial domination like China. But unlike elsewhere in the region, radical currents quickly became a dominant force in the Vietnamese anticolonial movement, and by the end of the 1930s, the ICP had become the primary actor in the struggle against colonial rule. In August 1945, when the wartime Japanese occupation of Indochina came to an abrupt end at the moment of Tokyo's surrender to the Allies, it was the ICP, and not its nationalist rivals, that took advantage of the opportunity by seizing power in Hanoi and declaring an independent republic.

By the late summer of 1945, then, the Vietnamese Communist movement had already won at least an initial victory in the struggle to define the future Vietnamese society. It remained to be seen, of course, whether the ICP would be able to maintain that advantage against its noncommunist rivals, not to speak of fending off the returning French.

At first, officials in Washington did not view the events in Indochina as a threat to U.S. national security. While not especially sympathetic to the Communist movement and its enigmatic leader, Ho Chi Minh, the Truman administration viewed the conflict essentially as a product of the colonial era and urged the French to reach a settlement with the leaders of the DRV. By 1949, however, the perspective from the White House had radically changed. As the wartime alliance between the United States and the Soviet Union was gradually replaced by the Cold War, Ho Chi Minh was transformed in the American mind from an enigmatic but essentially nonthreatening figure into a dangerous agent of international communism. His movement ceased to be interpreted as a legitimate product of French colonial oppression and was increasingly viewed as a tool of the Kremlin, to be opposed and defeated at all costs.

Why the United States became committed to thwarting a Communist victory in Vietnam is an essential part of this story and will merit our attention later in the book. But it is important to keep in mind that U.S. officials would not have turned their anxious eyes to Indochina had not Ho Chi Minh and his colleagues already raised the specter of a dynamic new Communist outpost in that vital part of the world. To investigate in more detail the factors that contributed to the striking success of the Communists in the immediate aftermath of World War II, an achievement which established the context for a generation of Cold War conflict in Indochina, let us turn briefly to the conditions that brought it about. Only if we learn more about the reasons for Communist success will we be able to understand why the United States lost in Vietnam.

CHAPTER 1

Roots of Revolution

In the winter of 1945–1946, Brigadier General Philip E. Gallagher returned from Hanoi, where he had served as chief of the U.S. liaison team with Chinese occupation forces in northern Indochina, and briefed U.S. officials in Washington on conditions in Vietnam. At that time, less than six months after the end of the war in the Pacific, the northern part of Vietnam had just come under a new provisional republican government led by the veteran Vietnamese revolutionary Ho Chi Minh. The southern part of the country was temporarily occupied by the British, who were in the process of returning the area to French colonial administration.

In his comments to U.S. officials at the briefing, General Gallagher was not unsympathetic to Ho Chi Minh and other leaders of his new government. The general remarked that he was impressed by their enthusiasm and their dedication, as well as by their native ability. But he was skeptical of the capacity of the new government to carry out its responsibilities in the unstable conditions of the immediate postwar period. Noting that the new leaders in Hanoi were naive and inexperienced, he predicted that, in competition with other governments in the area, they would "lose their shirts."[1]

General Gallagher's comments about the naiveté and inexperience of the Vietnamese people and their new leaders were not unusual. In fact, they reflected a view that was characteristic of the attitude of many Western observers at the time—that the Vietnamese did not yet possess the capacity to govern themselves. President

[1] *United States-Viet-Nam Relations, 1945–1967* (Washington, D.C.: GPO, 1967), 8, pt. B.II, pp. 53–55. Hereafter *USVN*. Others were more impressed with Vietnamese military capabilities than General Gallagher and predicted that they would be able to use guerrilla warfare successfully against the French.

5

Franklin Roosevelt himself, certainly an outspoken advocate of the concept of self-determination for all peoples, had assumed that after the end of World War II, Vietnam would require a period of tutelage before receiving its full national independence.

BIRTH OF A CIVILIZATION

What is striking about that assumption is not merely its condescending tone, in keeping with the "white man's burden" mentality of the time. But it also reflected a general ignorance of Vietnam, which had existed as an independent state for over 1000 years prior to the French conquest, fully 900 years before the signing of the American Declaration of Independence.

In fact, the history of Vietnam as an organized society goes back considerably further. First emerging as a coherent community in the Red River Valley sometime during the first millennium B.C., this embryonic Vietnamese state was conquered by the Chinese Empire in 111 B.C. and did not regain its independence until the tenth century A.D. From that date, with the exception of a brief period of Chinese occupation in the fifteenth century, the Vietnamese state grew into one of the more powerful and dynamic empires in Southeast Asia until it was subjugated by the French in the late nineteenth century. While the current generation of Vietnamese leaders may have lacked personal experience in administering an independent state, their forebears were hardly novices at the art of statecraft.

Vietnam's relationship with its larger neighbor to the north was a complicated one, and even today it exerts a major impact on the national psyche. On the one hand, ten centuries of Chinese rule did not erase memories of Vietnamese independence. If anything, the sense of national identity appears to have been sharpened by the experience. The collective memory of the long struggle against Chinese domination forms a powerful theme in Vietnamese history, and most of the nation's heroic figures—from the famous Trung sisters, who led a rebellion against the Chinese occupation in the first century A.D. to Le Loi and his chief adviser, the Confucian statesman Nguyen Trai, who drove out Chinese invaders centuries later—are identified with the national effort to protect Vietnam against invasion from the north.

On the other hand, Vietnamese society was significantly altered

TRƯNG·VƯƠNG

U GIÁC HÁN

Ò ĐỊNH

TRƯNG TR

TRƯNG

The Trung Sisters, who led a Vietnamese rebellion against Chinese rule in the first century A.D.

by its long and direct acquaintance with Chinese civilization, generally considered to be the most advanced in Asia. During the many centuries when it was an integral part of the Chinese empire, Vietnam was introduced to Chinese political and social institutions, religion and philosophy, art, literature, music, and the Chinese language. The educated Vietnamese elite wrote to each other in literary Chinese, and Chinese characters were adopted as the written script for Vietnamese.

Even after the restoration of independence in the tenth century A.D., Vietnamese institutions were patterned after the Chinese model. Vietnamese monarchs discovered that Chinese political mores and rituals provided a sense of majesty and legitimacy to the state, while Confucian social ethics, imported from the north, helped to shape industrious, docile, and loyal subjects. In civil service examinations patterned after those offered in China, aspiring young Vietnamese eagerly displayed their knowledge of the Confucian classics in the competition for positions in the bureaucracy. To the uninitiated, Vietnam must have seemed like a smaller copy of the Chinese imperial model, and indeed, elite culture in Vietnam was deeply impregnated with Chinese influence. But under that veneer, Vietnamese society retained many distinctive features, while its ruling elite and the monarchy—although accepting a patron-client relationship with the "elder brother" to the north—remained fiercely determined to protect the state from Chinese domination.

MARCH TO THE SOUTH

After the tenth century, the Vietnamese state, known at the time as Dai Viet, or "Great Viet," gained steadily in wealth and power. While the country did not possess abundant natural resources, the Vietnamese people, most of whom were rice farmers living in the fertile delta of the Red River, were hard-working and talented. As the population increased, pressure intensified to find new land for cultivation. Blocked to the north and west by forest-covered mountains, the Vietnamese began to expand southward along the coast of the South China Sea. During several centuries of intermittent conflict with the neighboring state of Champa, located directly to the south along the central coast, the Vietnamese carried out their historic March to the South. The Cham, a trading people unrelated in ethnic origin and language to the Vietnamese, had had little contact with China, and had been more strongly influenced by Indian civilization. After Muslim merchants became increasingly active in the regional spice trade in the fourteenth century, the Cham converted to Islam.

For several hundred years, the rivalry between Dai Viet and Champa continued without decisive advantage on either side. By the sixteenth century, however, Dai Viet had not only conquered Champa but had also seized the vast Mekong River delta from the nearly defunct kingdom of Angkor, the once-glorious predecessor of Cambodia. By 1700, Vietnamese authority extended from the Chinese border in the north to the tip of the Camau peninsula on the Gulf of Siam. Like the United States in the nineteenth century, the

Vietnamese state had realized its "manifest destiny." While the Vietnamese monarch continued to declare a tributary relationship to his "elder brother," the emperor of China, he adopted similar imperial pretensions in his dealings with neighboring rulers in Southeast Asia.

Unfortunately for the Vietnamese, territorial expansion had its price. Shaped like a giant letter S along the eastern rim of the Southeast Asian mainland, the expanded Vietnamese state lacked the territorial cohesion that it had possessed when it was concentrated in the Red River delta. Factionalism among princely families at court led to civil war in 1613 and the division of the kingdom into two separate warring states in the north and the south. Vietnam would remain divided for two centuries.

The southward march and consequent division of the country exerted a lasting impact on Vietnamese society. As Dai Viet expanded southward, thousands of Vietnamese peasants from densely populated villages in the Red River delta migrated from their original villages and established new communities in virgin farmlands scattered throughout the spacious but marshy delta of the Mekong River. Nourished by the ready availability of land in their new surroundings, as well as by the favorable climate, these migrants gradually developed a new frontier spirit far removed from the traditional ways practiced in their ancestral villages far to the north. Where northerners were conservative in their social attitudes, cautious in their economic behavior, and inclined to accept the primacy of the community over the interests of the individual, southerners tended to be more independent-minded, more entrepreneurial in spirit, and more fractious and individualistic in their social relations. A cultural divide had opened up that was destined to have profound effects on the later course of Vietnamese history, and indeed has not healed to this day.

In the early nineteenth century, an energetic member of the ruling house in southern Vietnam successfully reunited the country under his rule and declared the founding of the Nguyen dynasty. As a demonstration of unity, he moved the imperial capital from its traditional location at Hanoi, in the Red River valley, to Hue, on the central coast halfway between the Mekong and Red River deltas. Such cosmetic actions, however, were not sufficient to heal the breach that had opened up during the two centuries of civil strife, and tensions between the northern and southern provinces continued to plague the Nguyen court throughout the next decades.

To make matters even more difficult, the new state (now called Vietnam, or "Southern Viet"), simultaneously faced a new challenge from abroad. European traders and missionaries had been active in Vietnam since the early seventeenth century, but the country lacked many of the spices that had generated profits in the Indonesian islands further to the south, and by 1700, when the Vietnamese court began to restrict foreign commercial and missionary activities, most European merchants had already abandoned the area, although French missionary interests continued to cater to the needs of the country's numerous Christian converts. In the early nineteenth century, however, the needs of the Industrial Revolution provoked the capitalist states of the West to turn once again to Asia, this time in search of cheap raw materials and consumer markets for their manufactured goods. With the Dutch in firm control of the East Indies, and the British newly entrenched in Burma and the Malay peninsula, the French turned to Vietnam as a toehold on the Southeast Asian mainland and a base of possible future expansion into southern China.

The first French effort to create its own "balcony on the Pacific" (to use a popular French phrase at the time) was only modestly successful. For years, the imperial court at Hue attempted to prohibit Christian missionary activities inside the country. In 1858, on the pretext of avenging the arrest of a French missionary by imperial authorities, a French fleet sailed into Da Nang harbor, along the central coast, in the hope of capturing the imperial capital of Hue, about 80 miles to the north. But when the attack stalled because of disease and unexpectedly strong resistance from the local population, the commander of the French expedition abandoned the effort. Shortly after, the French launched a new attack in the region of the Mekong River delta and rapidly seized control of several provinces near the commercial center of Saigon (present-day Ho Chi Minh City). In 1862, an emissary of the Vietnamese court signed a peace treaty which ceded several provinces in the area to the French. The latter thereupon transformed their new acquisition into the colony of Cochin China, with its capital at Saigon.

Prodded insistently by merchant and missionary interests, the French government hoped to use its control over the estuary of the Mekong River as a means of seeking a water route into southern China, thus gaining access to the vast Chinese market. In 1863, to facilitate the exploration of the river, the French established a protectorate over neighboring Cambodia, which had already fallen under the joint suzerainty of Vietnam and the kingdom of Thailand, to the west. But when French explorers discovered that the Mekong was not navigable as far as the Chinese border, French imperialist interests turned to northern Vietnam. In the early 1880s, having found another pretext to justify military action, the French conquered the remainder of the country and divided it into two separate protectorates: Tonkin, comprising the area of the Red River delta, and Annam, consisting of the provinces along the central coast. The Vietnamese monarch in Hue was permitted to retain a nominal degree of sovereignty, but actual power resided with the French. A few years later, the French established a fourth protectorate over the neighboring kingdom of Laos to serve as a buffer zone against British advances into northern Burma. By the end of the century, all five territories—one colony and four protectorates—were united into a single Indochinese Union and placed under French administration.

THE FRENCH CIVILIZING MISSION IN INDOCHINA

In justifying their conquest, official sources in Paris claimed that France was carrying out a "civilizing mission" (*mission civilisatrice*) in Indochina. France would introduce the fruits of advanced Western civilization—democratic institutions, capitalist economics, modern technology, and French culture—to its subject peoples in Indochina, thus enabling them to compete in a social-Darwinist world of "survival of the fittest." No one expressed French objectives more eloquently than Governor General Albert Sarraut, who remarked to a Vietnamese audience in France before departing for his new post in Indochina in 1917: "I want to give you the instrument of liberation which will gradually lead you toward those superior spheres to which you aspire."[2]

In actuality, French motives were much more self-serving than Sarraut had implied. Certainly those "superior spheres" did not include the restoration of full national independence. The original impulse for French expansion into the region was, above all, the

[2] Quoted in Georges Garros, *Forceries humaines* (Paris: André Delpeuch, 1926), p. 51.

FRENCH INDOCHINA

CHINA

Red R.

Cao Bang

TONKIN

Black R.

Dien Bien Phu

Hanoi

Haiphong

Gulf of Tonkin

HAINAN

Mekong R.

Luang Prabang

V I E T N A M

LAOS

Vientiane

THAILAND

Mekong R.

Huê

Tourane

A N N A M

Bangkok

CAMBODIA

Tonle Sap

Phnom Penh

COCHIN CHINA

Saigon

Gulf of Thailand

| 0 | 150 mi. |
| 0 | 93 km |

SOUTH CHINA SEA

desire for economic profit. For the French, as for most capitalist nations in the West, colonies served as a source for cheap raw materials and a consumer market for manufactured goods produced in European factories.

But in the nineteenth century, as in our own day, economics often has political implications. Colonies were not only a hedge against the disastrous vicissitudes of the capitalist economic cycle; they were also a potential source of military power and a symbol of national wealth and grandeur. The pursuit of colonial possessions became a national pastime throughout the Western world, and at the end of the century culminated in a frenzy of territorial acquisitions (in Africa in the mid-1890s, for example, and in China a few years later), when European governments seized territories simply to prevent them from falling into rival hands. The French themselves were provoked into seizing Indochina partly out of fear that it would otherwise be occupied by the Germans, the Japanese, or the United States.

Unfortunately, the desire for financial profit and national grandeur all too often collided with the "civilizing mission" officially proclaimed in Paris. Anxious to preserve their colonial possessions as a market for manufactured goods produced in their own factories, the French discouraged the emergence of an indigenous industrial and commercial sector in Indochina that could compete with French imports. Determined to keep the price of imported raw materials as low as possible, French colonial entrepreneurs kept wages low for workers on rubber plantations or in coal mines along the coast of Tonkin. Although a small industrial sector did take shape, it was primarily oriented toward the export market and dominated by European interests or by Indian and Chinese entrepreneurs whose ancestors had operated in the area for centuries.

Nor did the colonial regime encourage the development of political institutions that were capable of reflecting the aspirations of the indigenous peoples of Indochina. All too aware that the creation of popular legislative assemblies would lead to demands for greater autonomy, or even for the restoration of national independence, French authorities were reluctant to introduce representative government or grant the franchise to the mass of the population. The first elected political bodies in Indochina, consisting of municipal councils in the major cities and assemblies at the provincial level, had only limited advisory powers and were composed almost exclusively of Europeans or of wealthy local elites willing to collaborate with the colonial regime. One prominent French politician admitted in an unguarded moment that the provincial assemblies had been established solely "for form's sake."

Defenders of the colonial regime stoutly maintained that French rule brought a number of benefits to the peoples of Indochina. The promotion of export crops such as rubber, coffee, tea, and rice helped to integrate Indochina into the global capitalist economy. The draining of the marshy lands in the Mekong River delta opened new fields for the cultivation of rice, and the French built modern roads and a railway that ran from Saigon to the Chinese border. Technological improvements such as these did provide material benefits to a small and privileged class of Vietnamese entrepreneurs, government officials, professionals, and landowners.

For the mass of the population, however, the consequences of colonial rule were generally unfortunate and often disastrous. For every urban merchant or landowner who profited from increased economic opportunities in the capitalist marketplace, there were dozens of rice farmers whose livelihood was threatened by the vicissitudes of that same market. As land became commercialized, peasants lost the security on the land that they had possessed under the traditional system, and those unable to pay rising taxes were forced to sell their land to moneylenders or to wealthy landowners. Even the new lands opened in the Mekong River delta, a development pointed to with pride by French officials, were a mixed blessing. These lands were sold to the highest bidder. Most plots were purchased by absentee landlords from Saigon, who rented the land out in small parcels to tenants at high annual rates of interest. Many could not pay the high rents and taxes and were forced to abandon the fields to seek jobs as landless laborers.[3]

Those who migrated to the cities were often little better off. Since the French did not actively encourage the development of a modern industrial sector, little employment was available for unskilled la-

---

[3] For a dramatic fictionalized account of the problem of poor peasants dealing with avaricious village power holders, see the excerpt from Nguyen Cong Hoan's novel *Buoc Dung Cung* [Dead End], in Ngo Vinh Long, *Before the Revolution: The Vietnamese Peasants under the French*, rev. ed. (New York: Columbia University Press, 1973), pp. 179–194.

borers except for low-paid factory workers, rickshaw pullers, or dockworkers in the port cities of Da Nang, Haiphong, and Saigon. On their meager earnings, most were forced to live in squatter settlements outside the main urban areas. Others sought work in the coal mines along the coast northeast of Hanoi or in the rubber plantations along the Cambodian border.

As in most European colonies, there were a few lucky ones. Well-meaning colonial administrators established a school system based on the stated objective of providing basic education for all and advanced learning to the small native elite. In actuality, only a minority of school-age children received more than the rudiments of education. There was a chronic lack of funds to establish schools throughout the union, but there was also the growing conviction among some French officials that exposure to Western ideas only encouraged hostility to the French colonial regime. Higher education, as one senior official sententiously observed, created "not one coolie less, but one rebel more." During the 1930s, only about 1 percent of the school-age population in Vietnam was enrolled in a school above the elementary level.[4]

The situation in Laos and Cambodia was somewhat different. Although both protectorates had come under varying degrees of Vietnamese influence during the precolonial period, they were culturally, ethnically, and linguistically quite distinct, both from Vietnam and from each other. Although all three were primarily Buddhist societies, neither Cambodia nor Laos had ever been occupied by China, and the primary cultural influence in both countries had come from India. These differences were accentuated rather than diminished under colonial rule. Lacking an abundance of available natural resources, both countries had come under French tutelage somewhat as an afterthought and served primarily as a buffer zone against Thailand, or British-controlled Burma. Having only limited economic and political interests in the two protectorates, the French simply established a skeleton administrative structure to preserve their colonial presence and then left them to their own devices.

---

[4] The speaker was French Governor General Martial Merlin. Statistics on education can be found in Nguyen Anh, "Vai net ve giao duc o Viet Nam tu sau dai chien the gioi lan thu I den truoc cach mang thang tam" [Education in Vietnam from the end of World War I to the August Revolution], *Nghien Cuu Lich Su* [Historical Research] 102 (September 1967):40. Hereafter *NCLS*.

A NATION IN PERIL

The imposition of colonial rule was a particularly traumatic event for the Vietnamese ruling elite. As French pressure intensified during the latter half of the nineteenth century, the imperial court at Hue became bitterly divided over how to respond to the threat from abroad. Some wanted to retreat to the hills and use traditional tactics of guerrilla warfare, previously applied against invaders from China, to fight the enemy to the bitter end. Others, fearful of the "fine ships and big guns" of the invaders, wanted to appease the French while attempting to introduce political and economic reforms to enable the empire to resist the enemy more effectively. As Nguyen Truong To, a member of the appeasement faction, remarked, to resist would simply be like pouring oil on a fire. Not only would it fail to put out the fire, but the blaze would burn more fiercely.[5]

The factionalism at court impeded any effective response to the problem and was ultimately disastrous. Emperor Tu Duc was well-meaning but indecisive, and when the French launched their first attack in 1858, he vacillated and temporized. After an unsuccessful effort to defeat French troops in the area of modern Saigon, the emperor had agreed to humiliating peace terms that ceded several provinces in the Mekong delta to the French in the hope of later persuading them to return the lost territories to imperial rule. But Tu Duc had miscalculated. The French had no intention of abandoning their foothold on the Southeast Asian mainland, as their later efforts to extend their influence northward graphically demonstrated.

The failure of the court to take the lead in resisting the French conquest placed patriotic Vietnamese in a dilemma. Should they follow imperial orders and refrain from active resistance to continuing French advances, or should they resist on their own initiative? That debate climaxed during the mid-1880s, when the French completed their takeover by establishing a protectorate over the northern provinces of the country. Although the court had agreed to the French terms, some leading civilian and military officials, led by the

---

[5] Nguyen Truong To, *Thien Ha Dai The Luan,* cited in Dang Huy Van, "Cuoc dau tranh giua phai 'chu chien' va phai 'chu hoa' trong cuoc khang chien chong Phap o cuoi the ky XIX" [The struggle between the resistance and appeasement factions in the struggle against the French at the end of the nineteenth century], *NCLS* 94 (1967):33.

Confucian scholar-official Phan Dinh Phung, decided to place patriotism before loyalty to the monarchy and took to the hills to organize resistance efforts. For the next several years, Phung and his followers carried on a bitter guerrilla struggle against the French colonial regime. To provide an aura of legitimacy to the movement, they persuaded the young emperor Ham Nghi, who had been placed on the throne by the French in the hope that he would serve their interests, to join them in their mountain headquarters and serve as a symbol of resistance for the movement, which adopted the symbolic title Can Vuong, meaning "Save the King."

Not all of the Vietnamese elite, however, opted to resist the French. Some bureaucrats resigned from office and retreated into private life, while others, whether out of political conviction or political expediency, decided to collaborate with the French. The disagreement between resistors and collaborators led to a celebrated exchange of letters between Can Vuong leader Phan Dinh Phung and Hoang Cao Khai, an old childhood acquaintance from his home village. Hoang Cao Khai wrote that although he understood his friend's motivation in taking up arms, continued fighting would only produce more hardship for the people.

> The subject I should now like to introduce is the suffering imposed upon our country. . . . Until now, your actions have undoubtedly accorded with your loyalty [to the king]. May I ask, however, what sin our people have committed to deserve so much hardship? I would understand your resistance, did you involve but your family for the benefit of a large number! As of now, hundreds of families are subject to grief; how do you have the heart to fight on? I venture to predict that, should you pursue your struggle, not only will the population of our village be destroyed but our entire country will be transformed into a sea of blood and a mountain of bones. It is my hope that men of your superior morality and honesty will pause a while to appraise the situation.

Hoang Cao Khai's words had no effect. While referring with fondness to their lifelong friendship, Phan Dinh Phung declared that his decision to resist the French was based on the traditions of the nation's glorious past. In his response, he lectured Khai on Confucian morality:

> I have concluded that if our country has survived these past thousand years when its territory was not large, its wealth not great, it was because the relationships between king and subjects, fathers

and children, have always been regulated by the five moral obligations. In the past, the Han, the Sung, the Yuan, the Ming [four of the great imperial dynasties in China] time and again dreamt of annexing our country and of dividing it up into prefectures and districts within the Chinese administrative system. But never were they able to realize their dream. Ah! If even China, which shares a common border with our territory and is a thousand times more powerful than Vietnam, could not rely upon her strength to swallow us, it was surely because the destiny of our country had been willed by Heaven itself.[6]

However laudable his intentions, Phan Dinh Phung's efforts to repeat the achievements of Le Loi and Nguyen Trai ended in tragedy and failure. His followers were driven into the hills, and by the time he died of dysentery in 1896, the movement had already begun to disintegrate. The French disinterred his body and scattered his bones in a gesture of contempt.

But the failure of Can Vuong movement did not spell the end of resistance to French rule, but only the end of its first phase. Shortly after the turn of the century, a new stage in the anti-French movement began, characterized by the abandonment of traditional ways and the adoption of Western ideas. The new stage was inaugurated by Phan Boi Chau, a well-known and widely respected Confucian scholar from central Vietnam. As a boy, Chau had been inspired by the activities of Phan Dinh Phung and his stalwart supporters to organize the youth in his home village into a local militia armed with sticks and bamboo spears. To his humiliation, the unit scattered when exposed to attack by a French military unit in the vicinity, and Phan Boi Chau was forced to flee amid a crowd of refugees. Later he would remark that the incident made him feel like "a boy building a tree house."[7]

After the defeat of the Can Vuong, Phan Boi Chau gradually realized that traditional methods could not deliver the Vietnamese people from their conquerors, and he became convinced that his country must adopt Western technology as well as political and economic institutions in order to resume its rightful role as an independent nation. In 1904 he organized the Modernization Society

[6] Cited in Truong Buu Lam, *Vietnamese Resistance against the French, 1858–1900* (New Haven: Yale University Press, 1967), pp. 121–128.
[7] Phan Boi Chau, *Doi Cach Menh Phan Boi Chau* [The revolutionary career of Phan Boi Chau] (Saigon, n.d.), p. 11.

Phan Boi Chau, Vietnam's first nationalist leader.

(Duy Tan Hoi), with the objective of driving the French from Vietnam. Phan Boi Chau might be considered the first modern nationalist in Vietnam, since he focused clearly on the nation rather than the ruling monarchy as the prime source of loyalty for the Vietnamese people, and he appealed to all Vietnamese regardless of age, sex, class, or religious preferences to unite in common struggle against the invader.

In pamphlet after pamphlet, in prose and in verse written in exile from Japan, Phan Boi Chau called on the Vietnamese people to rise up in a national effort to throw out the French. In *Viet Nam Vong Quoc Su* ("A History of the Downfall of Vietnam"), written in 1905 for publication in a journal in southern China, he appealed to his compatriots to live up to the glorious traditions of the past. In a shorter pamphlet entitled *Tan Viet Nam* ("New Vietnam"), he described a new society that would be based on the Western model. Deploring the "slave mentality" that was the consequence of 2000 years of Chinese cultural domination, he argued that only violent struggle promised the realization of success. "In a world of snakes," he lamented, "who speaks with the tongue of Buddha?"

Yet Phan Boi Chau's message was filled with ambiguities. Although a supporter of westernization, he was also convinced that the Vietnamese were a deeply conservative people, and he therefore selected a dissident member of the royal family to serve as a figurehead for his organization and the chief of a state in a projected constitutional monarchy. Moreover, although his basic appeal was for the spirit of self-reliance, "like a tiger protecting her cubs," Phan Boi Chau recognized that under existing conditions, Vietnam could not achieve national liberation without the assistance of a powerful foreign sponsor. He first sought aid from Japan. Then, when that appeal was rejected, he turned to Sun Yat-sen's Revolutionary Party in China. When Sun's movement appeared to have won a major victory by overthrowing the Manchu dynasty in October 1911, Chau changed his party's program from advocating a constitutional monarchy to advocating a democratic republic.[8]

Despite his efforts, Phan Boi Chau's approach, like that of his great predecessor Phan Dinh Phung, did not win universal acceptance among his compatriots. Although Chau contended that only violent resistance could successfully evict the French, some of his contemporaries argued that the real enemy of the Vietnamese people

[8] Phan Boi Chau, *Tan Viet Nam* [New Vietnam], reproduced in *NCLS* 78 (September 1965). The comment about a tiger protecting her cubs is from his *Viet Nam Vong Quoc Su*, printed in its original Chinese version in *Chung-Fa Chan-cheng* [The Sino-French War], vol. 7 (Shanghai: Jen-min ch'u-pan she, 1957), p. 537.

was not the French but their own outworn traditions. A prominent exponent of his view was Phan Boi Chau's friend and namesake, Phan Chu Trinh. Like Chau a respected Confucian scholar from central Vietnam, Trinh was convinced that the Vietnamese should exploit the presence of the French by allowing them to carry out their civilizing mission and then to withdraw. Trinh felt that Chau's reliance on the traditional monarchy and its supporters could not succeed. In a letter to the French governor general, Paul Beau, in 1906, Trinh conceded that colonial rule had brought many benefits to Vietnam, such as roads, bridges, and railways. But it had also given rise to government corruption, and French officials treated the people with contempt. He appealed to Beau to introduce Western political institutions, education, and modern technology and then transfer power to an independent Vietnamese government. If so, he stated, France would possess the everlasting gratitude of the Vietnamese people.[9]

In the eyes of his friend Chau, Trinh's expectation that the French would live up to their civilizing mission was naive. To Trinh's criticism that he was relying on the past to build the future, Chau retorted that trying to establish a democracy with the people's current level of ignorance would be like urging a child to run before the bones in his legs had been solidly formed. "First," he wrote to his friend, "we must unite to achieve national liberation. Then, if in ten years you bring up your reformist ideas, I will be the first to applaud.[10]

The ongoing debate between Phan Boi Chau and Phan Chu Trinh is worth discussing here because it symbolized one of the most fundamental dilemmas faced by patriotic individuals living under colonial rule, not only in Vietnam but throughout the region. What was more important, national independence or institutional reform? Could colonial powers be compelled to live up to their civilizing mission? Could patriotic forces achieve liberation without first carrying out basic changes in their societies? Such questions led

---

[9] Letter to Paul Beau (*Thu gui Toan Quyen Beau*) is located in a Vietnamese-language version in *NCLS* 66 (September 1964). For the original French version, see *Bulletin de l'Ecole Française d'Extreme Orient* (March-June 1907):166–175.
[10] Chau's letter to Phan Chu Trinh is quoted in Dang Thai Mai, *Van Tho Phan Boi Chau* [Essays and Poems of Phan Boi Chau] (Hanoi: Van Hoa, 1960), pp. 156–157.

to acrimonious debates and sometimes to splits within nationalist organizations throughout the region. They would plague the nationalist movement in Vietnam for three generations.

As far as Chau and Trinh were concerned, the dilemma was not resolved in their lifetime, although certain facts became clear. Chau discovered that more than dedication and love of country were needed to create an effective movement to oppose colonial power. After years of fruitless activities, in 1925 Chau was arrested by the French while living in China. Tried and convicted of sedition in Hanoi, he was placed under house arrest in Hue until his death in 1940. In the meantime, Phan Chu Trinh learned that persuasion and reason had little impact on the French. In 1908 he was arrested for taking part in a peasant demonstration against high taxes and, after a brief period of imprisonment in Vietnam, was forced to live in exile in France. He did not return to Vietnam until 1925, only a few months before he died of cancer. His funeral in Saigon was the occasion of mass mourning and popular demonstrations throughout the country.

FRENCH COLONIALISM ON TRIAL

During his travels throughout Vietnam to recruit supporters for the Modernization Society, Phan Boi Chau had made the acquaintance of a scholar-official from Nghe-Tinh province in central Vietnam by the name of Nguyen Sinh Sac. An official of the imperial government who resigned his position in protest against the creation of the French protectorate, Sac invited Chau to visit his home in Kim Lien village, not far from the provincial capital of Vinh, to discuss the means of liberating Vietnam from colonial rule. In the course of their discussions, Chau invited the son of his host, a young man by the name of Nguyen Tat Thanh, to join his movement, which at that time still had its headquarters in Japan.

The young Thanh, who would later be known to the world as Ho Chi Minh, was ambitious and fiercely patriotic, but he refused Chau's offer. Later a biographer would cite Ho as remarking that seeking assistance from Japan would be like driving the tiger out the front door while welcoming the wolf in the back. In 1908, while attending high school in the imperial capital of Hue, the young man took part in peasant antitax riots in central Vietnam. Dismissed from school for such activities, he taught briefly and then took employment with a French steamship company as a cook's assistant. Leaving Saigon in 1911, he spent the next several years at sea. He would not return to his native land for a generation.[11]

During the next several years, Nguyen Tat Thanh traveled throughout the world. He spent several months in the United States, where he worked in Boston and New York City and apparently made a short visit to the South, a trip which provoked his anger at the treatment of African Americans. When World War I broke out in 1914, he abandoned his career as a seaman and settled in Great Britain. It may have been there that he first became aware of the ideas of Karl Marx. At war's end he was in France, where he lived with Phan Chu Trinh in Paris and worked as a photo retoucher.

In France he soon became involved in political activities. In 1919, under the assumed name of Nguyen Ai Quoc ("Nguyen the Patriot"), he appealed to Allied leaders gathered at the peace conference in Versailles, demanding self-determination for colonial peoples in accordance with U.S. president Woodrow Wilson's famous Fourteen Points, which called for the building of a postwar world that would be safe for democracy. The appeal was ignored by the Allied leaders, but it caused a stir in the Vietnamese exile community in Paris and brought Nguyen Ai Quoc (as he would henceforth be known) to the attention of his contemporaries as a figure to be reckoned with in the Vietnamese nationalist movement.

In that same year, Nguyen Ai Quoc joined the Parti Socialiste de France (PSF). But he was disturbed by the lack of concern displayed by many of his French comrades for the problems of the colonies. He was also initially confused by the debates that were taking place within the party over the radical message of Soviet leader V.I. Lenin, who in 1917 had led his Bolshevik Party to victory in the October Revolution in Russia. Lenin had just formed a new organization called the Communist International (generally known as the Comintern) to promote the cause of world revolution. During the summer of 1920, Nguyen Ai Quoc read a tract entitled *Theses on the National and Colonial Questions* that Lenin had just presented to the Second Comintern Congress in Moscow. Lenin proposed a strategy calling for future communist parties in colonial areas to ally

---

[11] Truong Chinh, *President Ho Chi Minh: Beloved Leader of the Vietnamese people* (Hanoi: Foreign Languages Press, 1966), p. iii.

with local middle-class nationalist elements in a common struggle against the ruling colonial regimes.

Lenin's goal was to link the class struggle in Western industrial societies with the anticolonial struggle in preindustrial colonial and semicolonial areas in Asia and North Africa. In classical Marxism, such economically backward societies would not be ripe for a socialist revolution until they had passed through the Industrial Revolution and entered the stage of capitalism, at which time a domestic working class (the proletariat in Marxist terminology) would become a significant proportion of the local population. According to Karl Marx, it was the proletariat, as the most alienated and oppressed class in a capitalist society, that would lead the socialist revolution against the capitalist ruling clique.

Such ideas had little relevance in the preindustrial societies of early twentieth-century Asia. But after coming to power in Russia, Lenin and some of his more prescient colleagues realized that rising anticolonial sentiment among Asian peoples could make them a worthy ally against world capitalism; in Lenin's view, without access to the markets and resources of their colonies, which guaranteed profits to the industrialists, the capitalist regimes of Europe were bound to collapse.

To link his beleaguered state with the rising force of anticolonialism in the East, Lenin thus proposed that communist parties based on the small local working class and radical intellectuals be formed in colonial territories. Although such parties would necessarily lack the experience and the mass support necessary to triumph on their own over the entrenched power of colonial regimes, with the support of angry peasants and patriotic elements within the urban middle class, they might hope to overthrow colonial governments and the decrepit traditional cliques that sometimes ruled in their name. Once that "first stage" of the revolution had been completed, Lenin argued, the local communist parties could then mobilize progressive elements, break with their erstwhile middle-class allies, and attempt to seize power on their own.

To the young Nguyen Ai Quoc, Lenin's program presented a persuasive strategy to assist the colonial peoples liberate themselves from foreign domination. In the summer of 1920, he joined other radical members of the PSF to create the Parti Communiste de France (PCF), which then joined the Comintern. During the next three years, Nguyen Ai Quoc became a respected and active member of the PCF,

Nguyen Ai Quoc at the Conference of Tours, which created the French Communist Party in 1920.

with a particular interest in promoting revolution in the colonies. To provide an organizational focus for Marxist revolutionary activities among colonial subjects living in France, he created a multinational organization called the Intercolonial Union and published a journal known as *Le Paria* ("the Pariah") to publicize the problems of colonial areas and the need for active efforts to seek their liberation. He published a number of articles in left-wing newspapers and wrote a scarifying attack on French colonial policies entitled *Le Procès du colonialisme français* ("French Colonialism on Trial").

Nguyen Ai Quoc with colleagues in Moscow during the 1920s.

In 1923, having become the most articulate advocate of colonial causes in the PCF, Nguyen Ai Quoc was invited to the USSR to study Marxist ideology and work at Comintern headquarters. Traveling in disguise as a rich Vietnamese tourist, he arrived in Moscow sometime during the summer and enrolled in the newly opened School for the Oppressed Peoples of the East (popularly known as the Stalin School), where he studied Marxism-Leninism. He also served as a delegate to the Peasant International (Krestintern), an organization sponsored by the Comintern to carry out Lenin's strategy of promoting revolutionary activity among the rural masses. Few in Moscow, however, apparently took Lenin's idea seriously. Many probably argued with Karl Marx himself, who had felt that the peasant was a naturally acquisitive being whose desire for land would always overcome his revolutionary instincts. In a speech at a conference of the Peasant International in 1924, Nguyen Ai Quoc appealed in vain to his listeners to take seriously the revolutionary potential of agrarian societies in Asia. In a later comment to a colleague, he laughingly referred to himself as a "voice crying in the wilderness."[12]

Still, Nguyen Ai Quoc must have made an impression on key members of the Comintern. In the fall of 1924 he was instructed to report to Guangzhou (Canton) to serve as an interpreter on the staff of the Comintern headquarters attached to Sun Yat-sen's government in southern China. Sun Yat-sen's Nationalist Party, or Guomindang, had just established a territorial base in Guangdong province, China. Although he was not a communist, Sun had agreed to the suggestion of the Comintern to ally his party with the Chinese Communist Party (CCP), which had been formed by radical intellectuals in Shanghai in the summer of 1921.

Arriving in Guangzhou in December 1924, Nguyen Ai Quoc immediately set out to accomplish his real task: the formation of the first genuinely Marxist revolutionary organization in Indochina. He had arrived at a propitious moment, for it was a time of rising political ferment, not only in Indochina but throughout the region. Sun Yat-sen's government was preparing to launch a military expedition to attack the warlords still in power elsewhere in the country. Meanwhile, inside Indochina a new wave of anticolonialist unrest was on the rise throughout many segments of Vietnamese society.

THE FATAL FLAW

The most visible manifestation of unrest was in Saigon and Hanoi, where radical intellectuals, students, and merchants, disillusioned by the failure of the French to carry out their "civilizing mission" in Indochina, had begun to organize political parties and groups. Their goal was to force the colonial regime to adopt reforms or, in the view of some, to grant independence to the country. The trial of Phan Boi Chau in Hanoi and the death of Phan Chu Trinh in Saigon set off emotional outbursts throughout Vietnam. At Trinh's funeral

[12] The most detailed account of this period of Ho's life in the English language is Yevgeny Kobelev, *Ho Chi Minh* (Moscow: Progress Publishers, 1989), pp. 60–76.

in April 1926, an estimated 140,000 people lined the route from Saigon to the burial ground near Tan Son Nhut Airport.[13]

More ominous for the French was the unrest that was beginning to spread from the educated elite to the general population. Factory workers, coal miners, and rubber tappers on the plantations along the Cambodian border were becoming increasingly restive at poor working conditions and low wages, while peasants were being whipsawed by rising taxes, official corruption, prohibitions on the manufacture of salt and alcohol, and land seizures by wealthy land-owners. During the late 1920s workers' strikes began to increase, while unrest in rural areas was becoming more and more common-place.

Had the emerging anticolonial forces in the big cities been able to tap into the latent discontent among the masses, they might have been able to mobilize a nationwide protest movement involving broad sectors of the Vietnamese population such as the uprising envisioned by veteran revolutionary Phan Boi Chau half a genera-tion earlier. Unfortunately, urban nationalists encountered serious difficulties in formulating their message and articulating it effec-tively to their rural compatriots.

One reason for their problem was the continuing disagreement within the movement over tactics and ultimate goals. Some were willing to seek change by reformist methods and were reconciled, to one degree or another, to a French presence into the indefinite future. The most visible manifestation of this point of view was the Constitutionalist Party, which was made up of a small number of affluent professionals in Cochin China. They argued in favor of efforts to improve economic conditions and increase Vietnamese participation in the political process, while transforming the French colonial empire into a broader body of autonomous states similar to the British Commonwealth.

If some sought a peaceful road to national liberation or a new and more equitable relationship with France, others agreed with Phan Boi Chau that only violent struggle would bring about true national liberation. Best known among the parties that adopted such an approach was the Viet Nam Quoc Dan Dang (VNQDD), or Vi-

---

[13] Tran Huy Lieu, *Tai Lieu Tham Khao Lich Su Viet Nam: Cach Mang Can Dai Viet Nam* [Research Materials on Vietnamese History: The Modern Revolution in Vietnam], vol. 4 (Hanoi: Van Su Dia, 1958), p. 99.

etnamese National Party, formed by a number of discontented intellectuals in Hanoi in 1927. The ideology of the VNQDD, like that of the Guomindang in China, emphasized the establishment of an independent republic on the Western model. It was highly nationalist and generally progressive in its political and economic views, but anticommunist in its ideological orientation. Its leaders were convinced that the French could only be evicted by force of arms.

Disagreements over means and ends, of course, existed in anticolonial movements throughout Asia. In the more successful cases, such as the Congress Party in British India, and the Indonesian Nationalist Party in the Dutch East Indies, leading figures were able to reconcile such differences while maintaining the semblance of a unified front against the common enemy. In colonial Vietnam, such differences could not be overcome. Members of the VNQDD contemptuously dismissed supporters of the Constitutionalist Party as collaborators, while the latter haughtily disapproved of the political and social radicalism of their more militant critics. Until the final French soldier and colonial bureaucrat departed from Indochina thirty years later, noncommunist nationalism would be unable to face the colonial regime with a solid front. It was a fatal flaw.

The nationalists also had problems in articulating their message to the Vietnamese people. Most of the active members of the anticolonial movement in the 1920s were members of the educated urban minority. Many were students and journalists. Some had studied abroad. A substantial number were descended from the traditional ruling elite. While sympathetic to the needs and aspirations of the poor, relatively few had a deep understanding of rural problems, and their message understandably tended to focus on their own concerns, such as freedom of speech and assembly, equal pay for equal work (a serious source of complaint among Vietnamese serving in the colonial bureaucracy), and greater native representation in the governing process.

For Nguyen Ai Quoc, such conditions represented both a challenge and an opportunity. From his base of operations in Canton (he was already well known to French security officials and could not risk returning to Indochina), he began to seek support within the Vietnamese exile community in southern China, where thousands of Vietnamese were studying, working on the railroad between Yunnan province and the Red River delta, or simply hiding from the French security services, the dreaded Sureté. Some had crossed the border to serve under the banner of the old patriot Phan Boi Chau, but the latter, even prior to his arrest by the French, had aged visibly. Although he was still viewed with respect by many of his compatriots, he had now lost much of his energy and more of his following, and young radicals increasingly branched out on their own to seek the overthrow of the French regime.[14]

Such was the case for the small radical group of Vietnamese exiles who called their organization the Tam Tam Xa (Association of Like Minds). The group had originally owed a general allegiance to Phan Boi Chau, but was now operating on its own. The association lacked any specific ideology; it was simply dedicated to the violent overthrow of French rule. In 1924, one of the members of the group, the young militant Pham Hong Thai, attempted to assassinate the French governor general of Indochina while he was visiting Guangzhou to seek the extradition of Vietnamese radicals to Indochina. The attempt failed, and Pham Hong Thai drowned in the river while attempting to escape. But the news of the abortive assassination swept through the region. The movement had its first martyr.

THE REVOLUTIONARY PATH

Shortly after his own arrival in Guangzhou, Nguyen Ai Quoc established contact with surviving members of the group and persuaded them to join his own new organization, the Viet Nam Thanh Nien Cach Mang Dong Chi Hoi, or Vietnamese Revolutionary Youth League. The RYL was not a formal communist party as such. In his own writings during the early 1920s, Nguyen Ai Quoc had recognized that the Vietnamese people still lacked political sophistication, while the local proletariat was too small and disorganized to form the basis for a sophisticated party based on the principles of Marxism-Leninism. He would need time to organize and teach his followers the complexities of Marxist doctrine and practice. The program of the RYL therefore avoided specifics and espoused in very general terms to the twin goals of national independence and a vague commitment to creating a future egalitarian society. In preparation for

---

[14] Many of these young radicals respected Phan Boi Chau but thought he was naive. For example, see Tran Huy Lieu, "Nho lai ong Gia Ben Ngu" [In memory of Phan Boi Chau], *NCLS* 47 (February 1963).

the formation of a formal communist party in the near future, Nguyen Ai Quoc introduced six of the most active and dedicated of his followers into a small subgroup called the Communist League to serve as the nucleus of a future communist party.

While in the process of forming the RYL, Nguyen Ai Quoc had resumed his acquaintance with the veteran patriot Phan Boi Chau. While on a visit to Beijing, Chau had met Leo Karakhan, the Soviet ambassador to China, and expressed a general interest in Marxist socialism. After returning to his residence in Hangzhou in central China, Chau met with Nguyen Ai Quoc and apparently agreed to serve as a symbolic leader for the latter's new revolutionary organization. But while en route to Guangzhou to confer with him on the details, he was suddenly arrested by French police in the railway station in Shanghai, and thenceforth returned to Indochina for trial. Accusations have since been made that Nguyen Ai Quoc betrayed Phan Boi Chau in return for the ransom money, but there is no persuasive evidence to support the charge. Chau himself believed that he had been turned in by one of his followers.[15]

For the next two years, Nguyen Ai Quoc attempted to build up the RYL, while introducing his followers to the intricacies of Marxist doctrine and practice. Members were given ideological and practical training at a training institute in a small rented building in downtown Guangzhou. Nguyen Ai Quoc was one of the regular lecturers, along with leading members of the CCP such as Zhou Enlai and Liu Shaoqi. Nguyen Ai Quoc wrote a short pamphlet entitled *Duong Kach Menh* ("The Revolutionary Path"), which provided a simplified interpretation of the coming world revolution and its relationship to the revolution in Vietnam and was used as a textbook for the class on Marxism. In the pamphlet, the author declared that national liberation could not be realized simply through isolated acts of heroism and self-sacrifice (a clear reference to the activities of the Association of Like Minds), but required an ideology and a plan. Such a program, he contended, was offered by the ideas of Marx and Lenin.[16]

[15] The charge is repeated in Robert F. Turner, *Vietnamese Communism: Its Origins and Development* (Stanford, Calif.: Hoover Institute Press, 1975). For Phan Boi Chau's view of the matter, see his *Phan Boi Chau Nien Bieu* [A chronological biography of Phan Boi Chau] (Hanoi: Van Su Dia, 1957), pp. 189–190.

[16] A complete version of *The Revolutionary Path* is contained in *Ho Chi Minh Toan Tap* [Complete Works of Ho Chi Minh], vol. 2 (Hanoi: Su That, 1981). Hereafter *Toan Tap*.

After the completion of their training program at the institute, graduates were taken to the gravesite of the martyred Pham Hong Thai, where they took an oath of loyalty to the cause of Vietnamese national liberation. Most then returned to Indochina to recruit new members for the RYL. A select few were sent to Moscow for additional training.

The RYL was an immediate success and gained wide support from radical youths in all three regions of the country. Most of the early members came from families belonging to the educated elite, although some inroads were made into recruiting from factories, plantations, and farm villages. The RYL leadership made an effort to establish cooperative arrangements with other nationalist parties such as the VNQDD, but for the most part it competed with such organizations for followers. By the late 1920s, it had over 1000 members and was viewed by the Sureté as the most serious threat to French rule in Indochina.

Why was the RYL so successful? In the first place, it was better organized than its rivals. It artfully combined the appeal of patriotism and social reform in a manner that could appeal to wide sectors of the populace, moderates as well as radicals, the affluent as well as the poor. In this respect, it undoubtedly benefited from the sophisticated strategy that had been formulated by Lenin several years before. Secondly, the RYL made a greater attempt than other parties to transcend regional differences and organized branches in all areas of the country, although the bulk of the leadership came from Nguyen Ai Quoc's native province of Nghe-Tinh. Finally, in Nguyen Ai Quoc it possessed a highly charismatic leader who could inspire trust and devotion from his followers and appeal to moderates and radicals alike. Nguyen Ai Quoc was also a gifted strategist who had the ability to articulate his message in a way that appeared to sum up the aspirations of the vast majority of his compatriots.

Sun Yat-sen died of cancer in 1925, and the alliance between the CCP and the Guomindang came to an abrupt end when Sun's successor, Chiang Kai-shek, slaughtered thousands of communist supporters in Shanghai in April 1927. Chiang cracked down on communist activities throughout southern China, and Nguyen Ai Quoc fled to Moscow. In his absence, the RYL began to experience the problem of internal fragmentation that had plagued its rivals. The chief source of dispute was ideological. Some members became increasingly critical of the tendency of the leadership to emphasize national over economic concerns and argued for a policy that placed more stress on class struggle than on national independence. They also called for heightened efforts to increase enrollment in the organization among workers and poor peasants.

Such proposals had been provoked in part by a change of approach in Moscow. The Leninist strategy of encouraging alliances between communist parties and local bourgeois nationalist groups had clearly backfired in China. The Comintern reacted by instructing communist parties to build new, more narrowly based alliances with only the most revolutionary elements among the peasantry and radical intellectuals. Communist parties were themselves to be "proletarianized" by being purged of their bourgeois elements and enriched by new members recruited from the local working class.

In the spring of 1929, the RYL broke up into contending factions, each claiming to represent the official policy of the Comintern. Early the following year, Nguyen Ai Quoc, who had been organizing Vietnamese residents in nearby Siam (now Thailand) went to Hong Kong to unite the squabbling factions into a single communist party. But he had by no means changed his views on the correct course of the Vietnamese revolution. Although the program drafted under his guidance at the meeting held in early February 1930 attempted to conform to Comintern guidelines for a "party of the working class," it also called for the formation of a common front that would include both middle-class intellectuals and middle peasants and rich peasants, small landlords, and capitalist elements as well. The so-called unity conference also directed the new party to make use of patriotic slogans aimed at the creation of an independent Vietnam, while at the same time attempting to establish contact with oppressed and working-class elements throughout the world. As a clear symbol of the underlying patriotic character of its message, the new organization was named the Dang Cong San Viet Nam (Vietnamese Communist Party, or VCP). A provisional Central Committee was appointed until formal elections could take place.[17]

If Nguyen Ai Quoc was attempting to reconcile existing Comintern strategy with his own views on the proper course of the Vietnamese revolution, he did not succeed. A few months after the

[17] Nguyen Ai Quoc had already decided on the name before the conference was convened. See Note by Nguyen Ai Quoc, January 6, 1930, in the Ho Chi Minh Museum in Hanoi.

unity conference, two members of the RYL who had been studying at the Stalin School in Moscow returned to Hong Kong with clear guidelines from the Comintern on the proper organization and line of the new party. At a meeting of the Central Committee in October, a new program was adopted which essentially reversed the decisions of the February conference and placed a clear priority on the issue of class struggle. Nguyen Ai Quoc's plan to seek support from middle-class and progressive-landlord elements was rejected, and his ideas were denounced as "mistaken and dangerous" by colleagues in party publications. Such ideas, they wrote, placed emphasis on the struggle for national independence at the expense of social revolution. To dramatize the new line, at Moscow's direction the October conference changed the name of the organization to Dang Cong San Dong Duong—the Indochinese Communist Party, or ICP.[18]

After the meeting, the leadership of the new party was turned over to the new Moscow-trained leadership, while Nguyen Ai Quoc remained in Hong Kong as a representative of the Comintern. The new party had appeared at a fateful moment. While the Central Committee was wrestling with the problem of establishing a proper ideological focus, a major revolt broke out in Vietnam. Angry workers and peasants rioted against declining economic conditions brought on by the advent of the Great Depression. In Nghe-Tinh province, desperate peasants, supported by local communist organizers, unseated the local authorities and formed peasant associations (called "soviets" in imitation of the workers' committees formed during the 1917 Bolshevik Revolution), which reduced land rents and in some cases divided up the land of wealthy landlords among the poor.

Party operatives had been active in the central coast region since earlier in the year, preparing for an anticipated revolutionary upsurge throughout Indochina. Faced with the quickening tempo of

---

[18] Full details of the October conference are not yet available to historians. But it seems clear that it rejected Nguyen Ai Quoc's program and adopted one more in conformity with the decisions reached at the Comintern congress in 1928. For a recent discussion by a Vietnamese historian in Hanoi, see Le Mau Han, "Ho Chi Minh voi ngon co doc lap dan toc trong cuong linh dau tien cua Dang" [Ho Chi Minh and the standard of national independence in the first program of the party], *Tap Chi Lich Su Dang* [Journal of Party History] 33 (May 1990):18–33.

unrest, they attempted to provide guidance and leadership to the peasant movement. But the French reacted swiftly and ruthlessly to the revolt, and by the spring of 1931 the agitation had been suppressed. The Nghe-Tinh revolt had confirmed Nguyen Ai Quoc's contention of the revolutionary potential of the rural populace, but it also demonstrated the need for careful preparation and the mobilization of support on a nationwide basis. Although there were scattered outbreaks of violence in factories and plantations elsewhere in the country, in general farmers and workers in Tonkin and Cochin China did not rise in support of their compatriots in the central provinces.

The lesson in the art of revolution was an expensive one. In the French crackdown that followed, most of the party leadership and many of its most active members were executed or sentenced to lengthy terms in prison. In June 1931, Nguyen Ai Quoc himself was arrested by British authorities in a general roundup of radical elements in Hong Kong.

For the next several years, the party was in a state of disarray. Unable to hold a meeting of the Central Committee inside Indochina, the party's few surviving leaders assigned direction of the party to two temporary committees based in China and Thailand. Because the party's internal apparatus had been shattered, the new committees were staffed primarily by students returning from the Stalin School in Moscow. For the time being, party strategy continued to reflect the hard-line approach that had been adopted at the October 1930 conference. Articles published in party journals criticized the "nationalist" tendencies of Nguyen Ai Quoc and other members of his faction and called for a narrowly defined line based on working-class leadership.

It was a change of mood in Moscow that brought this sectarian phase of the Vietnamese revolution to an end. By 1935 Soviet policymakers had begun to react to Adolf Hitler's rise to power in Germany, and at an August Comintern congress all member communist parties were ordered to adopt a broader view of the united front. Not only should they begin to seek greater support from peasant and middle-class elements; they should also join forces with ruling authorities in colonial areas against the common danger of world fascism.

At first, some members of the ICP were reluctant to follow the new guidelines, which appeared to them to betray the cause of world revolution. But eventually the party closed ranks around the new approach and soon tasted its benefits when the colonial government in Indochina, under instructions from Paris, permitted the ICP and other nationalist organizations to function on a semilegal basis, so long as they did not promote violence. Communists were elected to the office on the Saigon Muncipal Council and published a newspaper called *La Lutte* ("The Struggle") without hindrance from the government. In succeeding years the ICP began to spread its popular base by forming self-help associations among the urban working class and organizing among the rural peasantry. Once again, the party had begun to play a prominent role in the Vietnamese nationalist movement.

Nguyen Ai Quoc had observed these events from Moscow, where he had gone after his release from prison in Hong Kong in 1933. There is little doubt that he would have liked to return to Asia to help protect his party from disintegration, but he was under suspicion by Stalin for his independent views on Marxist doctrine, and his activities were restricted to menial administrative chores and writing occasional articles on topics of general concern. Certainly he must have approved the new approach to the united front that was adopted at the 1935 Comintern congress, although he was permitted to attend the meeting only as an observer.

In 1939, he wrote an open letter to the ICP leadership explaining the new policy. What was needed, he said, was a comprehensive Indochinese Democratic Front that embraced not only workers and peasants but the middle class and progressive French citizens as well. If such elements were left out of the united front, they could be pushed into the hands of the Japanese fascists, who had invaded China in 1931, thus strengthening the influence of reactionary elements throughout the world. The ICP, he concluded, "must not demand that the front accept its leadership, but must show itself to be its most loyal, active and sincere member." Only when the broad masses of the population began to recognize the correct policy and leadership of the ICP could it claim leadership over the movement. By the time he wrote those words, Nguyen Ai Quoc had already returned to China to prepare for the next stage of the Vietnamese revolution.[19]

---

[19] Nguyen Ai Quoc's report is presented in an English-language translation in Bernard B. Fall, *Ho Chi Minh on Revolution* (New York: Praeger, 1967), pp. 131–132.

CALL TO ARMS

As the decade of the 1930s came to an end, the ICP had begun to return to the program that had originally been adopted by Nguyen Ai Quoc during the 1920s. It was just in time, because the world was clearly on the verge of a new era of widespread instability. In August 1939, the Soviet Union signed a nonaggression pact with Nazi Germany. The sudden move provoked a crackdown on Communist activities in Indochina by the French colonial authorities, and party leaders were forced to flee from their base of operations in the outskirts of Saigon. To the north, China and Japan were now at war. At a meeting of the reconstituted Central Committee held in a secret location near Saigon in November, party leaders called for a general uprising to achieve national liberation from colonial rule.

> All comrades must close ranks! Unite one thousand as one! Rise to realize the anti-imperialist national united front! Rise to overthrow the imperialist yoke! Seize independence, liberty, freedom, equality, peace, and happiness! The future is ours![20]

But within weeks of the meeting, most of the members of the Central Committee had been arrested by the French, and party members in the three regions were forced to act on their own.

In the summer of 1940, Japan demanded that the French close the border between China and Indochina to prevent the shipment of goods to the Nationalist government of Chiang Kai-shek, which was now headquartered in Chongqing in central China. In September, Tokyo demanded the right to station troops in northern Indochina and punctuated its demand with a sudden attack on French forces along the Sino-Vietnamese border. The new French government at Vichy capitulated to the Japanese demands.

Communist leaders along the frontier organized guerrilla units who briefly resisted the invaders and then faded into the mountains to preserve their strength and consolidate a liberated base area. Shortly after, the ICP's regional Committee for the South, taking

---

[20] Only recently has the 1939 meeting received credit for having been the first to raise the standard of national liberation. Previously the honor had gone to the Central Committee meeting held at Pac Bo in May 1941. The full resolution of the 1939 meeting is not available in English. For a Vietnamese-language version, see *Van Kien Dang* [Party Documents], vol. 2 (Hanoi: Institute of History on the Party, 1978), pp. 26–88.

advantage of rising popular discontent in both urban and rural areas of Cochin China, launched an uprising against French rule in Saigon and the neighboring Mekong River delta. The uprising was ruthlessly suppressed, and several key leaders from the Central Committee were seized and executed.

By now the party organization was in a state of considerable disarray. The regional committee in Tonkin had convened a meeting in October to consult with a delegate from the Committee for the South and evaluate the latter's proposal for the uprising in Cochin China. Members of the Tonkin regional committee opposed the plan on the grounds that it was too risky, but the visiting delegate from the south was arrested by the French before he could report back to his colleagues in Saigon. Now the regional committee in Tonkin decided to constitute itself as a temporary Central Committee until formal party elections could be held. Truong Chinh, a leading member of the Tonkin regional committee who had been active in party affairs since the early 1930s, was selected as provisional general secretary, the most influential position in the party.[21]

While ICP leaders inside Indochina struggled desperately to keep abreast of the rapidly changing situation, Nguyen Ai Quoc was in China, serving in various capacities with Chinese Communist Party units in different parts of the country while awaiting an opportunity to resume contacts with his colleagues in the Central Committee. He had left the USSR in the summer of 1938, having finally received approval from the Comintern to return to Asia to resume direction of the party. After stopping briefly at CCP headquarters in Yenan, he went on to southern China, where he worked at a club run by the Communist Party's Eighth Route Army in Guilin and published articles in a local newspaper extolling the virtues of the most recent united front between the Nationalists and the Communists against Japan. In the spring of 1940 he was finally able to establish contact with Pham Van Dong and Vo Nguyen Giap, two promising young ICP members who had been sent to China by the Central Committee to organize a party base in the area. At first,

---

[21] The events surrounding the Saigon uprising and the formation of the new Central Committee in Tonkin are poorly known and are only now being discussed and analyzed by Vietnamese historians in Hanoi. For a general overview, see *Histoire de la Révolution d'Août* (Hanoi: Foreign Languages Press, 1977), pp. 19–22. Descended from a prestigious scholar-gentry family in Tonkin, Truong Chinh (real name Dang Xuan Khu) had joined the RYL in the 1920s. After a term in prison, he was released in 1936 and became active in journalistic activities on behalf of the party.

Nguyen Ai Quoc planned to send them to Yenan to serve as a liaison with CCP headquarters, but as events in Indochina evolved, he changed his mind and instructed them to remain in southern China to reorganize the party's activities in the area.

Nguyen Ai Quoc's most immediate concern was to establish cooperative arrangements with the leading members of other Vietnamese anticolonial organizations operating in China. He took up the challenge on two levels. On the one hand, he sought alliances with all nationalist groups opposed to French rule and the Japanese occupation of Indochina, even though they might not agree to the party's ultimate goal of a communist society. As a vehicle for such activities, he arranged for members of the ICP to take part in the Vietnamese Liberation League, formed by Chinese authorities to assist them in undermining the Japanese occupation of Indochina. In conformity with the strategy that he had outlined in his article in 1939, Nguyen Ai Quoc did not insist that the ICP play a leading role in the Liberation League. But he did initiate plans for a separate united front of anti-Japanese groups in which the party would play a leading part, although its dominant position would be disguised in order to maximize its appeal to moderates. This second organization was eventually to be known as the Viet Nam Doc Lap Dong Minh, or League for the Independence of Vietnam, but was popularly known as the Vietminh.

The Vietminh was formally established in May 1941 at a meeting of the ICP Central Committee in the small mountain village of Pac Bo, near the Chinese border. Like its prototype, the Revolutionary Youth League, the Vietminh sought to win the support of both moderate and radical elements by espousing the dual goals of national independence and social reform. But in line with Nguyen Ai Quoc's firm belief that national liberation was the most crucial problem currently facing the Vietnamese people, he placed primary emphasis on the former goal. This overriding focus on patriotic themes was reflected in the name of the organization, which not only stressed the issue of independence but replaced the term *Indochina*, used in the name of the party, with the more emotionally charged word *Vietnam* in the united front. In a proclamation issued to the Vietnamese people after the close of the meeting, Nguyen Ai Quoc attempted to evoke the image of past glories.

> Dear fellow-countrymen! A few hundred years ago, in the reign of the Tran, when our country faced the great danger of invasion by

Yuan armies, the elders ardently called on their sons and daughters throughout the country to stand up as one to kill the enemy. Finally they saved their people, and their glorious memory will live forever. Let our elders and patriotic personalities follow the illustrious example set by our forefathers. . . .

At present national liberation stands above everything. Let us unite and overthrow the Japanese, the French, and their lackeys in order to save our people from their present dire straits.[22]

As had been the case with the RYL, the program of the Vietminh did not entirely ignore economic issues. But the appeal to land-hungry peasants was deliberately muted in order to avoid alienating wealthy landowners and other affluent members of Vietnamese society. The previous party program, which had called for the confiscation of land from big property owners, was replaced by the more limited one of reducing land rents and seizing the property of French imperialists and their Vietnamese collaborators. But the policy shift was only tactical. According to the resolution issued at the close of the meeting, the problem of class struggle would continue to exist. At the present time, however, "the nation has prime importance, and all demands which are of benefit to a specific class but which are harmful to the national interests must be subordinated to the survival of the nation and the race."[23]

The immediate goal of the front was thus to build a movement for national independence that could not only earn the support of the Vietnamese people but also the sympathy of the Allied powers. Victory would symbolize the triumph of the first stage of the revolution and usher in a broad-based government composed of several classes but dominated by the ICP. There would then be ample time to move toward the proletarian or socialist stage of the revolution. In the meantime, Nguyen Ai Quoc gambled that broad elements within the population would enthusiastically support the cause.

The ultimate goal of the new united front, of course, was to

---

[22] An English-language version of the appeal is in *Ho Chi Minh: Selected Writings* (Hanoi: Foreign Languages Press, 1977), pp. 45–46. The original Vietnamese version is in *Toan Tap*, vol. 3, pp. 147–149. Nguyen Ai Quoc's appeal to patriotic sentiment is reminiscent of Stalin's effort to mobilize the Russian people against the German invasion in June 1941.

[23] Tran Huy Lieu, *Lich Su Tam Muoi Nam Chong Phap* [A History of the Eighty-Year Struggle against the French], vol. 2 (Hanoi: Van Su Dia, 1958), p. 71.

assist the ICP in its struggle for power. During its meeting in November 1939, the party Central Committee had set the stage by calling for an armed uprising to seize power and restore national independence. As we have seen, party operatives along the Sino-Vietnamese border had already initiated steps to create a liberated area in the mountains of northern Vietnam—known in Vietnamese as the Viet Bac, or "northern Viet"—as a base of operations against the French. At the same time, a number of leading party members had begun to discuss the tactics that should be applied in the coming struggle for independence. One such was the promising young party activist Vo Nguyen Giap. Born to a scholar-gentry family in northern Vietnam in 1908, Giap had been educated at the University of Hanoi and joined the party during the mid-1930s while employed as a history teacher at a lycée in Hanoi. Like several of his colleagues, Giap had read Mao Zedong's works on the use of guerrilla tactics against Japanese occupation forces in China, and he became convinced of the relevance of such a "people's war" approach in Vietnam.

Nguyen Ai Quoc had been an advocate of guerilla warfare since the 1920s, when he had observed CCP units using such tactics against the Chinese warlords. After his return to China in 1938, he had ample opportunity to assess Mao Zedong's strategy against the Japanese, and later translated a number of Chinese tracts on guerilla tactics into Vietnamese for use in training Vietminh cadres. Mao Zedong's use of liberated areas as a base of operations to build up the strength of insurgent forces also caught his attention, and he undoubtedly noted its potential relevance to conditions in Vietnam.[24]

As important to Nguyen Ai Quoc as the kind of strategy to adopt was the question of when to put it into effect. Vietnam was a small country occupied by two powerful enemies. It did not possess the advantage of size that had enabled the Chinese Communists to set up a large base area in northern China and then maintain it for years against a powerful adversary. A similar area inside Vietnam would be too exposed to military attacks either by the Japanese or by the French, and could therefore only be established during the final stage of the struggle. At the same time, a premature uprising

---

[24] Ho Chi Minh, "Cach danh du kich" [Tactics of guerrilla warfare], *Toan Tap*, vol. 3, pp. 163–209.

could lead to severe repression by the enemy, which could destroy the movement just as the promise of national liberation had grown bright. Nguyen Ai Quoc frequently cautioned his headstrong colleagues against excessive haste and argued that the best time to strike would be at the point when Japan was on the verge of defeat by the Allied powers. In the meantime, the party could strengthen its political base by building a Vietminh network throughout the country while simultaneously creating armed units that, in due time, would launch local insurrections in preparation for the final seizure of power in the major cities. Thus appeared an element in Vietnamese Communist strategic thinking that played a key role in revolutionary planning down to the final uprising in Saigon in 1975—the concept of *thoi co*, seizing the right opportunity.

In the months following the Pac Bo meeting, the party began to form guerrilla detachments in the mountains of northern Vietnam. Much of the population in the region of the Viet Bac was composed of mountain peoples who had always resented efforts by the lowland Vietnamese to dominate them. By displaying a sensitive concern for the local customs and traditions of the indigenous people, the Vietminh were able to win support in many minority regions. A number of leading members of the movement were of minority extraction. Others married women of minority extraction and adopted the dress and customs of the local population.

Nguyen Ai Quoc returned to China to set up training camps for his followers and pull together the fragile alliance between the Vietminh and other anti-Japanese groups operating in the area. It was on one of those visits that he was arrested by local Chinese authorities and placed in prison once more. For several months he was out of contact with party leadership, and reports reached Vietnam that he had died in captivity. But he was able to inform his closest colleagues that he was still alive by means of secret letters written with disappearing ink.

In August 1943, Nguyen Ai Quoc was released from captivity by order of the Chinese commander Zhang Fakui. The circumstances of his release have always been somewhat mysterious, but there is some evidence that General Zhang, although fully aware of Nguyen Ai Quoc's communist affiliation, hoped to take advantage of his popular appeal in the Vietnamese exile community to mobilize the Vietnamese against the Japanese occupation forces in Indochina. Shortly after his release, Nguyen Ai Quoc resumed his efforts to form a broad united front to drive the Japanese and French from

Indochina. He now began increasingly to use a name that later became familiar to the entire world: Ho Chi Minh.[25]

A key element in Ho Chi Minh's evolving strategy was to win the support and recognition of the Allied powers for his movement when the war came to an end. A directive issued to all units two weeks after the Japanese attack on Pearl Harbor declared that Vietminh policy would be to cooperate with China and to establish relations with Great Britain and the United States. If the latter agreed to assist the revolution in Indochina, the directive declared, the Vietminh front should be willing to offer them concessions and unite with them on a conditional basis. If the Allies decided to assist in the return of the French, the Vietminh should be prepared to fight alone.[26]

It was in that spirit that in 1943 Ho Chi Minh first initiated contacts with U.S. military intelligence units in southern China. He offered the assistance of his own organization in providing intelligence information on Japanese troop movements in Indochina, as well as helping to rescue Allied fliers shot down during missions over the area. In letters written to President Franklin D. Roosevelt, Ho requested in return U.S. recognition of the Vietminh as the legitimate representative of the Vietnamese people. American officials forwarded his letters to Washington without comment.

In Washington, U.S. intelligence analysts were initially somewhat confused about the plethora of Vietnamese antifascist and anticolonial organizations operating in southern China. That, of course, accorded with Ho Chi Minh's strategy. Although he was hopeful that "progressive forces" in the United States would be sympathetic to Vietnamese demands for independence, he was well aware that the United States was a capitalist country and hoped to avoid unnecessarily alienating the Roosevelt administration in the delicate period ahead.

Ho Chi Minh's shell-game tactics had only limited success, for

---

[25] Nguyen Ai Quoc had apparently first used the name Ho Chi Minh to establish an alias during his trips across the Sino-Vietnamese border prior to his arrest. According to Zhang Fakui, he was identified by that name while he was in prison in China. Zhang contends that he knew Ho Chi Minh was a Communist, but released him because he felt he could be useful in building up an anti-Japanese organization of Vietnamese exiles living in south China. See Zhang Fakui's oral interview held in the Columbia University Library.

[26] "Cuoc chien tranh Thai binh duong va trach niem cua kip cua Dang" [The Pacific war and the tasks of the party], in *Van Kien Dang*, vol. 3, pp. 292–293.

knowledgeable U.S. observers were well aware that the mysterious Ho Chi Minh was in fact none other than the veteran revolutionary Nguyen Ai Quoc. Whether that had any effect on U.S. policy is not clear. President Roosevelt was sympathetic to the desire of the Vietnamese people for independence and had frequently expressed his opposition to the restoration of French colonial rule in Indochina. But both the British and the French had resisted FDR's plans to set up trusteeships in former colonies, and by early 1945 Roosevelt had begun to weaken in his resolve. In any event, he had no intention of becoming politically involved in the region until the end of the Pacific war. Ho Chi Minh's letters to the White House were therefore not answered. But Ho did succeed in establishing a cooperative arrangement with local U.S. intelligence units in China and the Vietminh received a limited number of weapons and communications equipment for their clandestine operations inside Vietnam. Major Archimedes Patti of the Office of Strategic Services (OSS, the predecessor of the CIA) was assigned as liaison to the Vietminh forces as the war came to an end. He and other U.S. officers helped to train a small Vietminh military force, known as "armed propaganda detachments" and placed under the command of Vo Nguyen Giap.[27]

THE AUGUST REVOLUTION

As the final months of the war gradually unfolded, events worked both in favor of and against the Vietminh. By early 1945, increasing numbers of French civilian and military personnel in Indochina were beginning to sympathize with Colonel Charles de Gaulle's Free French movement, which had just dispatched an official to southern China to represent its interests in the area. In March, the Japanese responded by abruptly abolishing the Vichy French colonial administration in Indochina and offering to restore independence to Vietnam under the puppet emperor Bao Dai. Despite the fact that the potential authority of his new government would be limited in key respects, and would not extend to Cochin China (Japanese officials

---

[27] For indications that U.S. analysts were aware that Nguyen Ai Quoc and Ho Chi Minh were the same person and that the Vietminh Front was dominated by the ICP, see Memo FE (Ballantine) to WE/EUR, dated August 23, 1945, in the *U.S. State Department Central Files.* Hereafter *Central Files.*

explained that Tokyo needed to maintain its control over the French colony for strategical reasons), Bao Dai accepted the offer. Some French civilian and military officials were able to escape abroad to serve with the Free French. The remainder were placed in detention.[28]

The abolition of the remnants of French colonial authority by Japan operated to the advantage of the Vietminh, since Japanese administrative control in Indochina was essentially limited to urban areas, while the French presence in the countryside quickly evaporated. This left a political and military vacuum which Ho Chi Minh's forces were quick to fill. Shortly after the Japanese coup d'état, key ICP leaders met under the direction of General Secretary Truong Chinh to make preparations for a general uprising designed to seize power at the end of the Pacific war. Their efforts to broaden the support for the movement were undoubtedly assisted by a widespread famine, which led to the death by starvation of thousands of Vietnamese in rural areas throughout the northern and central parts of the country. The original cause of the famine was bad weather, but its effects were exacerbated by the refusal of Japanese authorities to release grain stocks to the local population. During the next several months, Vietminh forces operating in the mountains surrounding the Red River delta began to intensify their efforts to seize control over rural areas and recruit followers from villages in regions under their control. Vo Nguyen Giap's tiny elite forces were now combined with other units in the country into a new Vietnamese Liberation Army (Viet Nam Giai Phong Quan).

In Cochin China, far removed from Vietminh headquarters in the mountains north of Hanoi, party operatives were forced to adopt a more political approach. The main base of Vietminh power was the Vanguard Youth (Thanh Nien Tien Phong), a broad popular organization with over 200,000 members that had been established under Japanese sponsorship but was actually under the secret guidance of the ICP through the clandestine communist Pham Ngoc Thach.

In one respect, world events operated to the disadvantage of the movement. In anticipation of an Allied invasion of Indochina during the final weeks of the war, Ho Chi Minh readied his forces to seize

---

[28] Bao Dai explained his decision to accept the Japanese offer in his *Dragon d'Annam* (Paris: Plon, 1980), pp. 103–104.

The First Armed Propaganda Brigades. Vo Nguyen Giap is at the left.

power in areas occupied by the Allies and then to seek recognition from them as the true representative of the Vietnamese people.[29] Unfortunately, the invasion never took place, as Allied forces by-passed the Southeast Asian mainland and struck directly across the Pacific toward the Japanese home islands. The Vietminh would be compelled to face the French alone.

The end of the war came with breathtaking swiftness. The first atomic bomb was dropped on Hiroshima on August 6. Two days later, by prearrangement with the Allies, the USSR declared war on Japan, while Soviet forces invaded Manchuria. The following day, a second atom bomb was dropped on the southern Japanese city of

[29] "Cuoc chien tranh . . . ," p. 292.

The Conference Hall at Tan Trao, where the Vietminh Front issued its call for revolution in August 1945.

Nagasaki. On August 14, the imperial government accepted Allied peace terms. The Pacific war was finally over.

The sudden collapse of Japan undoubtedly caught Ho Chi Minh and his colleagues by surprise. The anticipated Allied attack on Indochina had never taken place. Instead, Allied leaders meeting at Potsdam in late July agreed that Indochina would be occupied by British and Nationalist Chinese expeditionary forces: the British to the south of the sixteenth parallel, the Chinese to the north. Their task would be twofold—to accept the surrender of Japanese military forces and to maintain law and order until a postwar administration in the area had been secured.

To their good fortune, ICP leaders were holding a major strategy session at Tan Trao, a small village in the mountains north of Hanoi, just when the news of the Japanese surrender reached Indochina. That meeting was to be followed by a conference of Vietminh representatives from all over the country. Confronted with this new situation, the Central Committee called for an immediate insurrection of all Vietminh forces throughout the country to fill the vacuum caused by the end of the war and bring into being an independent republic under the leadership of the Vietminh Front. Using the name Nguyen Ai Quoc for the last time, Ho Chi Minh issued a public appeal for a general uprising to the Vietnamese people.

Dear fellow countrymen! The decisive hour has struck for the destiny of our people. Let all of us stand up and rely on our own strength to free ourselves. Many oppressed peoples the world over are vying with each other in wresting back independence. We should not lag behind.

Forward! Forward! Under the banner of the Viet Minh, let us valiantly march forward![30]

During the next few days, Vietminh forces seized power in villages and towns throughout the northern and central provinces of the country. In most cases, the insurgents met with little or no resistance, and local authorities simply handed over the seal of office on the demand of resistance leaders. In Hanoi, however, the situation was somewhat more complicated. A provisional government loyal to Emperor Bao Dai had been formed a few days before the Japanese surrender; it hoped to make the case with the Allies for recognition as the legitimate government of the country. To compel this government to resign, Vietminh cadres disrupted government-sponsored meetings held in the baroque National Theater in downtown Hanoi, while demanding a transfer of power to the Vietminh Front as the representative of the victorious Allies. On August 18, militia units from neighboring villages marched into the center of the city and joined forces with urban shock troops under the command of the ICP. In a bloodless coup they seized control of government offices from Japanese authorities.

It remained to remove the last tattered remnants of legitimacy from the old regime. In late August, a Vietminh delegation arrived in the imperial capital of Hue to demand the abdication of Emperor Bao Dai in favor of the new republic. Bao Dai was reluctant to accede but, according to one Vietminh source, he was informed bluntly that he could either lose his throne or lose his head. Bao Dai stepped out of the imperial palace and formally announced his abdication.[31]

On September 2, leading members of the new Provisional Republic of Vietnam gathered in Ba Dinh Square, a spacious wooded park near the governor general's palace in Hanoi. On a platform erected for the occasion and dressed in a simple khaki uniform, his feet shod in rubber thongs made from bicycle tires, President Ho Chi Minh presented a short speech to the thousands of people gath-

[30] For an English-language version of the call for the general uprising, see *Ho Chi Minh: Selected Writings*, p. 50.

[31] Bao Dai's version of the event is in *Dragon d'Annam*, pp. 120–123.

Ho Chi Minh, on the raised platform in the background, declares Vietnamese independence at Ba Dinh Square in early September 1945.

ered in the square. To the few Americans in the audience, his opening words were startling.

> "All men are created equal. They are endowed by their Creator with certain unalienable Rights; among these are Life, Liberty, and the pursuit of Happiness." This immortal statement appeared in the Declaration of Independence of the United States of America in 1776. In a broader sense, it means: All the peoples on the earth are equal from birth, all the peoples have a right to live and to be happy and free.

These, Ho announced, are "undeniable truths" and have been accepted as such by the French people themselves.

> Yet for eighty years, the French government has abused them by violating our Fatherland and oppressing our fellow citizens. Today we are determined to oppose the wicked schemes of the French imperialists, and we call upon the victorious Allies to recognize our freedom and independence. Vietnam has the right to enjoy freedom and independence and in fact has become a free and independent country. The entire Vietnamese people are determined to mobilize all their physical and mental strength, to sacrifice their lives and property in order to safeguard their freedom and independence.[32]

[32] For an English-language version of the speech, see *Ho Chi Minh: Selected Writings*, pp. 53–56.

The Vietminh had struck with lightning swiftness to take advantage of the disarray of the Japanese and the absence of the French. But their triumph was only a limited one. In Cochin China, the party apparatus had been virtually destroyed by the French after the abortive revolt in the fall of 1940 and had staged only a partial recovery during the war years. While Pham Ngoc Thach's Vanguard Youth provided the Vietminh Front with a firm political base of operations, competition from other nationalist parties was strong. The Vietminh also encountered problems in winning support from adherents of two prominent religious sects, the Cao Dai and the Hoa Hao, that had won popularity in various parts of Cochin China since the prewar period. The Cao Dai (meaning "high tower"), a syncretic faith containing elements of several major religions, had originated in the 1920s among civil servants in Saigon and later spread to rural areas near the Cambodian border. The Hoa Hao was an offshoot of Buddhism and the brainchild of the "mad monk" Huynh Phu So, who founded the new faith in the late 1930s in the lower reaches of the Mekong River delta. Both sects flourished in the frontier village environment of colonial Cochin China, while its leaders staunchly resisted all forms of external domination, whether by the French or by the Vietminh.

To maximize their influence in the region, Vietminh operatives in Cochin China joined forces with anti-French groups to form a provisional Committee of the South (Uy Ban Nam Bo) to negotiate with the British expeditionary forces on a transfer of power to local authority. But the commander of the arriving British troops, General Douglas Gracey, interpreted his instructions as calling upon him to return power to the French. Gracey ignored the demands made by the Committee of the South, and after bloody riots broke out in Saigon between Vietnamese and European residents, his expeditionary forces, beefed up by French troops just released from Japanese prisons, drove Vietnamese resistance forces out of Saigon. The Committee of the South established a new headquarters in the countryside and began to wage a guerrilla struggle against the French. Rivalry with the religious sects plagued Vietminh efforts in rural areas, a problem that was compounded when Huynh Phu So was assassinated, apparently at the hands of Vietminh operatives.

In the meantime, the French presence was augmented by the arrival of new units beginning in October, while Ho Chi Minh's new government in Hanoi provided assistance to the insurrection by infiltrating military units from the north. By the end of the year, Vietnam was divided into a communist north and a noncommunist south, with French forces trying to restore control over all of Indochina. It was an eerie preview of the war to come.[33]

THE MANDATE OF HEAVEN

To Ho Chi Minh and his colleagues, the August Revolution (as their sudden ascent to power is now described in official histories of the party) confirmed their conviction that the Vietminh Front had been accepted by the majority of the Vietnamese people as the legitimate representative of their national aspirations. The seizure of power in Hanoi was legitimized by the abdication of the emperor in Hue to the new representatives of the people. In the words of one sympathetic French historian, the Vietminh had earned the Mandate of Heaven, the traditional Confucian concept which served to legitimize imperial rule over Vietnamese society. It now remained only to obtain the consent of the Allied powers.[34]

To many outside observers, however, the issue was not quite so clear-cut. The Vietminh victory was a triumph in a vacuum, achieved in the chaotic conditions at the end of the war. The Vietminh Front claimed to represent all patriotic forces in the country, yet many of the nationalist parties operating in southern China during the war had refused to cooperate with the Vietminh and were about to arrive with Chinese occupation forces to stake their own claim to power. Moreover, the Vietminh had yet to prove their case by winning recognition from the Allies and defeating the French. Appeals by Ho Chi Minh to solicit recognition from the leading Allied powers remained unanswered.

In addition, some might point out, it was a triumph under false

---

[33] The attitude of the British government in these affairs has never been totally revealed. Some sources have charged that the British commander of the Southeast Asia Command (SEAC) in Ceylon, Lord Louis Mountbatten, had ordered Gracey to restore French colonial authority. One British Embassy officer remarked to U.S. officials at the time that London hoped for negotiations between the French and moderate Vietnamese elements.

[34] That French historian was Paul Mus. For a discussion, see John T. McAlister Jr. and Paul Mus, *The Vietnamese and Their Revolution* (New York: Harper & Row, 1970), pp. 17–18.

pretenses. The program that had been announced by the Vietminh congress in mid-August had called for moderate political and economic policies that could appeal to a wide constituency. Yet party documents make it clear that this was meant to be only a transitional stage until such time as the ICP leadership decided to embark on the next phase of socialist transformation. Although many Vietnamese might be expected to approve of the published program, the party had not divulged its full intentions to the people.[35]

Still, the Vietminh Front had made a case that it was the best organized movement in Vietnam and would do its utmost to meet the immediate needs of the people. It moved swiftly to deal with the widespread famine that still stalked the land since the previous winter. It had won approval from the masses in the northern and central provinces on the widespread assumption that it had the support of the Allies, an impression that Ho Chi Minh assiduously sought to foster. In the meantime, the party's Vietnamese rivals, as always, were divided and appeared to lack a concrete plan to deal with the challenges of the moment. The French had been discredited by their past performance and their failure to protect the area from Japanese conquest. If any organization appeared to possess the right to represent the Vietnamese people in the postwar era, it was the new government proclaimed by the mysterious figure named Ho Chi Minh in Ba Dinh Square.

[35] For the Front's new domestic program, see King C. Chen, *Vietnam and China, 1938–1954* (Princeton: Princeton University Press, 1969).

CHAPTER 2

The War of Resistance against the French

Ho Chi Minh's decision to seize power in Hanoi prior to the return of the French was based on the expectation that the victorious Allied powers, and especially the United States and the Soviet Union, would prevent the restoration of French colonial rule in Indochina. But for once, the veteran revolutionary had miscalculated: none of the Allied leaders replied to his appeals, and none stepped forward to prevent the return of the French. In the early fall, Washington announced that it had no objection to the restoration of French sovereignty in Indochina so long as the French government undertook to respect and carry out the provisions of the UN Charter regarding dependent territories. Moscow made no comment.

What had happened to dash Ho's hopes? Some historians have said that President Truman was more afraid of the expansion of communism than his predecessor, and in the long view, that contention is undoubtedly correct. Roosevelt was convinced that the evil of colonialism was one of the underlying causes of the war in the Pacific, and he had frequently remarked that after the restoration of peace, the peoples of Indochina should be placed under an international trusteeship until such time as they were prepared to become fully independent. Under pressure from the British and the French, as well as from European specialists in the State Department, he had weakened in his opposition to the return of the French, and at the Yalta Conference in February 1945 he had grudgingly agreed that colonial territories should be placed under UN trusteeship only at the voluntary decision of the colonial power that had controlled the country prior to World War II. But he confided to intimates that he would insist that the French promise ultimate independence for the peoples of Indochina. His successor, lacking FDR's visceral dislike of European colonialism and undoubtedly more concerned about the deterioration in U.S.-Soviet relations, tacitly abandoned Roosevelt's insistence on eventual independence in return for a pledge that the French would grant increased political freedoms to the Indochinese peoples within the framework of General de Gaulle's proposed French Union.

When the French resorted to force in Cochin China in the fall of 1945, however, Asian specialists in the State Department became concerned that such actions could exacerbate the situation and place the United States on the wrong side of history. They proposed that additional French troops not be sent to Indochina pending the formation of an independent commission to evaluate the situation. But European specialists, pointing to the growing influence of the French Communist Party, were able to head off the proposal. In the words of one senior State Department official, "the setting up of an international commission can only lead to one result—the eventual ejection of the French from Indochina. This would be bad for the French and the West and generally bad for the Indo-Chinese themselves." At the insistence of the Office of European Affairs, letters from Ho Chi Minh were not forwarded to the White House.[1]

Ironically, it seems probable that similar motivations were behind Moscow's failure to respond to Ho Chi Minh's appeal for support. Southeast Asia was low on the Kremlin's list of foreign policy priorities, while the appearance of a government dominated by the PCF in Paris would seriously undermine any plan by the United States to organize an anticommunist alliance among the nations of Western Europe. Moreover, Soviet leader Joseph Stalin had long harbored suspicions of Ho Chi Minh for his unorthodox views on Marxist-Leninist doctrine, and had no particular desire to see the rise of an independent-minded Vietminh government in Southeast Asia.

FORGING A NEW REPUBLIC

In the meantime, the new government in Hanoi faced an intimidating challenge in consolidating its own authority. The country suffered from severe economic problems. The famine that had struck

---

[1] A memo to this effect can be found in the State Department Central Files. For the quote, see *Central Files*, Memo, Bonbright to Matthews (EUR), October 2, 1945.

during the winter of 1944–1945 had cost the lives of an estimated 1 million Vietnamese. Foreign observers reported that in some regions of the country, thousands of dead bodies lay unattended by the roadside. Diplomatic sources in Hanoi estimated that an additional 1 million people were likely to die within the next few months. To make the problem worse, the severely underdeveloped Vietnamese economy lacked both capital and technology.

It soon became clear that Ho Chi Minh would attempt to deal with his problems by adopting a moderate stance in both foreign and domestic affairs. In the weeks following the declaration of independence in early September, the new government moved quickly to broaden its base of support throughout the political spectrum. It announced its intention to abolish the head tax and allow the free entry of rice from the southern provinces into the north. It seized the property of those individuals identified as imperialists or collaborators with the colonial government, but it confirmed the concept of private property and made no reference to the ultimate creation of a communist society.

The new government's political message was similarly tailored to appeal to a broad audience. It announced that general elections based on universal suffrage would be held to elect a National Assembly (Quoc Hoi), which would be the supreme political body representing the sovereign will of the Vietnamese people. To reassure moderate elements, official sources declared that the new government, now formally known as the Democratic Republic of Vietnam, or DRV, would be comprised not solely of workers and peasants (the program adopted during the sectarian period in the early 1930s) but of a broad alliance of all patriotic classes in the country, including progressive elements from the bourgeoisie and the landed gentry.[2]

The new government faced equally crucial challenges in foreign affairs. There were two immediate problems: how to deal with the presence of Chinese occupation forces north of the 16th parallel, and how to respond to the French conquest of the south. The first problem was complicated by the fact that some senior officers in the Chinese military command had close relations with Vietnamese na-

---

[2] "Mat tran cong nong hay mat tran dan toc thong nhat," *Cuu Quoc* [National Salvation], September 21, 1945. At that time, the newspaper *Cuu Quoc* was the official mouthpiece of the party.

tionalists, many of whom had spent the war in China and were now returning to Vietnam in the company of Chinese troops. In the weeks after their arrival, relations between the provisional government and senior Chinese military commanders were tense. In a clear effort to placate the Chinese, Ho Chi Minh agreed in November to guarantee a minimum of seventy seats in the National Assembly to members of political parties not affiliated with the Vietminh, regardless of the outcome of the elections. That same month, in a ploy to reduce suspicions among moderates and foreign observers as to the orientation of the ICP, the party formally announced its dissolution as a political organization and reformation in less threatening form as a "Marxist study group." Official histories of the party later conceded that the ICP continued to exist in clandestine form, but the move may have briefly allayed suspicions among its rivals, and it certainly served to realize a fragile accommodation with the Chinese high command.[3]

As to the second problem, the French had refused to recognize the new government in Hanoi but had agreed to hold discussions on a peaceful resolution of the dispute. Talks between Ho Chi Minh and French representative Jean Sainteny opened in the autumn of 1945. They were complicated by the Vietminh-sponsored resistance movement that was still underway in Cochin China. Ho Chi Minh was under intense pressure from militant elements within his own government to deal with the issue and could hardly afford to ignore the plight of his compatriots in the south. On the other hand, open support for the insurgency could lead to bitter hostilities between the French and the DRV and thus imperil the delicate negotiations underway in Hanoi. For the moment, Ho Chi Minh counseled his colleagues to be patient, while advising Vietminh leaders in the south to adopt guerrilla tactics until he could find other ways to bring the conflict to an end.[4]

Initially, Ho Chi Minh may have hoped for U.S. assistance in mediating the Franco-Vietminh conflict in the south. If so, he was

[3] For a reference to the party retreating into secrecy, see *Lich Su Dang Cong San Viet Nam* [A History of the Vietnamese Communist Party), vol. 1 (Hanoi: Su That, 1984), p. 475.
[4] See "Truong ky khang chien" [Protracted war], *Cuu Quoc*, September 10, 1945, and October 10, 1945.

disappointed. Washington expressed irritation over the failure of the French to take measures to reduce tensions in the area, but it took no action to pressure Paris to change its policies. In early March, after intense and lengthy negotiations, Ho reached a preliminary accord with Sainteny. The French agreed to recognize the new government of Vietnam as a "free state," with its own army, parliament, and finances. In return, Vietnam granted the French the right to maintain a cultural and economic presence in the north and to station 15,000 troops there to protect French interests in the area.

The most difficult problem in the negotiations was the status of Cochin China. The southern provinces, including the commercial metropolis of Saigon, had been ceded to the French as a colony in perpetuity. But Ho Chi Minh insisted on the unity of the three regions as a matter of principle and stated that no agreement could be reached without an understanding from the French on the status of Cochin China as an integral part of Vietnamese territory. In the end, he and Sainteny reached a compromise: a plebiscite would be held in all three regions to determine whether the population wished to affiliate with the new free state or make a separate arrangement with France.[5]

The Ho-Sainteny Agreement was not universally popular among the Vietnamese, and some militant elements criticized Ho Chi Minh for caving in to the French on key points related to Vietnamese sovereignty. But eventually he was able to persuade his party to accept the need for compromise, and the National Assembly, which had been elected in January, approved the agreement. It now remained to finalize the results in peace talks, scheduled to be held in France during the summer.

THE DRIFT TO WAR

From the start, the negotiations encountered difficulties. During talks held in the mountain resort of Dalat in April, French and Vietnamese representatives disagreed on several key issues. But the heart of the problem was the future of Cochin China, where French

---

[5] For a cable from the U.S. mission in Indochina reporting the Ho-Sainteny agreement, see *Central Files*, Telegram, Saigon to Department of State, March 7, 1946.

colonial interests, supported by collaborator elements among affluent sectors of the Vietnamese bourgeoisie, conspired to evade the
provisions of the treaty calling for a plebiscite to ascertain the wishes
of the people regarding their future. Georges Thierry d'Argenlieu,
a retired admiral and former Jesuit, was the newly appointed French
high commissioner (the new title for the old position of governor
general). He was a staunch defender of the colonial enterprise and
firmly resisted any efforts to detach the area from French control.
Neutral observers predicted that any plebiscite on the issue would
be close.

Additional problems arose during formal negotiations that began at the palace of Fontainebleau, south of Paris, in the early summer. Although he was not an official member of the Vietnamese
delegation, Ho Chi Minh traveled to France to attend the conference
as a private observer, clearly hoping to use his contacts with leading
members of leftist parties in Paris as a means of achieving a satisfactory settlement. But it soon became apparent that an agreement
based on the Ho-Sainteny talks was no longer possible. In the interim
since the signing of the preliminary agreement in March, a new
government had been elected in Paris which was less inclined to
compromise on the colonial issue. French delegates at the conference
thus made it clear that the provisions in the March agreement calling
for autonomy and the possible unification of the three regions was
a dead issue. That viewpoint was underscored in June, when High
Commissioner d'Argenlieu convened a second conference at Dalat,
in the central highlands of southern Vietnam. The conference was
attended by conservative forces in Cochin China who rejected unity
with the projected free state in the north and promptly voted to
create a separate Cochin Chinese Republic that would make its own
arrangements with the French.

Outraged by French duplicity, the Vietnamese delegation left
the conference in protest, and the talks were adjourned. But Ho Chi
Minh was all too aware of the weakness of his government and
armed forces and remained in Paris for several weeks in order to
avoid a total breakdown of the talks. In visits to the American Embassy, Ho appealed for Washington's assistance in persuading the
French to moderate their stand, but U.S. Ambassador Jefferson Caffery, although mildly sympathetic, was noncommittal, and Washington made no effort to intervene. In September, Ho Chi Minh finally
accepted a modus vivendi, whereby the two sides agreed to avoid

armed conflict while attempting to return to negotiations at the beginning of the new year.[6]

After signing the temporary agreement, Ho Chi Minh returned to Vietnam. But for unexplained reasons, he chose to travel by sea and did not arrive in Hanoi until several weeks after his departure. Some have speculated that Ho's motive was to allow passions to cool in Hanoi, where anger had erupted at his willingness to sign a compromise agreement. Ho also discovered that during his absence from Vietnam, relations between the Vietminh and the various non-Communist factions, notably the VNQDD and the Dong Minh Hoi (Vietnamese Revolutionary League, or VRL, which had been formed with the support of Zhang Fakui in south China in 1943), had rapidly deteriorated. In midsummer, clashes between the two sides took place repeatedly, and the government eventually cracked down on the activities of rival party organizations, arresting some and inducing many others to flee to China.

The breakdown of relations between the Vietminh and their rivals led to many charges and countercharges that have continued to this day, and the truth of the matter may never be divulged. But reports by contemporary observers suggest that the responsibility for the rupture lay on both sides. Leading nationalist elements connected with the VNQDD and the VRL may have deliberately attempted to provoke the government in order to create problems. But the tension may have been exacerbated by Ho Chi Minh's replacement, Vo Nguyen Giap, the minister of the interior for the DRV and a fiery militant who lacked Ho Chi Minh's delicate touch in politics.[7]

After his return to Hanoi, Ho Chi Minh attempted to soothe ruptured feelings and was apparently able to obtain general support from within his own party for his tactics. But with the departure of many non-Communist nationalist leaders, the previously broad base of the government had been badly eroded. Perhaps in tacit recog-

---

[6] Ambassador Caffery reported that Ho Chi Minh had behaved in a dignified and "tactful" way at the conference. See *Central Files,* Cable, Paris to Department of State, September 16, 1946. The lack of action in Washington provoked the Office of Southeast Asian Affairs to suggest that the State Department should press the French on the need to abide by the spirit of the March 6 convention. See Office Memo, Moffat to John Carter Vincent, August 19, 1946.

[7] Some French sources in Hanoi blamed the VNQDD for the dispute. See *Central Files,* Telegram, Hanoi to Secretary of State, June 16, 1946.

nition of this fact, Ho reorganized the cabinet, which was now composed almost exclusively of members of the Vietminh and two recently created puppet organizations, the Democratic and the Socialist parties. French intelligence sources reported that Ho Chi Minh was now increasingly under the domination of militant elements who had no desire to compromise with the French and argued that war was the only solution.[8]

Having achieved at least a fragile consensus among his colleagues on the desirability of avoiding a full-scale war, during the fall of 1946 Ho Chi Minh continued his maneuvers to prevent a breakdown in relations with the French. But the task became increasingly difficult, as armed clashes between the two sides were now taking place with increasing frequency. In late November the French tried to seize control of Haiphong harbor, the port that serviced the needs of the Red River delta, in order to prevent the Vietnamese from importing weapons from China. When clashes broke out, French naval vessels shelled the native quarter of the city, killing thousands of civilians.

Concerned at the drift toward war, the Truman administration sent Abbot Low Moffat, an Asian specialist in the State Department, to speak with Ho Chi Minh in Hanoi and evaluate the allegedly communist character of the government. Intelligence sources were reporting that the DRV was in direct contact with Moscow and CCP headquarters in north China, and that Soviet and Chinese advisers were training the Vietminh armed forces. The U.S. consul in Saigon warned Washington that if the Vietminh drove the French out of Cochin China, Cambodia and Laos would be under direct threat from the menace of international communism. It was perhaps the first reference to what would later be popularly called the domino theory.[9]

Ho Chi Minh complained to Moffat of French provocations and openly asked for U.S. assistance to prevent Vietnamese militants

---

[8] French sources in Hanoi now began to speculate on the existence of moderate and radical factions within the DRV regime. Some contended that against his will, Ho Chi Minh was dominated by hard-liners. A U.S. diplomatic representative reported rumors of a split within the ICP in October. Such a split has never been confirmed. See *Central Files*, Saigon 409 to Washington, October 18, 1946. For additional comments, see Phillipe Devillers, *Histoire du Vietnam de 1940 à 1952* (Paris: Editions du Seuil, 1952), *passim*.

[9] *Central Files*, Telegram, Saigon (Reed) to Department of State, November 7, 1946.

from taking over his government. He even offered to provide the harbor of Cam Ranh Bay, on the coast of central Vietnam, to the United States as a naval facility. Moffat was noncommittal and reported the conversation to Washington, adding that Ho Chi Minh was increasingly being pressured by leftist members of the Vietminh movement.[10]

Was Ho Chi Minh seriously hoping to avoid war with the French, or were his activities simply a ruse to delay the outbreak of hostilities and buy time to prepare for the inevitable confrontation? Of course, the Hanoi government had much to gain from delaying the breakdown of negotiations, and during the fall of 1946, the DRV feverishly attempted to build up its armed strength to prepare for war. Yet Ho also had good reasons to look for a peaceful solution to the dispute. In the first place, his government could hope for only limited assistance from external sources, and as Moffat reported to Washington, Ho must have felt "desperately alone." The Soviet Union was clearly focusing its own attention on the fragile political situation in Paris; it hoped to avoid any eventuality which could hinder the formation of a new French government dominated by the PCF. As for the Chinese Communists, Hanoi's other potential source of assistance, they were now preoccupied with their own civil war with the Nationalist government of Chiang Kai-shek. Ho Chi Minh's best hope was that political conditions in France would eventually lead to the formation of a leftist government in Paris that would offer better terms to the Vietnamese. For the moment, that possibility was worth waiting for.

During the fall, however, increasingly aggressive actions by the French military, culminating in the Haiphong incident in late November, may have convinced Ho and his colleagues that a military showdown could not be avoided. At the end of the month, Ho ordered Vo Nguyen Giap to begin preparations for the withdrawal of key government and economic facilities to Tan Trao, the village in the mountains north of Hanoi from which he had issued his appeal for a national insurrection over a year ago.

But Ho was still not ready to accept the inevitability of war. In early December, a new French government under Socialist prime minister Léon Blum was elected to power in Paris. Blum was an

---

[10] Moffat's report is in *Central Files*, Saigon (Moffat) to Washington, December 12, 1946.

advocate of a peaceful solution to the Indochina crisis and immediately announced that a commission would be sent to Hanoi to
seek a settlement of the dispute. On December 15, as tensions in
Hanoi increased, Ho sent a last-minute appeal to Paris, but the
message was delayed in transit, possibly by deliberate action in
Saigon. On December 19, Vietminh units attacked French installations and residential neighborhoods throughout the city, while regular troops retreated to previously prepared positions in the mountains surrounding the Red River delta. Shortly after, Ho's
last-minute appeal arrived in Paris.

Why the Vietminh government launched its attack just when a
new, more sympathetic government had come into office in Paris is
a question that has never been satisfactorily answered. Some historians have speculated that bellicose elements in Ho's government
deliberately provoked armed clashes with the French and thus
forced his hand. French sources in Hanoi reported at the time that
Ho was opposed to war but had lost control over his party to a
militant faction led by Vo Nguyen Giap. There were even rumors
of a coup to remove him from power. Without further evidence, all
such hypotheses must remain speculative.[11]

PEOPLE'S WAR

The outbreak of war in December 1946 faced the Vietminh with
some excruciating decisions. The August Revolution had been an
essentially nonviolent affair, combining popular demonstrations in
the cities with a bloodless seizure of power in rural areas. Such a
strategy had been appropriate at a time when forces hostile to the
revolution were in a state of disarray. But in the months that followed the end of the Pacific war, the French had regrouped and
were now militarily superior in both numbers and firepower to the
Vietminh. While there were unverified reports of the presence of
Soviet or Chinese advisers with Vietnamese units, Ho's government,
for the moment at least, would have to fight alone.

[11] For an interesting analysis of possible reasons for the attack in Hanoi, see Stein
Tonnesson, 1946: Déclenchement de la guerre de l'Indochine (Paris: l'Harmattan, 1987).
Also see Central Files, Memorandum of Conversation with Emperor Bao Dai (Hanoi),
January 27, 1950.

The Vietminh clearly required a strategy appropriate to the new situation. They found their answer in the Chinese strategy of people's war. Mao Zedong had formulated the concept after the famous Shanghai Massacre of April 1927 had brought an end to the party's united front with Chiang Kai-shek's Nationalist Party. Mao was convinced that the Chinese revoluton had to be waged not according to the Bolshevik model of an urban insurrection based on the power of the proletariat but in the countryside, where restive peasants, lacking the acquisitive instincts of their European counterparts, could be mobilized to provide active support to the forces of social revolution. Mao's strategy called for a three-stage process, beginning with the creation of liberated base areas in inaccessible regions of the country, leading to a second stage of equilibrium when revolutionary units began engaging in selective attacks on enemy installations, and culminating in a general offensive to seize power in the major cities. That strategy was already being applied by the CCP in the civil war that had just broken out in China.[12]

In late December, three days after the outbreak of the Franco-Vietminh conflict, Ho Chi Minh publicly announced that his government would adopt the Maoist model of people's war in its struggle against the French. Characteristically, Ho did not elaborate on the process but left it to ICP General Secretary Truong Chinh, already emerging as the chief ideologist of the party, to place the concept in a Vietnamese context. In a treatise that would later be known in the West as *The Resistance Will Win*, Truong Chinh declared that even though conditions in Vietnam were different in several respects from those in China, the Maoist three-stage model held considerable significance for the Vietnamese revolution. Much of his short book, in fact, was virtually a verbatim repetition of Mao's ideas on revolutionary strategy in China. But Truong Chinh pointed out that, when appropriate, Vietminh leaders would adapt Maoist ideas to local circumstances. For example, he noted that external factors, notably the role of major world powers, would probably play a greater role in the Indochinese conflict than in China. He also implied that the DRV might use the tactic of what he called "false

---

[12] Mao Zedong's ideas on guerrilla warfare are discussed in detail in his "Problems of strategy in the guerrilla war against Japan." An English-language version is contained in *Selected Military Writings of Mao Tse-tung* (Peking: Foreign Languages Press, 1972).

negotiations" to weaken the enemy's will while Vietminh strategists prepared their forces for the final general offensive against the French.[13]

During the spring of 1947, the Vietminh began to unveil their new strategy. While Vietminh forces fought fiercely to protect the remnants of their fragile foothold in the Red River delta, Ho Chi Minh appealed to the French to agree to a cease-fire and a resumption of the peace talks. The situation in Paris, however, was more complex. High Commissioner d'Argenlieu's increasingly hard line had provoked strong criticism in France, and in March he was replaced by Emile Bollaert, a Radical Party politician who liked to resolve disputes by conciliation. But Bollaert's task would not be easy, for some leading members of the French government were no longer interested in a peaceful solution to the crisis and were determined to impose a settlement based on superior force.

Bollaert apparently embarked on his new task with an open mind toward the possibility of a peaceful solution. On his arrival in Indochina, he began negotiations with former emperor Bao Dai, who was now living in exile in Hong Kong. Bollaert hoped to persuade Bao Dai to serve as chief of state in a new non-Communist government that would cooperate with the French against the Vietminh. He also sought to resume contacts with Ho Chi Minh by sending the well-known Indochina specialist Paul Mus to consult with the Vietminh leader on a peaceful solution to the conflict. Mus was sympathetic to the Vietminh cause, but he was hamstrung by his message, which demanded that Ho's forces lay down their arms before peace talks were resumed. In refusing the offer, Ho Chi Minh remarked, "There is no room for cowards in the French Union. If I should accept such terms, I would be one."[14]

In the meantime, the French planned a major operation against Vietminh units hiding in the mountains north of Hanoi. Rumors of the projected campaign surfaced during the late summer and provoked a testy response from Washington, which advised the French not to seek to resolve the problem by force. Paris reassured the White House that it had "no plans" for a major military offensive against

[13] Truong Chinh, "The Resistance Will Win," contained in Bernard B. Fall, ed., *Primer for Revolt* (New York: Praeger, 1963).

[14] A report of Paul Mus's interview with Ho by a U.S. diplomatic official is contained in *Central Files*, Hanoi to Department of State, June 20, 1947.

Women guerrillas serving in the Vietminh armed forces against the French.

the Vietminh. But in October, French paratroops were dropped into the mountains near the Vietminh redoubt at Tan Trao. Ho Chi Minh and his colleagues were barely able to evade capture, but after a few weeks the French withdrew from the mountains and returned to the delta.

With the door to a peaceful settlement temporarily closed, the Vietminh had little alternative but to seek victory by violent action. But they soon discovered that they had much to learn about how best to put their new strategy of people's war into operation. Some inexperienced commanders were reckless in their use of troops and fought to hold their positions even at the cost of heavy casualties. In other instances, Vietminh units fled from the battlefield in disarray without making provisions for preserving order and rejoining the struggle at a later date. Many Vietminh officers had little understanding of the different roles assigned to guerrilla, regional, and main force units, while civilian cadres often failed to mobilize support for the army by providing the people living in liberated areas with a clear-cut message of the long-range goals of the revolution.[15]

By the end of 1947, the Vietminh had begun to get a better grip on the situation. They had learned, first of all, that in a small country

[15] Greg Lockhart, *Nation in Arms: The Origins of the People's Army of Vietnam* (Wellington: Allen & Unwin, 1989), chap. 6.

like Vietnam they could not hope to carve out a large and invulnerable liberated base area (the French attack on Vietminh headquarters in October had demonstrated that), but must rely instead on a more fluid strategy involving shifting liberated zones and a war of constant movement.[16]

Secondly, they learned the importance of creating a movement in which all elements in the population, including women, children, and the elderly, contributed to the common cause. The French often facilitated this effort by mistreating the local people in the course of their military operations. In an autobiographical account of her life in wartime Vietnam, Le Ly Hayslip recalls a song which her mother sang to her during her childhood in a village in central Vietnam.

> In our village today
> A big battle was fought,
> French kill and arrest the people;
> The fields and villages burn,
> The people, they run to the winds:
> To the north, to the south,
> To Xam Ho, to Ky La.
> When they run, they look back;
> They see houses in flames.
> They cry, Oh, my God—
> Our houses are gone—
> Where will we lay our heads?
> In our village today,
> A big battle was fought.
> Old ladies and children,
> Were sent straight to hell.
> Our eyes fill with tears
> While we watch and ask God:
> Why is the enemy so cruel?

It is little wonder that the region was sympathetic to the Vietminh, and was later called "Pinkville" by American soldiers.[17]

One type of noncombatant was the "combat mother." According to the memoir of one Vietminh soldier, combat mothers "are for

---

[16] Ibid, pp. 189–193.
[17] Le Ly Hayslip, with Jay Wurts, *When Heaven and Earth Changed Places* (New York: Plume, 1990), p. 4.

the most part older women who consider it an honor to adopt a soldier of the people's army during the duration of the war. The entire family of the mother of the combatant serves as an adopted family for the young soldier or the cadre stationed in the sector." In cases where a unit was forced to disperse because of enemy attack, the family would be expected to take in the "adopted son" and protect his identity by dressing him in civilian clothes and presenting him as a close relative.[18]

Through such policies as these, the Vietminh gradually consolidated their hold over the vast countryside. Vietminh strength was even imbedded in areas ostensibly controlled by the French, so oftentimes villages controlled by the enemy during the day lapsed into Vietminh hands at night. By these tactics of feint and deception, the Vietminh appeared to be everywhere at once. As Truong Chinh described it in an article written in 1947, "If the enemy attacks us from above, we will attack him from below. If he attacks us in the North, we will respond in Central or South Vietnam, or in Cambodia and Laos. If the enemy penetrates one of our territorial bases, we will immediately strike hard at his belly and back, . . . cut off his legs [and] destroy his roads."[19]

Such a strategy led to increasing frustration on the part of French commanders, who complained that they never knew who or where the enemy was. In the phrase of the time, "the night belongs to the Vietminh." "If only," lamented one French officer, "the Vietnamese would face us in a set battle, how we should crush them!" It was a lament that would later be echoed by the Americans.[20]

A GIFT FOR PRESIDENT HO

In early 1949, the French finally came to terms with Bao Dai. In an agreement signed at the ornate Elysée Palace in Paris in March, the former emperor consented to form a government that would coop-

[18] Ngo Van Chieu, *Journal d'un Combattant Viet-minh* (Paris: Editions du Seuil, 1957), p. 142.

[19] Truong Chinh, article in *Inner Life,* contained in *Cuoc Khang Chien Than Thanh cua Nhan Dan Viet-Nam* [The Sacred War of the Vietnamese People], vol. 1 (Hanoi: Su That, 1958), p. 239.

[20] Lucien Bodard, *The Quicksand War* (Boston: Little, Brown, 1967), p. 47.

erate with the French in prosecuting the war against the Vietminh. The Elysée Accords, however, did not provide for total independence. Although Bao Dai's government, formally called the Associated State of Vietnam (ASV), had authority over local affairs, the French retained control over national defense and foreign affairs and would continue to play a major political, economic, and cultural role in Vietnam. Similar governments were established in Laos and Cambodia.

To Bao Dai, now chief of state of the new government, the continued French presence was disagreeable but unavoidable, since his new government was in no position by itself to pose a serious military threat to the disciplined and increasingly well armed Vietminh forces. Moreover, the French had finally conceded to Bao Dai what they had never conceded to Ho Chi Minh, abandoning their claim to a separate colony of Cochin China. After nearly 100 years, the three regions of the country were finally reunited under a single Vietnamese administration.

One of the French goals in setting up the ASV was to provide patriotic Vietnamese with an alternative to the Vietminh. Paris hoped that support for the so-called Bao Dai solution would permit the formation of a Vietnamese army—to be known officially as the Vietnamese National Army, or VNA—that would relieve the French Expeditionary Forces from carrying the entire burden of the war. By mid-1949, the first units of the VNA began to take shape. At first, they were commanded by French officers, but a native officer corps was already in the planning stage.

The French also hoped that the Elysée Accords would result in military and economic assistance from the United States. The war was becoming an increasing burden on French finances, and politicians in Paris were anxious to convince the Truman administration that what was taking place in the rice paddies of Indochina was a matter of concern to the entire free world. At that time, France was receiving military assistance from the United States for its part in the new North Atlantic Treaty Organization (NATO), but not for its operations in Indochina.

At first, the French had little success in inducing the United States to provide support for their war effort. Although officials in Washington, sensitized by the impending defeat of the Nationalist government of Chiang Kai-shek in China, were showing greater anxiety over the communist character of the Vietminh leadership, many felt that the crux of the problem remained the reluctance of the French government to give the Vietnamese people something to fight for. Through the end of 1948, the White House steadily refused French requests for direct assistance.

The signing of the Elysée Accords initially made little difference in Washington's attitude. Bao Dai was viewed by many U.S. observers as a playboy with little potential for providing a nationalist alternative to Ho Chi Minh. As for the so-called Bao Dai solution, it was seen in Washington as a French ruse to disguise the fact that the Franco-Vietminh conflict was in essence still a colonial war. Many patriots in Vietnam agreed, and withheld their support for the new government. When approached in the spring of 1949 for military and economic aid, the Truman administration indicated that Paris would have to take additional steps before the United States would be willing to untie its purse strings and add its prestige to the struggle.

On several occasions during the spring and summer of 1949, President Truman's new secretary of state, Dean Acheson, bluntly informed the French that U.S. aid would be dependent upon the granting of additional powers to the new Bao Dai government and a public statement by the French that the ultimate goal was formal independence for all the states of Indochina. This, however, Paris refused to do, on the grounds that the French public would be unwilling to bear the burden of the struggle unless French national interests were protected. As had happened in the months immediately following the end of the Pacific war, European and Asian specialists in the State Department disagreed over the proper approach to adopt. Asian specialists called on the White House to use the French request for aid as a bargaining chip to extract further concessions from Paris, while Europe experts contended that the French could do no more in light of the state of public opinion. By midsummer, Acheson had begun to tilt markedly toward the latter view.

Washington's chief concern was that the impending Communist victory in China could spill over into Southeast Asia. The French fed those fears by providing U.S. diplomatic officials with intelligence reports of growing Chinese assistance to the Vietminh as units of the Chinese People's Liberation Army (PLA) arrived on the Sino-

Vietnamese frontier. Such reports indicated that treaties had already been signed between China and the DRV regarding both military assistance and the stationing of Chinese advisers inside Vietnam.[21]

Some U.S. officials suspected that much of this information had been concocted by the French to lure Washington into taking a greater role in the Indochinese conflict, and it is highly likely that such was the case.[22] On the other hand, there is ample evidence that the Communist victory in China did lead to a substantial increase in Chinese aid to the Vietminh. In April, Radio Vietminh announced that units of the PLA had arrived at the border and were already providing "important support" to the DRV. In the fall, the new Chinese government confirmed it. In a speech given in November to a trade union congress in Beijing, CCP Politburo member Liu Shaoqi, once an occasional lecturer at the Vietnamese training institute in Guangzhou, declared that his government would give active support to insurgent forces in Southeast Asia, while specifically mentioning the Vietminh. Early the following year, Ho Chi Minh went to Beijing and initialed an agreement that provided Chinese military assistance and advisers to the struggle in Indochina. Radio Vietminh began to proclaim that the DRV had adopted the Chinese model as a means of realizing final victory. U.S. diplomatic sources reported that the two countries had agreed to create a combined general staff and to merge their military high command in the event of a general war.[23]

The Communist victory in China represented a major boost to Vietminh prospects, and they were quick to take advantage of it. In the late summer of 1949 the first embryonic Vietminh division was created. Early the following year, U.S. diplomatic sources reported that Vietminh leaders had begun to discuss plans for a general offensive to inaugurate the final stage of people's war against the French. Further confirmation came in August, when the U.S. mission in Saigon sent a captured document to Washington purporting to deal with the projected campaign, which was scheduled to take place

[21] For example, see *Central Files*, Saigon to Secretary of State, August 15, 1950. A later cable, Saigon 1577 to Department of State, March 9, 1951, cites evidence that cooperation between the Vietminh and the CCP had begun as early as 1945.

[22] According to the French journalist Lucien Bodard, many French intelligence reports were fabricated by the French to arouse greater concern in Washington. See Bodard, *The Quicksand War*, p. 228.

[23] *Central Files*, Saigon 150 to Department of State, September 11, 1950.

not as a single battle but as a series of stages. "Final victory," the document said, "cannot be attained either on a single front, or in a single battle. The General Counteroffensive will have to be divided into several stages, campaign will follow campaign, victories and defeats will alternate. We may meet with adversity but Final Victory will be ours." Defense Minister Vo Nguyen Giap elaborated on these ideas in a short book published by DRV sources later that year.[24]

The reports of growing Chinese assistance to the Vietminh aroused concern in Washington. Some interpreted it as an ominous forecast of a spreading tide of bolshevism throughout mainland Southeast Asia, an eventuality that could send shock waves as far as the Middle East and Japan. The Joint Chiefs of Staff and the newly created National Security Council (NSC) began to allude to the alarming possibility that a Communist victory in north Vietnam could deprive the U.S. of vital natural resources and destabilize the position of the free world throughout the region. The pronounced Vietminh shift toward the Chinese Communists also attracted attention and confirmed the views of those who saw Ho Chi Minh as a surrogate for the forces of international communism.

The fear of communist expansion in the region was felt not only in Washington but in other world capitals as well. In Paris and London, the Communist victory in China represented a serious threat to European colonial possessions in Southeast Asia. Both governments requested that the Truman administration take part in joint staff talks as a means of achieving a common military response in the event of direct Chinese intervention in the Franco-Vietminh conflict. But Washington, despite its growing anxiety over the deteriorating situation in Asia, was reluctant to become directly involved in Indochina, which it viewed as essentially a French responsibility. The Joint Chiefs, noting that the United States lacked the military forces to take an active role in the defense of the Asia mainland, recommended against such staff talks on the grounds that they might commit the United States to military action in the region.

As the new year opened, the Truman administration appeared

---

[24] *Central Files,* Saigon to Secretary of State, August 21, 1950; *Central Files,* Peking to Secretary of State, Feb. 25, 1950; Vo Nguyen Giap, *Nhiem Vu Quan Su Truoc Mat Chuyen Sang Tong Phan Cong* [The Military Task in Preparing for the General Counteroffensive], (Hanoi, 1950).

determined to avoid intervention in the spreading conflict in Indo-china. In a highly publicized speech at the National Press Club in Washington, Secretary of State Dean Acheson confirmed that U.S. policy was to avoid direct involvement of American combat forces on the mainland of Asia, while restricting such efforts to the island perimeter stretching from Japan to the Philippine islands.

At the same time, however, the White House was prepared to offer greater assistance to the French in a struggle which Washington now declared was crucial to the security interests of the United States. In February, after lengthy deliberations with the French and other friendly governments, the administration announced diplo-matic recognition of the new ASV as the legitimate government of Vietnam. Shortly after, economic and military aid missions were sent to Indochina to discuss the nature of U.S. assistance to the French and the new Vietnamese government.

Thus, the Truman administration was already committed to ac-tive aid to the French in Indochina before the outbreak of the Korean War in June. Although the North Korean invasion of South Korea strengthened U.S. fears of a unified effort by Moscow and Beijing to promote revolution throughout Asia, it also put a heavy strain on limited U.S. military resources in the Pacific and made the Joint Chiefs even more reluctant to commit such forces to additional re-sponsibilities in the region. In late June, in an immediate response to the beginning of the Korean conflict, the administration increased the level of U.S. assistance to the French in Indochina but fended off requests from Paris for a more direct involvement.

While Western governments grappled with the rising atmos-phere of crisis in Asia, Vietminh strategists sought to take advantage of their new ally. In September 1950, Vietminh units attacked French border posts in the mountainous area near the Chinese frontier. The border offensive was a spectacular success. Attacking at regimental strength for the first time, Vietminh units mauled French convoys trying desperately to evacuate exposed positions along the frontier. The French high command had been caught by surprise—General Marcel Carpentier, commander of French forces in Indochina, had commented to a U.S. diplomat that the first clashes were a "purely local action"—and abruptly abandoned their position on the border except for a single post at Mao Khe, near the Gulf of Tonkin. Radio Vietminh announced that a new stage of the general counteroffen-sive would be launched in early 1951, and that the Vietminh

Ho Chi Minh and Vo Nguyen Giap plan the 1950 border offensive.

army would be in Hanoi for Tet, the Vietnamese New Year. It was, said the broadcast, "the gift that it will give President Ho for Tet."[25]

The autumn border offensive was a severe psychological blow to the French. An atmosphere of dread permeated the European community in Hanoi, where rumors circulated that all French dependents would soon be evacuated. The U.S. mission reported that 50 to 70 percent of the population in the city supported the Vietminh. In the hope of reinvigorating the French effort, Paris replaced its senior personnel in Indochina. General Carpentier, whose cautious

[25] Ngo Van Chieu, *Journal*, p. 141.

and passive attitude had aroused strong criticism in Paris, was re-placed by General Jean de Lattre de Tassigny, who brought with him the reputation of being an aggressive and flamboyant leader. French officials undoubtedly hoped that the new French commander could serve as a tonic for flagging spirits in Indochina.[26]

The long-anticipated Vietminh general offensive was launched in January 1951, when 15,000 Vietminh troops descended from the mountains on the fringe of the Red River delta to launch Chinese-style "human wave" attacks on French posts at Vinh Yen, about 30 miles northwest of Hanoi. Had French units not held their ground, the war might have been over then and there and Ho Chi Minh might have celebrated Tet in Hanoi. Fortunately for the French, General de Lattre reacted decisively, rushing strategic reserves to the area and launching air sorties against Vietminh units with sup-plies of napalm bombs newly imported from the United States. Au-thor Ngo Van Chieu, then a member of the Vietminh, provides us with a horrifying description of the results.

> Our division had attacked since the morning. From a distance three *hirondelles* [swallows] grow larger. They are airplanes. They dive, and hell opens before my eyes. Hell in the form of a large egg container falling from the first plane, then a second, which lands to my right, near the road where there are two machine guns. An intense flame which seems to spread for hundreds of meters, sows terror in the ranks of the fighters. It is napalm, the fire which falls from the sky.
>
> Another plane approaches and spews more fire. The bomb falls behind us and I feel its fiery breath which passes over my entire body. Men flee, and I can no longer restrain them. There is no way to live under that torrent of fire which runs and burns all in its route.[27]

The attack at Vinh Yen was driven back at the cost of an esti-mated 6000 Vietminh dead. But Vo Nguyen Giap was not finished. In succeeding weeks, additional attacks were launched at other points along the perimeter of the Red River delta. The fighting was

---

[26] On the other hand, some French officers reportedly asked for transfers on the ground that they could not serve their demanding new superior. Carpentier himself told a U.S. diplomat that de Lattre was too impulsive. See *Central Files*, Saigon 1067 to Secretary of State, December 14, 1950. For rumors of the impending evacuation of French dependents, see *Central Files*, Hanoi 132 to Secretary of State, October 17, 1950.
[27] Ngo Van Chieu, *Journal*, p. 154. For a different English-language translation, see Bernard B. Fall, *Street without Joy* (Harrisburg, Pa.: Stackpole Press, 1964), pp. 35–38.

bitter, and General de Lattre's own son was killed in action, but the assaults were blunted again and the French held. For the moment, Ho Chi Minh would not receive his New Year's gift.

PROTRACTED WAR

The failure of the delta offensive was undoubtedly a severe disappointment to Vietminh leaders—and perhaps the first clear indication that Chinese tactics were not always appropriate to conditions in Vietnam. Vo Nguyen Giap was rumored to have undergone harsh criticism from his colleagues. At a meeting of the party's Central Committee in March, a more cautious approach was adopted. From then on, Vietminh strategy would focus on the attempt to disperse French forces in defensive positions throughout Indochina so that they could be attacked and destroyed piecemeal while Vietminh leaders waited for war weariness to take its toll on enemy morale. The world was now to be introduced to the Vietnamese concept of protracted war.[28]

The new Indochina-wide strategy placed a sharper focus on Laos and Cambodia, which would now inevitably become a larger part of the war. Until the late 1940s, these two protectorates had played only a limited role in Vietminh calculations. At the direction of the Comintern, Laos and Cambodia had been included in the area of ICP responsibility since the formation of the party in 1930. At a meeting held in Macao in 1935, party leaders had proposed the future formation of a "federation of soviet republics" in all three countries, to be given the formal name of the Indochinese Federation (Lien Bang Dong Duong) and to operate under Vietnamese guidance. In practice, however, organizational work among the indigenous Lao and Khmer peoples in the two protectorates had been minimal, since they were assumed to lack a strong sense of political and national awareness.[29]

But the Pacific war led to significant changes in the political and

---

[28] For a discussion of the resolution of the Central Committee, see *Khang Chien Than Thanh*, vol. 2, p. 22. The resolution placed most of the blame for the new situation on the increased assistance to the French provided by the United States, but one knowledgeable Vietnamese source recently informed me that Vietminh leaders had indeed been overcofident of victory prior to the failure of the 1951 general offensive.

[29] For the records of the Macao conference, see *Van Kien Dang (1930–1945)*, vol. 1 (Hanoi: Ban Nghien Cuu Lich Su Dang Trung Uong, 1977), pp. 461–668.

social conditions in the two protectorates. The disruption of French authority, combined with Japanese promises of future independence, aroused aspirations for self-rule among members of the traditional Lao and Khmer aristocratic elite, and as the war came to a close, embryonic nationalist organizations began to take shape in both countries.

The growing desire for statehood among educated groups in Laos and Cambodia created a dilemma for Vietminh strategists. On the one hand, it heightened the potential appeal of communism among radical elements in both countries, while simultaneously enhancing the possibility of expanding the struggle against French colonialism throughout all of Indochina. To take advantage of such sentiments, in the late 1940s the party began to expand its organizational efforts in both countries. At the same time, however, the rise in nationalist sentiment also gave birth to new tensions within the communist movement, as Khmer and Lao members became increasingly conscious of their own national aspirations and restive at the dominant role played by ethnic Vietnamese within the party and the Vietminh Front. By the end of the decade, such individuals had begun to voice their demands for the creation of independent parties and revolutionary fronts to represent the interests of the Lao and Khmer peoples. The force of their arguments was strengthened when the French granted associated statehood to royal governments in both countries after the Elysée Accords in 1949.

In February 1951, party leaders attempted to respond to such demands by replacing the ICP with three separate parties, a Vietnam Workers' Party (VWP) in Vietnam, and people's revolutionary parties in Laos and Cambodia. The concept of the Indochinese Federation was also replaced by a new vision calling for the creation of three independent states united in a symbiotic relationship to preserve the fruits of their common revolution. Party documents made it clear, however, that the Vietnamese would continue to play a guiding role.[30]

During the months following the end of their abortive 1951 general offensive, Ho Chi Minh and his lieutenants put their new strategy to the test. In the far northwest, Vietminh units began to

---

[30] For the official reasons why the party was now renamed the Vietnam Workers' Party, see Truong Chinh, *Selected Writings* (Hanoi: Foreign Languages Press, 1977), p. 434.

operate actively among minority tribal peoples in the region, seizing district capitals in heavily forested mountainous regions that had previously been under the control of the French. The French had treated these areas as separate from those inhabited by the ethnic Vietnamese and allowed them to remain under the authority of their traditional leaders, few of whom had any sympathy for communism. But Vietminh operatives had worked among minority peoples in the mountains north of the Red River delta since the formation of the Vietminh Front in 1941, and a number of ICP members were of minority extraction. In some areas, notably in districts near the Chinese border, the party had considerable success in "winning hearts and minds" among the local population.

The Vietminh also began to undertake more active efforts in neighboring Laos. A guerrilla force called the Pathet Lao was organized to provide a Laotian counterpart to the Vietminh Front, and a leading member of the Lao royal family, Prince Souphanouvong, was placed at the head of the movement to give it increased stature. By 1952, Laos had become a crucial element in Vietminh strategy. Following the tortuous routes that snaked through the rugged mountains of northwestern Tonkin, Vietminh units gradually extended their activities into northern Laos and even briefly threatened to seize the royal capital of Luang Prabang.

Insurgent forces were less active farther to the south. Cochin China had become a relative backwater in the war since early 1950, when an offensive ordered by the local Vietminh commander, Nguyen Binh, had been dealt a bloody defeat at the hands of the French. Nguyen Binh allegedly had a tendency to operate independently of directives from the party leadership in the Viet Bac, and in 1951 he was assassinated, reportedly at the order of the party, while being escorted to the north to report to the high command. From that time on, Vietminh activities in the southern provinces declined for the remainder of the war, although some units were active among tribal peoples in the central highlands.[31]

The setback encountered during the abortive Red River delta offensive in early 1951 undoubtedly created problems for the revolutionary cause. According to U.S. intelligence sources, the decision

---

[31] The 1950 offensive in the former colony of Cochin China is briefly described in Bodard, *The Quicksand War,* pp. 190–191. Several sources report that Nguyen Binh was killed at the order of his superiors because of his failure to follow orders.

Ho Chi Minh's house in the Viet Bac during the war against the French.

to turn to the strategy of protracted war caused severe morale problems in Vietminh ranks, and many left liberated areas to return to the cities. Some Vietminh followers were unhappy with the constant bombing, the "volunteer" work, and the economic hardship encountered in liberated areas. Some intellectuals complained of the need to undergo "self-criticism" to cleanse their minds of bourgeois sentiments, while peasants sometimes resisted conscription into the armed forces or labor units. Still, even U.S. observers conceded that the bulk of the population supported the Vietminh. Ho Chi Minh, said one report, was seen everywhere. Dressed as a simple peasant and frequently walking barefoot, he appeared in villages, in the rice fields, at meetings, or even on the battlefield to urge his followers on. Countless Vietnamese wanted to be the adopted sons and daughters of Uncle Ho, as he was apparently fond of calling himself.[32]

[32] For an estimate of Vietminh popular support, see *Central Files*, Hanoi 34 to Department of State, March 25, 1952.

Many Vietminh followers undoubtedly drew courage from the conviction that they were no longer alone. Virtually the entire area along the Chinese border was now in Vietminh hands, and a steady supply of arms and equipment was coming down from China. There were an estimated 250,000 Chinese troops in the provinces immediately north of the border, providing a constant menace to the French and undoubtedly provoking nightmares among policymakers in Paris and Washington. The French had now abandoned their efforts to crush the insurgency and adopted a more limited strategy, hoping to control the lowlands and thus deprive Vietminh forces of access to rice and new recruits in the most heavily populated parts of the country. But Chinese provisions and advisers were now moving across the frontier unmolested, and supply routes and even airfields to handle the traffic were being constructed at several points on both sides of the border. Other routes connected the Red River delta with central Vietnam.

In an effort to disrupt enemy communications, in the late fall of 1951 General de Lattre ordered the seizure of the town of Hoa Binh, on the southern fringe of the Red River delta. French military planners considered Hoa Binh a keystone in the Vietminh communications network between the delta and regions farther south and hoped to reduce the flow the supplies and troops to enemy units operating in the north. It was one of de Lattre's last decisions before resigning his command to return to France. A few weeks later he was dead of cancer.

Vietminh strategists recognized the French occupation of Hoa Binh as a threat to their supply route from the south and decided to contest the French control of the city. After a bitter battle that cost the Vietminh an estimated 55 percent of their attacking force of over 40,000 troops, the French finally withdrew in February 1952. Although some foreign observers praised the decision as a prudent one, U.S. diplomat Donald Heath conceded that it had been a political and psychological reversal for the French.[33]

---

[33]*Central Files,* Saigon 1689 to Department of State, February 29, 1952. A Vietminh analysis of the situation is in "Tinh hinh va nhiem vu moi" [The new situation and tasks], in *Communist Vietnamese Publications,* a microfilm series issued by the Library of Congress in Washington, D.C. The latter source described the French attack on Hoa Binh as an opportunity that could lead to a general French defeat. For estimates on troop losses in the battle, see *Central Files,* Office Memo, John Allison to G (Matthews), February 28, 1952, and Bernard B. Fall, *Street without Joy,* p. 60. Allison said that one of the reasons the French decided to abandon the area was that the Vietminh had set up alternate routes of supply.

The deteriorating situation in Indochina led to a steady decline in morale on the part of the French and their Vietnamese supporters. By now even the Red River delta was not secure. The French had built a string of pillboxes (popularly known as the "de Lattre line") to protect the area from Vietminh infestation, but insurgent units simply bypassed the French posts and infiltrated the area at will. Only the city of Hanoi was truly secure, and pessimistic observers feared that it too could fall in three to four months.[34]

Washington observed the bleak situation in Indochina with dismay, but appeared unwilling to increase its assistance to the French. The White House was increasingly disenchanted with French policies, as well as with the failure of the Bao Dai government to earn the support of nationalist elements among the population, and seemed preoccupied with conveying to Beijing that direct Chinese intervention in the war in Indochina would lead to immediate U.S. retaliation. A proposal to that effect was opposed vigorously in both London and Paris, as British and French officials feared the possibility that the conflict in Indochina would escalate into global war. During the presidential campaign of 1952 in the United States, Republican Party candidate Dwight D. Eisenhower had pledged that his administration would seek to "roll back" the Iron Curtain and defend the forces of freedom everywhere. If such was the case, the French might hope that a more receptive attitude toward their pleas for help would prevail in an Eisenhower White House.

In talks between French and U.S. officials during the early months of 1953, the new Eisenhower administration agreed to increase American aid to French Indochina, provided that France came up with a more effective way to prosecute the war. The result was the Navarre plan, a product of the newly appointed commander of the French forces in Indochina, General Henri Navarre. Under heavy pressure from Washington, General Navarre presented the Americans with a vague but ambitious plan to take the offensive and defeat Vietminh forces in Indochina during the dry season of 1955. Although skeptical of the plan's success, the Joint Chiefs of Staff gave it their blessing, and in late summer the administration agreed to bankroll the increased French effort. By the end of 1953, the United

---

[34] *Central Files,* Saigon to Department of State, March 5, 1952; *Central Files,* Hanoi 527 to Department of State, February 5, 1952.

States was paying an estimated two-thirds of the entire cost of the war.[35]

A HISTORIC CAMPAIGN

In late November 1953, French paratroop units were airlifted to the isolated mountain capital of Dien Bien Phu, less than 20 miles from the Laotian border in the northwestern corner of Vietnam. Dien Bien Phu had been seized by the Vietminh in 1952. It served as the linchpin of their plan to pressure French positions in Laos, since the town sat astride the sole route between the Red River delta and northern Laos. General Navarre reasoned that French control over the town would reduce the ability of the Vietminh to ship troops and supplies into northern Laos. If Ho Chi Minh should decide to attack the base, he explained, so much the better. The base would be well defended and could serve as a "meat grinder" to impose high casualties on the attacking forces. Some U.S. observers expressed skepticism about the French plan to divert badly needed troops and material to such an isolated corner of the war, but some visiting U.S. civilian and military observers, such as General John "Iron Mike" O'Daniel, voiced the opinion that the base could be held against whatever the Vietminh could launch.[36]

Since the failure of their 1951 offensive, Vietminh strategists had concentrated on dividing French forces throughout the Indochina theater while seeking vulnerable areas susceptible to attack. As Navarre had contended, the Vietminh had already decided to attack Lai Chau, a small mountain outpost about 30 miles north of Dien Bien Phu, and had moved some of their main force to the area in preparation for the assault. The French airdrop at Dien Bien Phu took place just as the Vietminh high command was meeting to present its 1953–1954 battle plan in the northwest to division commanders. Informed of the French move, Vietminh leaders now decided to

[35] General Navarre described and defended the plan in his memoirs. See Henri Navarre, *Agonie de l'Indochine* (Paris: Plon, 1956).
[36] Navarre contended that the seizure of the town had also prevented a Vietminh attack on the nearby French post at Lai Chau. See *Central Files,* Saigon 897 to Department of State, November 27, 1953. For the initial U.S. report on the operation, see ibid., Hanoi 310 to Department of State, November 23, 1953. Also see Navarre, *Agonie de l'Indochine,* pp. 161–162.

C H I N A

0   150 mi.

0   93 km

Pac Bo

V I E T
B A C

Lai Chau

Phong
Saly

Dien Bien
Phu

Tan Trao

Vinh Yen

Hanoi

Hoa
Binh

Hon Gay

Haiphong

Sam Neua

Luang
Prabang

L
A
O
S

*Gulf
of
Tonkin*

Vinh

Vientiane

Dong Hoi

T H A I L A N D

Huê

Da Nang

Hoi An

C A M B O D I A

*Tonle
Sap*

**NORTH VIETNAM DURING THE
FRANCO-VIETMINH CONFLICT**

shift the focus of their own upcoming campaign to Dien Bien Phu. An attack on the town would present some logistical problems, since it was farther away than Lai Chau from the Vietminh supply source in south China, but the hilly terrain surrounding the town provided a number of advantages to an attacking force. Moreover, a French defeat there could have a significant impact in Paris. After long deliberation, they decided to attack the base with three Vietminh divisions sometime in early 1954.[37]

During the autumn of 1953, however, the most significant developments in the Indochina conflict were taking place not on the battlefield but on the political front, where there were incipient signs of a possible negotiated settlement of the war. A cease-fire had ended the Korean conflict in July. This inevitably fanned antiwar sentiment in France, where criticism of the "dirty war" in Indochina had become increasingly pronounced as the likelihood of victory had receded. French government officials had begun to hint at the possibility of a negotiated settlement as early as the spring of 1952. Now, in October 1953, senior officials in Paris openly declared that they would welcome discussions on a compromise settlement.

The Eisenhower administration was strongly opposed to the idea and made its views known to Paris. When the French pointed out that the United States had negotiated a settlement in Korea, administration officials responded that the conflict in Indochina was strikingly different from the one in Korea. The latter, they argued, was located on a peninsula, and a defeat there would not lead inevitably to a communist takeover of neighboring countries. In Indochina, a victory for the Vietminh could have an incalculable effect on the free world position throughout the entire region.

But Washington's arguments had little effect in Paris, where the government of Prime Minister Joseph Laniel was under intense pressure from French public opinion to seek an end of the war. In Oc-

---

[37] For a Vietnamese account of these decisions, see the article by Hoang Van Thai in *Vietnam Courier*, March 1984. According to a Chinese historian, sources in Beijing indicate that the attack on Dien Bien Phu was suggested to the Vietnamese by Chinese advisers. See Qiang Zhai, "Transplanting the Chinese Model: Chinese Military Advisers and the First Vietnam War, 1950–1954," in *The Journal of Military History*, 57 (4) (October 1993), p. 708. The author does concede that Chinese advisers had made a mistake in recommending to Vo Nguyen Giap an all-out attack on French strongholds in the Red River delta in early 1951. See p. 714. I am grateful to John Prados for pointing out this source to me.

tober, Laniel declared that France would not hesitate to seek a compromise peace if it could be arranged, and in succeeding weeks a number of reports surfaced in Paris that the French government was anxious to bring the conflict to an end.

Significantly, conciliatory signals were emanating from other world capitals as well. In Moscow, the death of Soviet dictator Joseph Stalin in March and the advent of a new party leadership under Georgi Malenkov had led to a reevaluation of Soviet foreign policy goals, and during the summer and fall, Soviet press reports began to hint that the conflict in Indochina should be solved by means of negotiations. Similar sentiments issued from Beijing, where there were clear signs that Chinese leaders, in the wake of their costly intervention in the Korean conflict, were anxious to focus on domestic concerns. In November, Foreign Minister Zhou Enlai declared that China would not be averse to a peace settlement in Indochina that followed the general guidelines of the recent cease-fire that had been concluded in Korea. Was peace in the offing?[38]

The spreading rumors of peace talks must have received a mixed reception at Vietminh headquarters in the Viet Bac. After the brief flurry of diplomatic exchanges in the spring of 1947, Ho Chi Minh and his colleagues had expressed little interest in a peace settlement, convinced that success at the conference table could come about only in conjunction with a more favorable situation on the battlefield. Efforts by the neutral governments of India and Indonesia to mediate the conflict had apparently run into a brick wall from the Vietminh. In the summer of 1951, when peace talks in Korea first got underway, Radio Vietminh had used the occasion to underscore its own tough line on bringing the conflict in Indochina to an end. There was a close parallel, it said, between the situations in Korea and Indochina. The cornerstone of any settlement in both cases was the preliminary withdrawal of all foreign troops (meaning, of course, the French Expeditionary Forces). American diplomatic observers concluded that Ho Chi Minh was not interested in a negotiated settlement.[39]

[38] *Central Files*, Moscow dispatch 307 to the Department of State, September 2, 1953; *Central Files*, Paris dispatch 795 to Department of State, September 15, 1953. For the Chinese attitude toward peace talks, see François Joyaux, *La Chine et le règlement du conflit en Indochine: Genève 1954* (Paris: Sorbonne, 1979), p. 91.

[39] *Central Files*, Saigon 236 to Department of State, July 27, 1951. For the apparent rejection of Indonesian proposals, see ibid., New Delhi 1890 to Department of State, January 31, 1951.

Vietminh leaders did not react quickly to the rumors of a ne-gotiated settlement in the fall of 1953. In early September, Ho Chi Minh said in a speech that peace could only come about through victory. That view was echoed by DRV Foreign Minister Pham Van Dong in an article in the weekly journal *Cominform* a few weeks later. The struggle against the French in Indochina, Dong said, "will continue until final victory." But in November, Ho Chi Minh sud-denly granted an interview to a reporter of the Swedish newspaper *Expressen.* In the interview, Ho remarked that the DRV would be willing to seek a compromise settlement at the conference table. A few days later, both Moscow and Beijing voiced their pleasure at the news.[40]

What had happened to change minds in the Vietminh camp? One possibility is that the USSR and China had applied pressure on the Vietminh to agree to a peace conference. At the moment, how-ever, there is no definitive evidence to that effect. Sources in Hanoi today assert that the DRV decided to attend the conference on its own initiative, and it is certainly possible, as author Carlyle A. Thayer has contended in his recent study entitled *War by Other Means,* that war weariness within the Vietminh ranks had convinced Ho Chi Minh and his colleagues that a compromise settlement was better than a continuation of the war.[41]

Whatever the case, it is clear that if peace talks did take place, Vietminh leaders wanted them to occur under the most favorable conditions possible. It was undoubtedly with that in mind that they responded to the French occupation of Dien Bien Phu in late No-vember. A Central Committee of the VWP pointed out in a resolu-tion issued shortly after the news reached Vietminh headquarters, "We must strengthen resistance war and destroy as much of the enemy's political strength as possible. Only then will the enemy be willing to negotiate on a peaceful resolution of the Vietnam problem, while respecting the democratic rights and independence of our people." If the French post at Dien Bien Phu could be overrun before or during the conference, it would not only help to reduce the ene-

---

[40] The text of the interview is reported in *Central Files,* Stockholm 463 to Department of State, November 29, 1953. A Vietnamese-language version is in *Toan Tap,* vol. 6, pp. 494–496. For an English translation, see Bernard B. Fall, *Ho Chi Minh on Revolution* (New York: Signet, 1967), pp. 232–234.

[41] Carlyle A. Thayer, *War by Other Means: National Liberation and Revolution in Vietnam, 1954–60* (Sydney: Allen & Unwin, 1989), p. 3.

Ho Chi Minh and his colleagues prepare the attack on Dien Bien Phu in 1954. From left to right: Le Duan, Pham Van Dong, Ho Chi Minh, Truong Chinh, Vo Nguyen Giap.

my's military capabilities but also have an electric effect on French and world public opinion and create a favorable climate for a satisfactory settlement at the peace table.[42]

A crucial prerequisite for Vietminh success at Dien Bien Phu, however, would undoubtedly be an increase in Chinese military assistance, and it seems likely that Ho Chi Minh may have conditioned his government's agreement to attend a peace conference on such an increase. During the years following the signing of the Sino-Vietnamese agreement in 1950, Chinese aid had been steady but relatively modest in size, averaging about 400 to 500 tons of military materiel each month. But according to French estimates, by July 1953 it had increased to at least 10,000 tons per month. During the winter of 1953–1954, Western intelligence sources reported a significant

---

[42] The quote is from Central Committee Decree no. 92, December 12, 1953, cited in *Lich Su Quan Doi Nhan Dan Viet Nam* (Hanoi: Quan Doi Nhan Dan, 1974), p. 536. Hereafter *LSQD*.

increase in Chinese equipment crossing the border, while senior Chinese military officers were rumored to be serving as advisers on the Vietminh general staff.[43]

Beginning in early 1954, three divisions of Vietminh troops, comprising about 40,000 combat troops and supplemented by about 15,000 support units, began to infest the hills surrounding the French base at Dien Bien Phu. Thousands of porters, many of them women recruited from villages in the districts surrounding the Red River delta (the Vietminh had discovered that women porters, known collectively as the "long-haired army," were more effective than their male counterparts), labored on foot over tortuous mountain terrain to transport heavy military equipment and provisions into the area. To induce peasants to provide such support, during the previous autumn the party had passed a new land reform program in liberated areas calling for the confiscation of the land of wealthy landowners for distribution among the poor. According to Vietminh sources, the program was a success, as thousands of peasants enlisted in the cause.

The attack on Dien Bien Phu, waged under the command of General Vo Nguyen Giap, began in mid-March. At first Giap, advised by senior Chinese military officers provided for the occasion, applied the familiar "human wave" tactics that had first been adopted by the Chinese PLA against UN forces in Korea. Vietminh units advanced en masse in an attempt to overrun enemy gun emplacements on the perimeter of the French base in the valley. But such tactics resulted in high casualties with only limited results. According to one U.S. diplomatic report, the Vietminh left nearly 2000 troops on the French barbed wire alone during the first few days of the campaign. With morale in the Vietminh ranks reportedly severely shaken, the human wave attacks ceased at the end of March, while Giap and his high command reevaluated the situation. A few days later, they adopted a new approach, patiently digging trenches along the perimeter of the base while Vietminh artillery units, in-

---

[43] A Vietnamese informant has told me that although Ho Chi Minh decided to seek a negotiated settlement on his own initiative, pressure from allies to accept such a settlement began to intensify beginning in early 1954. For one estimate of Chinese assistance to the Vietminh during this period, see the CIA report entitled "Probable Developments in Indochina through mid-1954," June 4, 1954, cited in *USVN*, bk. 9, pp. 46–57.

stalled in tunnels dug into the mountains surrounding the base, pounded French defenses and gradually made the airfield unusable.[44]

In the meantime, diplomats scurried back and forth in world capitals to set the stage for the peace talks, scheduled to begin at Geneva in early May. In attendance would be representatives from France, Great Britain, China, the USSR, and the United States, as well as the DRV and the three associated states of Vietnam, Laos, and Cambodia. The latter two countries had been granted total independence by the French the previous year. The Eisenhower administration had agreed to attend the conference, but was convinced that a peace settlement would be a disaster and hoped that the French could be dissuaded from abandoning the war effort. The French were playing their own double game with Washington, however; they attempted to use the threat of U.S. intervention as a means of strengthening the French position at Geneva, thus inducing the Vietminh to reduce the scale of their own demands. In late March, as the situation at Dien Bien Phu became increasingly perilous, the Laniel government sent General Paul Ely, chief of the French General Staff, to Washington to request U.S. air strikes on Vietminh gun emplacements at Dien Bien Phu. Eisenhower was unwilling to commit U.S. combat forces to the conflict unless the French agreed to join a multilateral alliance of major Western nations to wage the war to a victorious conclusion. As a condition of possible U.S. military involvement in the war, he also demanded a promise from Paris to grant total independence to Vietnam at the close of the conflict.

The looming prospect of peace talks at Geneva made a decisive Vietminh victory at Dien Bien Phu ever more pressing. By mid-April, Vo Nguyen Giap's new approach, which had been given the slogan of "steady attack and steady advance," had begun to pay off. As casualties among the defenders increased and the airfield became unusable, the French were forced to supply the base by airlift. By the end of the month, the Vietminh had tightened the noose around the base and began to overrun the firebases along the perimeter. Despite high casualties (the French claimed that over 50 percent of

[44] Georges Boudarel, "Comment Giap a failli perdre la Bataille de Dien Bien Phu," *Le Nouvel Observateur*, April 8, 1983; Thayer, *War by Other Means*, p. 3. For the Chinese view, see Qiang Zhai, "Transplanting the Chinese Model," pp. 709–710.

Raising the Flag of Victory at Dien Bien Phu, May 1954.

the final Vietminh assault force was composed of raw recruits), the Vietminh pressed on, and the camp finally surrendered on May 6, literally on the eve of the discussions at Geneva.[45]

PEACE AT GENEVA

The fall of the French base at Dien Bien Phu provided Vietminh leaders with the favorable conditions on the battlefield that they had been seeking. In keeping with the news, Pham Van Dong, head of the DRV delegation at Geneva, presented stiff demands: international recognition of the full sovereignty and national independence of all three Indochinese states; the withdrawal of all foreign military forces; and elections to be held under local supervision. Furthermore, he demanded that delegations representing the revolutionary movements in Laos and Cambodia (the Pathet Lao and its Cambodian counterpart, the Khmer Rouge) be seated at the conference was the legitimate representatives of the peoples of the two states.

During the next few weeks, intensive discussions were held on the key issues involved in a peace settlement. A consensus was reached on the advisability of dividing Vietnam into two separate regroupment zones in the north and south, representing the forces

---

[45] The most dramatic account of the battle of Dien Bien Phu, though now somewhat dated, is Bernard B. Fall's *Hell in a Very Small Place* (New York: Vintage, 1966).

supporting the Vietminh and the Bao Dai government respectively. An International Control Commission (ICC) would be created to police the settlement and maintain the peace until elections could be held in the two zones to create a united Vietnam under a single government. But where would the dividing line between the two zones be placed? How would the ICC be composed? When would the elections take place, and how would they be administered?[46]

Eventually, the DRV delegation, undoubtedly under heavy pressure from Chinese delegate Zhou Enlai, reluctantly agreed to offer a number of key concessions. It abandoned its demand for the seating of delegations from the revolutionary movements in Laos and Cambodia, on condition that the two countries be neutralized and no foreign bases be permitted on their territory. On Vietnam, it agreed to the establishment of a demilitarized zone (DMZ) at the 17th parallel (Pham Van Dong had originally demanded the 13th parallel, farther to the south), thus dividing the country into two roughly equal parts, with the Vietminh to the north and the non-Communist elements to the south. In return, the conference recognized the principle of Vietnamese national unity. A political declaration drafted at the close of the conference called for national elections to be held two years after the final conclusion of the Geneva accords. Consultations between representatives of the two zones were to be held in the summer of 1955, and the elections were to be supervised by a tripartite ICC composed of representatives from Canada, Poland, and India.

Such conditions were undoubtedly difficult for many Vietminh leaders to swallow. Supporters of the insurgent movement in South Vietnam, who would now be placed at least temporarily under an enemy administration, were particularly angry at what they considered the betrayal of the cause of Vietnamese independence and national unity. It was presumably in an effort to enlist Ho Chi Minh's support for the compromise settlement that Zhou Enlai met with the DRV leader near the Sino-Vietnamese border in early July. Ho apparently agreed to the broad terms of the settlement, including a recognition of the sovereignty and territorial integrity of all three

---

[46] Many observers had assumed that Vietminh leaders would opt for a cease-fire in place rather than the creation of two clearly demarcated regroupment zones. For possible reasons why they preferred the latter alternative, see Duiker, *The Communist Road to Power in Vietnam* (Boulder, Colo.: Westview Press, 1981), p. 164.

nations of Indochina, in return for a Chinese commitment to provide increased support to the DRV, now about to return to Hanoi.[47]

Even so, it is likely that Zhou Enlai's arm-twisting at Geneva infuriated Vietnamese delegates at the conference, and probably revived long-standing suspicions among Vietnamese leaders that Beijing had its own designs in the area. While party leaders swallowed their anger in order to maintain close ties with their ally, their resentment remained under the surface and, as we shall see later, reappeared in a particularly vocal form after the end of the Vietnam War.[48]

Vietnamese Communist leaders in Hanoi, and their followers in the southern provinces, were not the only ones who had doubts about the advisability of signing the Geneva accords. Across the table at the conference hall at Geneva, representatives of the Bao Dai government were adamantly opposed to the agreement, which would divide their country on the altar of Cold War expediency. While the ASV was not a signatory to the document that established the cease-fire, the Bao Dai delegation at Geneva refused to give its assent to the political declaration, which called for holding national elections throughout the country within two years after the signing of the accords.

The Eisenhower administration was only slightly less unhappy with the results of the conference. From the outset, Washington had misgivings about attending the conference. The French were clearly in an unfavorable military situation as the conference convened and would inevitably be forced to make a number of concessions to their

[47] The details of the talks between Zhou Enlai and Ho Chi Minh have never been divulged, but it is likely that there was some hard bargaining involved. According to one writer, Zhou persuaded the Vietnamese leader that a continuation of the conflict, combined with efforts by the DRV to strengthen its influence in Laos and Cambodia, could antagonize other countries in the region. The announcement at the close of the talks that both countries declared their respect for the sovereignty and territorial integrity of Laos and Cambodia suggests that China was concerned about Vietminh plans for a militant alliance of all three Indochinese states after a revolutionary victory throughout the area. See Thayer, *War by Other Means*, p. 10, citing D. R. SarDesai, *Indian Foreign Policy in Cambodia, Laos, and Vietnam, 1947–1964* (Berkeley: University of California Press, 1968, p. 48. Also see Duiker, *China and Vietnam: The Roots of Conflict* (Berkeley: Institute of East Asia Studies, 1987), p. 30.

[48] For Vietnamese charges against Chinese behavior at Geneva raised after the end of the war, see *The Truth about Vietnamo-Chinese Relations over the Last Thirty Years* (Hanoi: Ministry of Foreign Affairs, 1979).

adversaries in order to bring about a cease-fire. President Eisenhower and his secretary of state, John Foster Dulles, were adamantly opposed to any concessions in the belief that they would only reward aggression and set the stage for further regional advances by communism in future years. As the peace talks opened in early May, the White House announced a series of strict conditions that it was prepared to insist upon as the price for its adhesion to any agreement. Among the more important prerequisites was that at least a part of the state of Vietnam could be protected from a possible Communist takeover after the close of the conference.

The problem was, Washington had few palatable alternatives. The French had insisted that they would only continue the effort in Indochina if there was a substantial increase in U.S. military assistance. During the last year of the war, the U.S. contribution totalled over $1 billion, but by March 1954, that was not enough for Paris. When the Eisenhower administration refused a French request for air strikes to save the French base at Dien Bien Phu, the Laniel government decided to opt for a peace settlement. By April, Eisenhower had decided that an unsatisfactory settlement at Geneva was preferable to unilateral U.S. intervention in the conflict. The United States refused to give its formal adherence to the final agreement, on the grounds that the call for national elections in the political declaration jeopardized the security of the non-Communist regroupment zone in South Vietnam, but it did announce that it "took note" of the accords and would not take action to disturb them.

THE BALANCE SHEET

For Vietminh leaders and their followers, the results of the Geneva conference must have been bittersweet. They had achieved international recognition of their right to rule the north, but at the expense of the division of the country into two separate zones and the continuation of the Bao Dai government in the south. To some, the cup of victory was half full; to others, it was half empty.

The barely concealed criticism from DRV sources that the Vietminh had been sold out by their allies was based in part on the assumption that the insurgent forces could have achieved a greater victory if they had received adequate support from China to continue the fighting. Could the Vietminh have done better had they fought on? Had they won the war on the battlefield only to lose it at the conference table? Or was the final settlement a realistic recognition of the balance of forces at the time? In recent years, Vietnamese sources have sometimes implied that after the fall of Dien Bien Phu in early May, victory was in their grasp. On the other hand, Soviet party leader Nikita Khrushchev (hardly a disinterested observer, as we shall see) recounted an alleged remark by Zhou Enlai at the time that the Vietminh were on the verge of collapse and desperately in need of a settlement at Geneva.[49]

We can never know the answer to this question, of course, since history does not permit second chances. But the evidence at hand suggests that neither contention is entirely justified. In the weeks following the fall of Dien Bien Phu on May 6, French officials conceded to U.S. observers that the overall situation in the Red River delta had become increasingly perilous, and that a determined assault by Vietminh units could result in the fall of Hanoi in a matter of weeks. There were multiple reports of Vietminh troop movements in the delta in May and June, but the attack never came. What had happened to delay the Vietminh? One possibility is that Vietminh leaders lacked the capability of realizing a decisive victory in the heart of the Red River delta. A decade later, one leading party member remarked that Vietminh forces lacked the strategic reserves at that time for a major attack on French positions near the capital. As Vo Nguyen Giap himself conceded, Dien Bien Phu had been a decisive but not a total victory.[50]

Even had the Vietminh been in a position to win a total victory in Indochina, of course, there was always the risk that the United States would decide to intervene. The fear of that possibility had been a major factor in deterring China from taking a greater part in the war, and the Eisenhower administration, as well as the French, had effectively played on that fear by carrying on public discussions of possible U.S. intervention in the conflict. Some historians have asserted that Eisenhower never intended to introduce U.S. combat

---

[49] Nikita Khrushchev, *Khrushchev Remembers* (Boston: Bantam, 1971), p. 477.

[50] See Vo Nguyen Giap's article in the *Vietnam Courier*, March 1984. Also see his alleged comment to Hungarian diplomat Janos Radvanyi that Dien Bien Phu was "the last desperate exertion" of the Vietminh army, cited in Thayer, *War by Other Means*, p. 3. For the comment about the lack of a strategic reserve, see Le Duan, *Thu Vao Nam* [Letters to the South] (Hanoi, Su That, 1986), letter of May 1965.

forces into the war, but documentary evidence suggests that had the negotiations collapsed, the White House might have felt compelled to provide naval and air forces in a multinational defense of the area. The possible use of such forces would have been even greater, of course, had there been a real likehood of a total Vietminh victory over the French. One can only assume, then, that Washington would have stepped in to prevent a total Vietminh victory throughout all of Vietnam.[51]

Such, at any rate, was the conclusion of Ho Chi Minh himself. In a meeting of the VWP Central Committee held a few days before the signing of the Geneva accords in mid-July, Ho appealed to his colleagues to accept the necessity of a compromise peace in Indochina, however unattractive the prospect. Some colleagues, he remarked, do not see the Americans behind the French and want to fight on. Ho's argument was persuasive. The resolution issued at the close of the meeting approved of the decision by party leaders to negotiate a compromise settlement, while setting forth new slogans of peace, national unity, independence, and democracy. For the moment, the struggle for national unity would be postponed.[52]

---

[51] For the argument that Eisenhower had no intention of introducing U.S. combat forces into the war, see Steven B. Ambrose, *Eisenhower*, 2 vols. (New York: Simon & Schuster, 1983–1984). For a different view, see David L. Anderson, *Trapped by Success: The Eisenhower Administration and Vietnam, 1953–61* (New York: Columbia University Press, 1991), p. 38.

[52] See *Van Kien Dang ve Khang Chien Chong Thuc Dan Phap* [Party Documents on the Resistance War against the French], vol. 2 (Hanoi: Su That, 1988), pp. 363–365, which cites the resolution of the Sixth Enlarged Plenum of the VWP, July 15–17, 1954. For Ho's speech at the plenum, see *Ho Chi Minh: Selected Writings*, p. 180.

CHAPTER 3

Building the North,
Looking to the South

In mid-October 1954, Ho Chi Minh and the remainder of the DRV government and party leadership returned to Hanoi for the first time in nearly eight years. According to reports by observers at the time, it was a festive occasion. The city was festooned with Vietminh flags and slogans, and organized processions took place before large and enthusiastic crowds in the downtown sections of the city. Ho Chi Minh himself did not appear in public until a week later, explaining in a brief speech that he had not wanted to waste his compatriots' time in an extended welcoming ceremony. Our mutual love, he said, "does not depend on appearance."[1]

But beneath the surface aura of euphoria, Ho and his colleagues must have realized that they faced a number of fateful decisions. What actions should they take to assist North Vietnam to recover from the long years of war and colonialism? Should they move expeditiously to destroy the legacy of the past and build the foundations of a socialist society, or should they adopt more moderate policies designed to improve the material standard of living to win the hearts and minds of the overall population? Could the regime win the gratitude of the urban and rural poor, who composed much of the nucleus of their support during the war against the French, while at the same time seeking to avoid alienating the more affluent sectors of the population? How should it deal with the issue of national elections and protect Vietminh supporters who had remained in the south? Should it assume that such elections would

---

[1] For a report of the welcoming ceremonies, see *Central Files*, Hanoi 278 to Department of State, October 10, 1954. Ho's speech is reported briefly in ibid., Hanoi 314 to Department of State, October 20, 1954.

DRV officials return to Hanoi after the Geneva Conference in October 1954.

take place as scheduled, or that a return to revolutionary war would eventually be necessary?

The question of the most immediate importance was how to consolidate power in Hanoi and revive the northern economy. Crucial to that task would be an effort to reassure the most productive sectors in the population, elements whose capital and expertise would be required to create the conditions for rapid economic development in the future. A few days before the signing of the Geneva accords, the DRV had issued an eight-point program designed to alleviate the concerns of moderates and thus avoid the mass exodus of noncommunist elements to South Vietnam as part of the exchange of refugees called for by the Geneva settlement. The program declared that the ownership and management of enterprises and public services previously run by the French or by the Bao Dai government would be turned over to the state. Otherwise, private wealth and property, including that which was in the hands of foreign nationals, would be respected. The government promised to respect freedom of religious belief. Civil servants employed by the Bao Dai regime who had remained in the north were instructed to report to the new revolutionary authorities on the assurance that they would not be punished if they had not taken up arms or otherwise resisted the new regime. But those who refused to report would be "severely punished."[2]

The regime's attempt to reassure the population living in areas previously controlled by the enemy was only partly successful. Eventually a total of over 800,000 refugees, an estimated two-thirds of the Roman Catholics, departed for the south. Many were members of the small but influential educated and professional class. Others were peasants from Catholic villages who departed en masse with their priests. Foreign observers reported that the restaurants, shops, and streets in the foreign residential areas of Hanoi were virtually deserted on the eve of the arrival of the DRV leadership.[3]

Crippled by the exodus, the northern economy was in dire straits. Most of the factories were shut, and many of the owners had left the country. One scholar has reported that in the port city of Haiphong, twenty-nine of the thirty French-owned factories had been closed. Fuel for motor vehicles was in short supply, and the railroads were not working. Much of the irrigation network had been destroyed by the French, and nearly 10 percent of the cultivated land in the Red River delta had been abandoned because of the flight of the local population to urban areas during the closing months of the war. In December, disastrous floods along the central coast raised the specter of a new famine, and the price of rice in the markets shot up rapidly.

At first the regime moved with caution in seizing control of the levers of economic power. There was ample precedent for a policy of prudence. After the end of the Russian civil war in 1920, the Bolsheviks under V.I. Lenin had launched a moderate program

[2] *Central Files*, Memo, "Vietminh policy toward captured cities," July 16, 1954.
[3] Many Vietnamese Catholics were allegedly lured to depart by warnings from their priests that "the Virgin Mary is leaving for the south." According to Mieczyslaw Maneli, a Polish representative on the ICC, hunger was also a major cause of the refugee exodus. See his *War of the Vanquished* (New York: Harper & Row, 1971), p. 38.

called the New Economic Policy (NEP), which permitted a continuation of private ownership in order to build up the productive forces in the Soviet economy. Only in 1928, four years after Lenin's death, did Joseph Stalin launch the first Five-Year Plan and inaugurate the phase of socialist transformation in the Soviet Union. China had followed a similar path in 1950, when Mao Zedong announced the program of New Democracy, characterized by moderate policies designed to build confidence among well-to-do farmers and reassure the urban bourgeoisie that its interests would not be threatened.

During the initial phase after Geneva, DRV leaders followed a similar pattern and moved slowly toward their dream of a socialist society. Although major industries were nationalized, farmland and most of the retail trade remained in private hands until the late 1950s. But there were already some signs of impending internal conflict. Attempts by the regime to extend the land reform program throughout the north ran into problems when doctrinaire elements, many of them apparently incited by Chinese advisers inspired by the example of the land reform program carried out in China, adopted a harsh approach to the issue of land redistribution. Not only wealthy landlords but also many families of modest means lost their land and sometimes their lives in a brutal class conflict produced by overzealous cadres in the countryside. Many of those punished had reportedly given loyal service to the Vietminh cause in the common struggle against the French. By early 1956 it became clear that the program had aroused widespread public hostility, and President Ho Chi Minh made a public confession that errors had been made in implementing the program. General Secretary Truong Chinh, widely believed to be a key supporter of the program, was relieved of his post, and a number of key officials who had administered the policy, including the minister of agriculture, were removed from their positions.[4]

---

[4] Truong Chinh remained a member of the Politburo, however, and four years later he was elected chairman of the Standing Committee of the National Assembly. The number of casualties incurred during the land reform program has always been a matter of dispute. Vietnamese sources privately confirm that the mistakes committed during the land reform program were a significant factor in raising doubts over the relevance of the Chinese model to the process of building a socialist society in the DRV. The most authoritative analysis of the land reform issue is Edwin Moise's *Land Reform in China and Vietnam* (Chapel Hill: University of North Carolina Press, 1983).

The regime also encountered problems in its treatment of Catholics. The eight-point program announced by the DRV during the Geneva conference had promised that freedom of religion would be honored in areas under its authority, and the government now established an officially sponsored Catholic Association to link them to the fate of the revolution. Nevertheless, despite an effort by Ho Chi Minh to bring about a conciliatory official policy toward religious groups in the DRV, some leading party members were dubious about the loyalty of Catholics to the new order, many of whom were persecuted because of their religious convictions. Resentment against the government in rural districts inhabited by Catholics spilled over during riots in central Vietnam in 1956 and led to a harsh crackdown by the regime.[5]

THE ISSUE OF NATIONAL ELECTIONS

A second question facing Party leaders was what to do about the South. The regime had already provided a temporary answer to the question by its decision to accept the compromise settlement hammered out at Geneva. By adhering to that agreement, the DRV tacitly agreed to accept the process laid out by the political declaration while concentrating on domestic reconstruction, in the hope that unity could be achieved by peaceful means.

There were undoubtedly a number of reasons for that decision. Western observers have sometimes remarked that DRV leaders knew from the start that the scheduled elections would not take place, and planned accordingly. In fact, however, there was general uncertainty in world capitals as to whether elections would be held, and many observers felt that it would be difficult to avoid holding them. There seems little doubt that a similar confusion reigned in Hanoi; some Vietminh leaders, reportedly including Ho Chi Minh himself, believed that the elections would occur, although they were well aware that they might not. There was, of course, every reason to hope that the elections would take place as scheduled. If the issue did come to a vote, party leaders were confident that, given the popularity of Ho Chi Minh as the recognized leader of the Vietnam-

[5] See Hoang Van Chi, *From Colonialism to Communism* (New York: Praeger, 1964), for details.

ese struggle for national independence, they would win majority support throughout the country.[6]

There were also practical reasons for accepting a delay in the struggle to complete reunification. With the DRV legally back in power in the north, party leaders would need to devote time and resources to the process of promoting economic development and building a socialist society. A breathing space would be especially crucial to modernize the North Vietnamese armed forces (now known formally as the People's Army of Vietnam, or PAVN) in case of a return to war. Finally, Hanoi had its allies to consider. Both Moscow and Beijing, each for its own reasons, desired a reduction in world tensions and had undoubtedly made it clear that, should the war resume, the DRV might be forced to fight on its own.

In the months that followed the signing of the Geneva accords, Hanoi prepared for the possibility of a peaceful road to reunification. Many of the party's most loyal followers in the south, variously estimated at between 50,000 and 100,000 people, were transported to North Vietnam as part of the transfer of refugees called for by the Geneva agreement. Many of the younger ones were placed in school or in a training academy to prepare for the possibility of reinfiltration into South Vietnam at a later date. Of those Vietminh supporters who remained in the south, some left the movement, while others were removed because of what was described in party documents as "low morale," "dubious political backgrounds," or unsatisfactory performance. Those who remained active, numbering some 15,000 individuals, were now deployed in a variety of ways. Some surfaced as members of local peace committees to promote the holding of national elections, while others were assigned to work in small mobile paramilitary organizations or organize and maintain a clandes-

---

[6] For an extended discussion of this issue, see Carlyle A. Thayer, *War by Other Means*, pp. 6–7. Jeffrey Race, in *War Comes to Long An* (Berkeley: University of California Press, 1971), p. 74, cites unnamed Vietminh elements in South Vietnam to the effect that they were skeptical that elections would be held. A senior official in Hanoi informed me recently that DRV officials definitely expected them to occur and were quite disappointed when they did not. An indication that party leaders expected the Geneva accords to be carried out is contained in a captured document entitled "A Party Account of the Situation in the Nam Bo Region of South Vietnam, 1954–1960," p. 41. Hereafter this source will be cited as "Party Account."

tine organization in the cities, towns, and villages of South Vietnam. The party clearly hoped to prepare for all contingencies.[7]

The most visible symbol of remaining Vietminh influence in the south took shape in the committees formed throughout the region to promote the holding of national elections. The most publicized of such organizations was in Saigon, the capital of the new government of South Vietnam, where a Saigon-Cholon Committee to Promote the Peace (Phong Trao Hoa Binh Saigon-Cholon) was established under the chairmanship of Nguyen Huu Tho, a lawyer and long-time supporter of the Vietminh. Tho had been arrested and jailed for seditious activities during the war against the French, but had never been directly identified as a member of the Communist Party. Other committees were formed in smaller market towns and rural villages throughout the country.[8]

Clearly, however, party leaders in Hanoi did not assume that the road to national unity would necessarily be a peaceful one. Although the movement's southern headquarters during the Franco-Vietminh conflict, known as the Trung Uong cuc Mien Nam (the Central Office of South Vietnam, or COSVN) was now replaced by a smaller regional Committee for the South, the party retained an underground network as well as several thousand well-hidden weapons, and soon began to establish contact with other dissident groups in the southern provinces, such as discontented members of the two religious sects, the Cao Dai and the Hoa Hao. The director of the new committee was Le Duan, a veteran party member from central Vietnam and now a member of its leading executive body, the Politburo. The son of a railway worker, he rose to Central Committee status in the late 1930s, but spent most of World War II in prison on the island of Poulo Condore, off the coast of Cochin China. After release from jail, Le Duan served as deputy director of COSVN during the war against the French. He was reported to be skeptical

---

[7] "Party Account," pp. 35–36. This source claims that there were 15,000 party members in the south prior to the cease-fire, and that there was a party chapter in virtually all villages outside of sect areas and among the minority regions in the central highlands.

[8] For a discussion of the Committee to Promote the Peace, see Tran Van Giau, *Mien Nam Giu Vung Thanh Dong* [The South on the Road to Victory] (Hanoi: Khoa Hoc, 1964). Cholon is a section of Saigon inhabited primarily by Overseas Chinese.

that the provisions of the Geneva accords calling for national elections would be upheld. Within the party leadership he was an influential spokesman for an activist policy to achieve national reunification at the earliest possible time.

Still, for the time being, the primary emphasis was placed on seeking reunification by peaceful means. As one source put it:

> Our goal, then, was not to overthrow the enemy government as during the resistance, but to force it, by means of struggles, to improve social welfare and carry out freedom and democracy. By this way the enemy administration would be changed gradually, and favorable conditions for the realization of independence and reunification through the fulfillment of the Geneva agreement would come about.[9]

It soon became clear that Hanoi's hopes for a peaceful road to unification on its own terms were misplaced. Leading figures in the new government in the south had no intention of permitting the remnants of the Vietminh organization to take part in legal political activities. The offices of the Saigon-Cholon Committee to Promote the Peace were closed down, while Nguyen Huu Tho and several other members of the committee were arrested and sent to prison. Similar actions were taken against local committees throughout the country.

At the head of the new government in Saigon was Prime Minister Ngo Dinh Diem, a veteran Vietnamese politician who had been appointed to the office by Bao Dai in June 1954, while the Geneva conference was still underway. The son of a court official in the imperial city of Hue, Diem had been active in politics for two decades and was known as a devout Catholic, a fervent anticolonialist, and a vigorous opponent of the Communists. In 1945 he had refused an offer by Ho Chi Minh to cooperate with the Vietminh. After hiding in the Canadian Embassy in Hanoi for several weeks, he escaped to South Vietnam, where he rejected an offer by Bao Dai to join the latter's own fledgling Associated State of Vietnam.

In 1950, Diem went to the United States, where he resided for a time in a Catholic seminary in New Jersey. Intensely interested in Vietnamese politics, he periodically consulted with State Department officials in Washington, usually at his own request. Many U.S.

---

[9] "Party Account," p. 39.

diplomats viewed him as devoted to his country but impractical and rigid in his views. Diem argued that only a Catholic could truly guarantee the success of a noncommunist government, but many U.S. officials were concerned that the Catholics, who represented a small and privileged sector of South Vietnamese society, could hardly hope to provide a unifying force for the fragile government in Saigon.[10]

Whether senior officials in the Eisenhower administration were persuaded at that time that Ngo Dinh Diem provided a possible solution to the problem of Vietnam is doubtful. But Bao Dai apparently thought that this was the case, and by his own account it was for that reason that, despite their mutual antipathy, he offered Diem the prime ministership in the early summer of 1954. Bao Dai was well aware that France was about to withdraw from Vietnam, and he hoped that the appointment of Diem would persuade the United States to step in as the new patron of the projected government in Saigon.[11]

Diem's appointment apparently did not play especially well in South Vietnam. According to Robert McClintock, the chargé d'affaires in the U.S. mission in Saigon at the time, the announcement of his appointment "totally failed to arouse enthusiasm [among the] Vietnamese people." Except for the region of his birth in central Vietnam, where many people respected him for his staunch integrity and patriotism, the reaction elsewhere was one of "indifference and skepticism." When U.S. Chief of Mission Donald Heath returned to Saigon, Diem appealed to him for assistance. In cables to Washington, Heath expressed his doubts about Diem, who, he said, was viewed as inept, unsympathetic to social reforms, and hostile to the religious sects. Heath concluded that the U.S. should support him, but only because there was "no one else."[12]

---

[10] For a typical comment by U.S. officials about Ngo Dinh Diem, see *Central Files,* Memo PSA (Bonsal) to FE (Allison), January 16, 1953. General surveys of his early career can be found in Robert Scigliano, *South Vietnam: Nation under Stress* (Boston: Houghton Mifflin, 1963), and Denis Warner, *The Last Confucian* (Harmondsworth, England: Penguin, 1964).

[11] It has been asserted that Diem was picked for the office at the insistence of the United States, but I have seen no evidence to that effect. For Bao Dai's account, see his *Dragon d'Annam,* pp. 325–328.

[12] *Central Files,* Saigon 304 to Department of State, July 23, 1954; ibid., Saigon 2819 to Department of State, June 18, 1954.

In Washington, the CIA was equally cautious. A National Intelligence Estimate (NIE) published just after the close of the Geneva conference predicted that the situation in South Vietnam would continue to deteriorate during the next several months and concluded that if national elections were held, the Vietminh would be almost certain to win. In the meantime, the author speculated, the latter would try to realize their goals by political and psychological means. Secretary of State John Foster Dulles was determined to act: "We do not wish [to] make it appear," he replied, "[that] Ngo Dinh Diem [is] our protégé or that we are irrevocably committed to him. On [the] other hand we do believe [that the] kind of thing he stands for is [a] necessary ingredient of success and we do not now see it elsewhere." Dulles reported that the administration was prepared to provide him with aid and a public statement of support.[13]

During the final months of 1954, Ngo Dinh Diem's situation in Saigon was perilous. A combination of leading members of the religious sects, pro-French elements sympathetic to Bao Dai, and French officials in Saigon conspired to bring about his replacement by someone more responsive to their wishes. The Eisenhower administration sent a high-ranking emissary, the president's personal friend and wartime colleague, General J. Lawton Collins, to Saigon to bolster Diem's authority and persuade his enemies to cooperate with the new government to stabilize the situation. But Diem was his own worst enemy and soon alienated key groups within South Vietnamese society by seeking to concentrate power in his own hands. Even General Collins suffered growing doubts about Diem's capacity to lead, and during the winter of 1954–1955 Collins advised the White House to cooperate with the French in seeking a new prime minister. But Diem had friends in Washington, notably Mike Mansfield, an influential senator from the state of Montana, and Colonel Edward Lansdale, a U.S. military officer who had earlier assisted Ramon Magsaysay in putting down a Communist-led insurgency in the Philippines. Both argued tirelessly that Diem, whatever his weaknesses, was the only Vietnamese politician with the determination and the credentials to wage a successful struggle

---

[13] *Central Files*, Department of State 610 to U.S. Embassy, Paris, August 18, 1954. The NIE, entitled "Present situation in South Vietnam," was dated August 13, 1954.

against communism and preserve an independent government in the South.

For the next several months, Diem held stubbornly to his course, asserting his authority over the sects and removing pro-French elements from positions of influence in the government. For a brief period in April, it appeared as though the centrifugal forces in South Vietnamese society would pull his government down, and at one point the White House—at Collins' urging—was on the verge of cooperating with the French in finding a replacement. But at the last minute Diem was able to suppress opposition elements among the sects, and resistance collapsed. Colonel Lansdale cabled jubilantly from Saigon that Diem had triumphed over his rivals, and the administration canceled its plans to replace him.

The decision to back Diem was not made without misgivings in Washington. Even President Eisenhower admitted to intimates that Diem had only a 50-50 chance of surviving, while Secretary of State Dulles remarked that, even if the Diem experiment failed, it would buy time for the U.S. to strengthen other areas of Southeast Asia against the anticipated expansion of international communism into the region. The administration had already made a tentative commitment to defend South Vietnam and the neutral states of Laos and Cambodia. In an "umbrella clause" of the new Southeast Asia Treaty Organization (SEATO), signed in Manila in September 1954, members of the new organization would consider an attack on any of the three Indochinese states equivalent to an attack on one of the signatories.[14]

In the United States, an organization called Friends of Vietnam was formed to drum up support for the new government, while Michigan State University signed a contract to help build up its

---

[14] SEATO was formed under U.S. sponsorship as a means of resisting the further expansion of communism in Southeast Asia. Members included the United States, the United Kingdom, France, Australia, New Zealand, Thailand, Pakistan, and the Philippines. The Indochinese states were not permitted to join the new organization because of the neutrality provisions prohibiting them from joining foreign alliances contained in the Geneva accords. SEATO did not require military action along the lines of NATO, but called on each signatory to respond to aggression in the treaty area "in accordance with its constitutional processes." See Leszek Buszuynki, *S.E.A.T.O.: The Failure of an Alliance Strategy* (Singapore: Singapore University Press, 1983).

administration and police forces. But it did not take long for Washington to encounter problems in establishing a cooperative relationship with Saigon. The first issue to arise was on the enforcement of the Geneva accords. Diem was obdurate on the subject of national elections. The Eisenhower administration wanted to avoid the elections, which it was convinced Diem would lose. But it hoped to persuade him to agree to consultations with North Vietnamese representatives, while placing such stringent conditions on the electoral process that Hanoi could not possibly accept. Diem, however, was adamant in his opposition to any form of elections, and when Hanoi appealed to Saigon to set up a meeting to discuss the issue, the latter refused. The White House hid its discomfort and gave Ngo Dinh Diem its public support.

The failure to hold elections caused relatively little stir at the time. Hanoi complained to Great Britain about Diem's behavior, and China demanded the convening of a new Geneva conference to resolve the issue. But there was little international support for resuming the talks, and when even Moscow failed to back the DRV strongly, the idea of a second conference was abandoned. For the time being, Ho Chi Minh and his colleagues had little choice but to swallow their frustration and hope that the road to peaceful reunification was still open.

The refusal of the Saigon government to hold consultations on national elections later became one of the most controversial issues in the Vietnam conflict. Critics of U.S. war policy argued that by backing Diem's decision, the Eisenhower administration had in effect weakened the legal case for U.S. assistance to South Vietnam and freed the DRV to ignore the terms of the accords. Defenders of the administration pointed out that Saigon was not in fact obligated to respect the terms of the political declaration, since the representatives of the Bao Dai government at Geneva had refused to adhere to the agreement. They further asserted that no country could be bound to conditions accepted by a past colonial oppressor and argued that free elections were in any case impossible in the north, which openly professed its adherence to the principles of Marxism-Leninism.[15]

---

[15] For a view critical of the U.S. decision, see Franklin Weinstein, *Vietnam's Unheld Elections* (Ithaca, N.Y.: Cornell University Southeast Asian Series, 1967).

COUNTERREVOLUTION IN THE SOUTH

Having suppressed the religious sects and dodged the issue of national elections, by the summer of 1955 Diem was ready to make use of U.S. assistance to build a viable noncommunist state in the south. His first task was to dispose of his chief rival, Chief of State Bao Dai. The latter had undermined his own already fragile reputation in the United States by conspiring unsuccessfully with pro-French elements to force Diem's resignation. With his own position more secure, Diem now plotted to seek Bao Dai's removal from the political scene. With little warning, in October he called for a national referendum to choose between himself and Bao Dai. The latter was then living in France and refused to contest the election, thus giving Diem a clear field to mobilize popular support for his own candidacy. In the referendum, engineered by his Machiavellian younger brother Ngo Dinh Nhu, Diem received over 98 percent of the total vote. Although on the face of it this was a convincing figure, the new U.S. ambassador in Saigon, Frederick Reinhardt, expressed his concern at Diem's political techniques, calling them "a travesty of democratic procedures." In some areas, Diem allegedly received more ballots than there were legal voters.[16]

Ambassador Reinhardt pleaded with Washington to press Ngo Dinh Diem to undertake political reforms aimed at creating a democratic society. But influential officials in the State Department argued that what was needed in South Vietnam was not so much democratic procedures as a strong government capable of suppressing the menace of communism. Such views were especially prevalent among Western scholars specializing in Asian affairs and undoubtedly reflected trends elsewhere in the region, where several embryonic democratic governments, shaken by racial, religious, and class tensions, had been overthrown and replaced by one-party governments or military rule. Secretary of State Dulles, no mean practitioner of realpolitik himself, agreed with such views. In his judgment, a strong and stable government was the most essential thing in South Vietnam. Constitutional procedures, he instructed the am-

---

[16] Saigon to Department of State, October 14, 1955, cited in *Foreign Relations of the United States, 1955–1957*, vol. 1, (Washington, D.C.: United States Government Printing Office, 1985), pp. 562–563. Hereafter *FRUS*.

bassador, "should be developed to the extent that they do not weaken central authority."[17]

Washington's preference for political stability over representative government was shared by Ngo Dinh Diem's entourage in Saigon. At U.S. urging, Diem moved toward creating a legal basis for his government. In 1956 a constitution was promulgated which created a republic (called the Republic of Vietnam, or RVN) based on a combination of the presidential and parliamentary forms of government. But Diem manipulated the system to provide himself, as president, with strong executive powers. The legislative branch, called the National Assembly, was dominated by representatives sympathetic to the regime, and opposition parties were not permitted. A progovernment political party, known as the Personalist Labor (Can Lao) Party, was established under the leadership of Diem's younger brother, the manipulative minister of the interior, Ngo Dinh Nhu.[18]

The heart of Ngo Dinh Diem's support came from his fellow Catholics, who numbered over 1 million in the late 1950s, about 7 percent of the total population of South Vietnam. Many of them had migrated from the northern provinces. Once in the South, they were resettled in relatively unpopulated areas in the mountains or in the suburbs around Saigon. There they were expected to provide a protective zone for Diem's government against possible Vietminh activities in rural areas. Generally better educated and more hostile to communism than their Buddhist or animist compatriots, Catholics were a bulwark of the Saigon government during its early years. It is not surprising that Diem tended to rely on them, as well as on other refugees from the North. According to one historian of the period, there were no southerners in his initial cabinet. Later, some were appointed to senior positions, but throughout the remainder of Diem's period in office the majority of officials in the bureaucracy were from the northern or central provinces.[19]

The Saigon regime also began to turn its attention to the issue of land reform. Cultivable land in South Vietnam had been parceled out on an inequitable basis at least since the arrival of the French nearly a century before, when vast tracts in the Mekong River delta

---

[17] *Central Files*, Secretary of State to Saigon, October 6, 1955.
[18] The Personalist Labor Party was not a mass party but a small elite core composed of bureaucrats and military officers sympathetic to the president.
[19] This information comes from Scigliano, *Nation under Stress*, p. 51.

had been opened up to the highest bidder. According to knowledgeable observers, less than 1 percent of the total population owned over half the cultivated land in the south. During the Franco-Vietminh conflict the Bao Dai government had failed to take significant action to remedy the situation, and in the winter of 1954–1955, Eisenhower's personal emissary, General J. Lawton Collins, had placed land reform high on the list of priorities of the new Saigon government.

It was soon clear, however, that Diem was not especially sympathetic to the idea. Not only did his family background preclude him from understanding the needs of the poor, but much of his active support came from absentee landlords in the cities and the landed gentry in rural areas. Although the Saigon regime, at U.S. insistence, eventually promulgated a land redistribution program, its provisions were not nearly as stringent as programs launched elsewhere in Asia and were easily evaded by wealthy landowners. Several years after the program had been put into operation, less than 10 percent of the land eligible for transfer had been put under new ownership.

As a result, the land reform program had little effect on the patterns of land ownership in South Vietnam. In one village studied by a U.S. researcher, out of 130 landowners, 31 were nonresident landlords who collectively owned over 50 percent of all the rice land in the village. The average farm was less than 2 hectares (a hectare is a little over 2 acres), while one-quarter possessed less than a single hectare, the amount of rice land generally considered necessary for subsistence. For tenants, rents amounted to an average of about 25 to 30 percent of the main crop. Although that figure was lower than it had been under the French, two-thirds of all farmers in the village were in debt.[20]

Diem's approach to the challenge posed by revolutionary forces in the south was military, rather than political and social. In the summer of 1955 he opened a so-called Denounce the Communists campaign which was designed to root out subversive elements throughout the country. Those arrested for antigovernment activities were sent to detention camps, where they were sometimes tortured or summarily executed. In January 1956 a presidential decree authorized "the arrest and detention of anyone deemed dangerous

[20] James B. Hendry, *The Small World of Khanh Hau* (Chicago: Aldine, 1964).

to the safety of the state and their incarceration in one of several concentration camps." Under the program, thousands of alleged opponents of the regime were sent to prison.

WHY ARE SOUTHERN COMRADES UPSET?

As South Vietnamese army units scoured the countryside and attempted to eliminate all resistance to Diem's rule, leaders of the Vietnam Workers' Party authorized their followers in the south to engage in limited self-defense efforts, and Vietminh elements began to fight back. Here is one account published in Hanoi.

> From the end of 1955 to 1956, as Diem stepped up his "Denounce the Communists" campaign, the hunt for patriots and former resistance members became fiercer. Finding it impossible to live and carry on the political struggle in the countryside the latter fled to former resistance bases such as the Plain of Reeds [southwest of Saigon], the U Minh jungle [between Bac Lieu and Rach Gia provinces on the Gulf of Thailand] or Resistance Zones D and C [north and northwest of Saigon]. Diem sent his troops after them. Cornered, they had to organize self-defense together with the local population. In their fight for survival the first units of the Liberation Army took shape, one or two companies in strength in some places and a battalion in others.[21]

The immediate reaction in Hanoi to Diem's belligerent stance, however, was generally cautious. In the summer of 1955, shortly after Saigon's refusal to hold consultations, the VWP Central Committee confirmed the existing policy of consolidating power in the north while seeking a peaceful road to national reunification with the south. Such an approach, however, did not sit well with some of the party's leading cadres in the south, who chafed under the restrictions imposed by Hanoi and began to argue that Diem's aggressive actions required a firm response. During the winter of 1955–1956, Le Duan warned the party leadership that a policy involving increased use of armed violence might be required to bring about the overthrow of the Diem regime and unification of the two zones.

---

[21] Ta Xuan Linh, "How Armed Struggle Began in South Vietnam," in *Vietnam Courier*, March 1974, p. 20, cited in *No Other Road to Take: Memoirs of Mrs. Nguyen Thi Dinh*, (Mai V. Elliott, trans.), Ithaca, N.Y.: Cornell University Date Paper Number 102, 1976), p. 12. For a more detailed analysis of DRV policy during this initial post-Geneva period, see Thayer, *War by Other Means*, chaps. 2 and 3.

In March, however, he was instructed to restrict the activities of the movement within the framework of the current guidelines until a long-term strategy could be worked out. But the mood of restiveness was also prevalent among refugees from the south now living in the DRV, many of whom occupied positions of responsibility in the party and the government bureaucracy and formed a vocal pressure group for the problems and aspirations of their compatriots in the southern provinces.

For party leaders in Hanoi, in fact, the appeal from their southern constituents for a more activist policy in the south had come at a particularly awkward moment. At the Twentieth National Congress of the Communist Party of the Soviet Union (CPSU) in January 1956, the new Soviet party chief, Nikita Khrushchev, had announced a new policy of promoting "peaceful coexistence" with the nations of the West. The Congress also approved a statement abrogating the Leninist view of the inevitability of violent class struggle and announcing the possibility of a peaceful transition to socialism in many countries. Moscow had undoubtedly passed those decisions on to the party leadership in Hanoi when Soviet Politburo member Anastas Mikoyan visited Hanoi just prior to the convening of a meeting of the VWP Central Committee in mid-April. According to press reports, Mikoyan stressed the importance of a strict observance of the Geneva accords and the need to seek reunification of the two zones of Vietnam through national elections.

The debate within the Central Committee must have been intense. Truong Chinh, who had attended the CPSU Twentieth Congress in January and was reported to have been in favor of continuing the policy of peaceful reunification, declared that there were

> some people who do not yet believe in the correctness of this political program and in the policy of peaceful reunification of the country, holding that these are illusory and reformist. The view of the CPSU 20th Congress on the form of transition to Socialism in different countries, and of the possibility of preventing war in the present era, has provided us with new reasons to be confident in the correctness of the policy of the Vietnamese Workers' Party and Fatherland Front in the struggle for national Reunification.[22]

[22] *Vietnam News Agency* (hereafter *VNA*), April 30, 1956. Mikoyan's speech was reported in *VNA*, April 7, 1956. According to Thayer, those "some people" probably included the party's senior commander in the South, Le Duan. See *War by Other Means*, p. 63.

In the end, the Central Committee agreed to follow Moscow's lead, but with some reservations. The final resolution issued at the close of the conference declared that the party continued to support the existing policy of promoting national reunification by peaceful means. But an added statement warned that although the party still believed deeply that this was a correct policy, "reactionary forces still exist in the other half of our country, and are still plotting to instigate war. We must therefore constantly enhance our vigilance and exert efforts to consolidate National Defense in order to meet all eventualities." In his own closing remarks at the conference, Ho Chi Minh was more explicit, noting that while in the modern era the road to socialism might sometimes be a peaceful one, in countries where the bourgeois class continued to control the police forces and the machinery of state, "the proletarian class still has to prepare for armed struggle."[23]

The April meeting of the Central Committee did not close the debate. For the remainder of the spring and summer, the discussion over policy in the south continued. To quiet the discontent, Ho Chi Minh wrote an open letter to "southern comrades" in an attempt to defend the government's policy of pursuing national reunification by peaceful means. The struggle, he warned, would be long and hard, and the south could not be liberated until the north itself was strong.[24]

But the passing of the scheduled date for national elections in mid-July 1956 led to a new eruption of disquiet. An article in the official party newspaper *Nhan Dan* referred to such discontent, remarking that "some people" were overly optimistic and impatient for a quick victory, while others were filled with pessimism and doubts. Some were "simple in their thoughts" and "thought that national elections would surely be held and then became pessimistic and depressed when the elections did not take place." Others were "reluctant to carry on a long and hard struggle" and hoped for

---

[23] Ho's speech is quoted in *USVN*, bk. 2, pt. IV.B.5, p. 47, and *VNA*, April 27, 1956. For a discussion, see Thayer, *War by Other Means*, p. 67. Also see *Cuoc Khang Chien Chong My Cuu Nuoc, 1954–1975: Nhung Su Kien Quan Su* [The Anti-U.S. Resistance War, 1954–1975: Military Events] (Hanoi: Quan Doi Nhan Dan, 1981), p. 27. Hereafter *CKC*.

[24] *Toan Tap*, vol. 7, pp. 453–457. For an English-language version, see Fall, *On Revolution*, p. 302.

unification by peaceful means. Such people fail to realize, the editorial concluded, that the best way is "to positively build up the North, positively to unite and struggle with perseverance and patience in the South, and not to be afraid of difficulties and hardship." Such statements, however, did not pacify the more ardent patriots within the regroupee community. In September, Pham Ngoc Thach, the former head of the Vanguard Youth organization in Saigon and now deputy minister of health, requested permission to return south to take part in the struggle. Two months later, the party newspaper *Nhan Dan* published another article entitled, "For what reason are the Southern comrades in work camps, state farms and enterprises upset?"[25]

But, as Ho Chi Minh's brief comment in his closing speech to the April conference had implied, some party leaders in Hanoi (perhaps including Ho Chi Minh himself) had already begun to reach the tentative conclusion that a policy of armed struggle might eventually be needed. In mid-June, the Politburo discussed the problem and issued a statement which concluded that it was "extremely important that we endeavor to build up the revolutionary forces" in the South. Although the primary form of struggle continued to be political in nature, it noted, that did not preclude the use of armed self-defense under certain circumstances. The statement called for the consolidation of existing self-defense units in the south and the building of revolutionary base areas. It only remained to determine how and in what circumstances the transition to a more aggressive approach must be applied.[26]

While senior party officials in Hanoi discussed strategy, a similar debate was taking place in the south. Although some cadres stationed in the southern provinces chafed under the restrictions applied by DRV leaders in the north and wanted a more direct military approach similar to that which had been applied during the war against the French, others wanted to retain the policy of seeking reunification by peaceful means. Le Duan, however, opposed the adoption of any strategy that relied wholly on either the political or

---

[25] *Nhan Dan* editorial, July 22, 1956. On Pham Ngoc Thach, see Ken Post, *Revolution, Socialism and Nationalism in Viet Nam*, vol. 2: *Viet Nam Divided* (Aldershot: Dartmouth Publishers, 1989), pp. 121–122. Pham Ngoc Thach later reportedly died of malaria while in South Vietnam. The reference to the September article in *Nhan Dan* is in ibid.
[26] *CKC*, p. 28.

the military approach, and instead advocated a combination of the two. In the summer of 1956, in an effort to influence the debate within the Politburo (and perhaps to bring unconvinced colleagues within the Committee for the South around to his views), he wrote a short report on conditions in South Vietnam entitled "The Path to Revolution in the South" ("Duong Loi Cach Mang Mien Nam"). In broad terms, the pamphlet argued in favor of continuing the existing policy of political struggle, but in a more activist manner (given by Le Duan the label of "revolutionary war") that would enable southern cadres to protect themselves against the repressive measures adopted by the Diem regime. Le Duan proposed a strategy that was less like Mao's strategy of people's war, which had been applied during the Franco-Vietminh conflict, and more like the strategy employed during the August Revolution, which used military and political techniques in a combined uprising in the towns and cities.[27]

The Politburo in Hanoi did not act immediately on Le Duan's proposals. The question was apparently raised for debate at a meeting of the Central Committee in September, but no decision was reached, and the issue was referred back to the Politburo for further consideration. It was discussed again by the Central Committee in December, but it seems clear that the regime was not yet ready to make a final decision on a problem of such transcendent importance. An editorial in *Nhan Dan* published after the December meeting noted that "we must not allow the winning over of the South to detract from the requirements of consolidating the North." On the other hand, directives were sent to the Committee for the South ordering the creation of secret military units and revolutionary bases in mountain areas. Party units in the south were now authorized to engage in selective terrorist operations to punish those who served the enemy cause and encourage fence-sitters to join the revolutionary movement. This compromise apparently served as the operational guidelines for the southern insurgent movement for the next two years.[28]

---

[27] The pamphlet is available as item no. 1002, in Race Documents, a collection of materials deposited by Jeffrey Race with the Center for Research Libraries, Chicago, Illinois. An English-language version is located in Gareth Porter, ed., *Vietnam: The Definitive Documentation of Human Decisions*, vol. 2 (Stanfordville, N.Y.: E. M. Coleman, 1979), pp. 24–30.

[28] See the reference to the meeting of southern leaders in December in *CKC*, p. 20. Also see the article by Bac Ngoc Anh in *NCLS* 196 (January 1981): 87.

In the meantime, a change in the party leadership sent a clear signal that the mood in Hanoi was shifting. Sometime early in 1957, Le Duan was relieved of his post in the south and appointed to a new position in Hanoi as acting general secretary of the VWP. President Ho Chi Minh had replaced Truong Chinh as general secretary after the latter's demotion a few months previously, but was apparently unable to bear the heavy workload required of the position and wished to concentrate on his presidential duties. With Le Duan in charge of the Politburo, southern comrades would now have a strong advocate in Hanoi.

Undoubtedly one of the factors preventing party leaders from shifting to a more activist mode in the south was the difficulty that it would present for Hanoi's relationship with its chief allies. China did not pose a serious problem. At least for the moment, Beijing did not want a return to the level of conflict in Indochina that had existed prior to the settlement at Geneva, but it had no apparent objection to a relatively low level of insurgency in the south. Such conditions, in fact, might actually enhance Hanoi's dependence upon Chinese assistance, while not increasing the risk of a direct confrontation with the United States. Sometime in 1956, Chinese leaders allegedly sent a telegram to their fraternal comrades in Hanoi advising them to restrict their activities in South Vietnam to Maoist-style protracted war and the mobilization of the masses. The opportunity for final victory, they advised, would only come when international conditions were ripe, a condition that might not occur for a decade or perhaps even for a century. Such advice could hardly have been welcome to Ho Chi Minh and his colleagues.[29]

The Soviet Union was a more serious stumbling block. Under the direction of new CPSU party chief Nikita S. Khrushchev, Moscow had become increasingly insistent in urging the Vietnamese to refrain from stoking the revolutionary fires in South Vietnam and had not been especially supportive in protesting Diem's refusal to hold national elections. In January 1957, the USSR suddenly proposed the admission of both Vietnamese states to the United Nations. This surprise announcement undoubtedly caused shock waves in Hanoi and resulted in the hasty exchange of high-level

[29] Hanoi released this comment as an excerpt from the telegram at a time when it was anxious to criticize China for the inconstancy of its support for the Vietnamese revolution. Therefore, this quotation must be treated with care. See *CKC*, pp. 34–35.

visitors in succeeding months. In November, Ho Chi Minh led a delegation to Moscow to attend the Congress of Delegates of Communist and Workers' Parties. The overall thrust of discussion at the conference was to emphasize the need for peaceful coexistence with the West, but the following reference was inserted into the conference communiqué: "In conditions in which the exploiting classes resort to violence against the people, it is necessary to bear in mind another possibility—the nonpeaceful transition to socialism. Leninism teaches and history confirms that the ruling classes never relinquish power voluntarily." It seems probable that the statement had been inserted at the request of Ho Chi Minh, since it closely resembled the remark made in the speech that he had presented to the meeting of the VWP Central Committee in April.[30]

AN EXTREMELY IMPORTANT MILESTONE

During 1957, the Diem regime intensified its efforts to suppress the movement in the south, to which it now began to apply the pejorative label Viet Cong (Vietnamese Communists, or VC). With U.S. assistance in the form of both equipment and training, the size and weapons capability of the South Vietnamese armed forces (to be formally known as the Army of the Republic of Vietnam, or ARVN) was increased, and governmental military units attempted to penetrate key areas occupied by resistance forces north and northwest of Saigon, as well as in the U Minh forest, in the heart of the Ca Mau peninsula. Many of the officers in the new armed forces had previously been trained for commanding positions in the Vietnamese National Army by the French.

By now there was a growing recognition in Saigon and Washington that the revolutionary movement could not be suppressed unless the resistance forces were isolated and prevented from maintaining contacts with the population. In Maoist parlance, the "fish" (the guerrillas) received their sustenance from the "sea" (the people in the countryside). Without that contact, the fish could not survive. If the guerrilla movement could be prevented from obtaining provisions and recruits from the villages, it would die of its own accord.

---

[30] For a reference, see *USVN*, bk. 2, pt. 51, fn. 171, and ibid, bk. 2, pt. IV.A.5, summary, p. 26.

To hasten this process, in 1958 the Saigon regime introduced a new program to fortify and defend villages from Communist infiltration and control. Known as "agrovilles," these new fortified hamlets were designed as population clusters larger than the natural village and strengthened with barbed wire and other fortifications to enable the villagers to defend themselves against enemy attack. Within the agrovilles, government agents and informers tried to identify and root out the enemy, some of whom had innocently surfaced during the months following the Geneva accords.

The ultimate objective of the agrovilles was to isolate dissident elements from their source of provisions and recruits in rural areas. Villagers were mobilized by the RVN to enroll in government-sponsored organizations like the Republican Youth and the People's Self-defense Militia to protect the community against infestation by subversive elements. As the situation was described by one Hanoi source:

> Nightly, people had to mount guard duty, and when they saw our cadres come to their villages, they would beat on their hollow bamboo stems to ring the alarm. In many villages, which had been in the center of four base areas during the resistance, our cadres, when they appeared, were encircled and hunted by screaming people. This situation causes suspicion and division even among our brothers.[31]

Party leaders in Hanoi were now forced to concede that Diem's vigorous action had served to stabilize his heretofore fragile regime and severely damage the morale of supporters of the Vietminh.

> The enemy at this time had completed the establishment of his ruling machinery from top to bottom, being able to build a tight espionage network and to form popular force units in every village. He was able to control each and every family by means of the house-block system [a Saigon-run security system according to which families throughout the country were organized into units of five and made jointly responsible for the loyalty of all of their members]. The movement's influence was so low that even the people's low-level struggles, such as the requests for relief or for loans to grow crops were labeled as "Viet Cong activities," and the enemy participants were intimidated and terrorized. At the

---

[31] "Party Account," p. 32.

same time, the enemy kept on systematically building his agro-villes, concentrating people in centers and hamlets away from remote areas and to zones near commercial [sic] centers, wide roads and waterways. He carried out a tight system of oppression in the rural areas. . . .

During this period, the people were somewhat perturbed and shaken even though they strongly hated the enemy and believed that the revolution would be victorious in spite of everything. Doubt in our struggle method and old views from the past were now revived and voiced more vigorously. People said that the struggles for "democratic and civil rights only lead to the prisons and to the tombs." and that "such struggles will end with everyone's death." In many localities people requested the Party to take up arms and fight back against the enemy.[32]

Directives from Hanoi had authorized southern commanders to organize themselves for self-defense, and even to selectively punish enemies of the revolution by means of assassination and intimidation, but it had provided no precise instructions on how to cope with the new challenge. With Le Duan now in Hanoi, the new leader in the south, Nguyen Van Linh, appeared momentarily uncertain about what tactics to adopt. Some units reacted passively, while others began to act on their own, organizing military units to launch counterattacks against government sweeps or intensifying terrorist actions against government informers or officials in local areas. But in the absence of an effective means of self-defense, the party organization was essentially defenseless. As the *Party Account* noted, the movement's military efforts between 1957 and 1959 "did not help the movement much" to counter the Saigon campaign.

By early 1959, the size of the party in the south had declined to about 5000 members. In some areas, the VWP organization was virtually wiped out. In the Saigon industrial suburbs of Go Vap and Tan Binh, for example, there were more than 1000 active cadres at the time of the cease-fire. After consolidation and the removal of inactive members, the local organization in 1957 was down to 385 members. By mid-1959, only one comrade remained active. Every member of the district leadership had either been killed or placed in prison. In the words of the *Party Account*, from its point of fragility

---

[32] Ibid., p. 26.

in 1954, the Diem regime had now reached "a relatively strong and stable position with centralized power."[33]

Official histories of the movement written in Hanoi single out key areas where local cadres began to adopt more active measures to defend themselves. In mid-1958, the party committee in Tay Ninh province, a rubber plantation area adjacent to the Cambodian border, decided to form a regional military command to direct self-defense military operations. The scattered resistance forces in the province were integrated into four companies and assigned the objective of creating two liberated base areas northeast and northwest of Saigon, known as War Zones C and D, respectively. In August, guerrilla units launched a sudden attack on a district capital in Tay Ninh province and briefly occupied it. Two months later a second attack took place on the U.S. military base at Bien Hoa, less than 20 miles north of Saigon.

In the meantime, similar developments were underway in the central highlands and along the central coast. In mid-1958 the party committee of Interzone V, a region that covered the bulk of the central highlands, declared:

> Having reviewed the situation in the Interzone and recently gained experience in Nam Bo [in western South Vietnam], we can combine limited armed struggle with political struggle. . . . We must know how to combine self-defense armed struggle or limited armed struggle under certain circumstances and to a certain degree, with the objectives of restricting fascism and expanding our military base.[34]

In late 1958 Le Duan embarked on a secret trip to South Vietnam to evaluate the situation and consult with party leaders in the southern region. On his return to Hanoi, he reported his conclusions to the Central Committee, which held its fifteenth plenary session the following January. It was clear that the southern strategy badly needed clarification. Diem's determined effort to root out dissident elements had met with considerable success, and the party's forces in South Vietnam were not only severely reduced in numbers but

---

[33] Ibid., pp. 37–38.
[34] *CKC*, p. 43, citing the summer-fall resolution of the party committee of Interzone V.

badly demoralized. It was, in the words of one prominent historian in Hanoi, the "darkest hour" of the revolution. Yet there were promising signs as well, for Ngo Dinh Diem had achieved political stability at a high price. In the view of leading party representatives in both zones, a growing percentage of the population in the south was now alienated from the Saigon regime and potentially ripe for revolution. It only remained to determine how to carry it out.

But that question placed party strategists in Hanoi in a quandary. Although efforts by the regime to strengthen the North Vietnamese armed forces had had some effect, the government had just embarked on an ambitious program to begin the transformation to socialism in the DRV. A plan to collectivize farmlands in the north was underway, and a three-year program to begin the process of socialist industrialization had just been announced. To make matters more difficult, neither of Hanoi's main allies could be expected to approve a decision to adopt a more activist policy in South Vietnam. Although Moscow's view has not been publicized, Chinese leaders continued to advise their Vietnamese comrades to move slowly on plans for reunification until the time was ripe.[35]

Official histories published in Hanoi declare that the Fifteenth Plenum of the VWP Central Committee was an "extremely important milestone" in the struggle for Vietnamese national liberation, because it marked the decision to resort to force to achieve victory in South Vietnam. According to the resolution issued after the conference but not publicized until many years later:

> The fundamental path of development for the revolution in South Vietnam is that of violent struggle. Based on the concrete conditions and existing requirements of revolution, then, the road of violent struggle is: use the strength of the masses, with the political strength as the main factor, combined with military strength to a greater or lesser degree depending on the situation, in order to overthrow the ruling power of the imperialist and feudalist forces and build the revolutionary power of the people.[36]

---

[35] See Hoang Van Hoan, "Distortion of facts about the militant friendship between Viet Nam and China is impermissible," *Beijing Review,* December 7, 1979, p. 15. For Le Duan's trip to the south in 1958, see *USVN,* bk. 4, pt. A.5, tab. 3, p. 56. Also see George Carver, "The Faceless Viet Cong," *Foreign Affairs* 44(3): 359–360.
[36] *CKC,* p. 49.

Party leaders at the fateful meeting of the Central Committee in January 1959, which decided to resort to a strategy of revolutionary war in the south.

The resolution affirmed that final victory in the south could only be achieved through a protracted, difficult, and heroic struggle. But it remained uncertain how to achieve it, and simply stated:

> In the process of difficult and complicated struggle, political struggle will be the main form, but because the enemy is determined to drown the revolution in blood, and because of the . . . revolutionary mood in the South, it will be necessary to a certain extent to adopt methods of self-defense and armed propaganda activities to assist the political struggle. . . . But in the process of using self-defense and armed propaganda units, it is necessary to grasp thoroughly the principle of emphasizing political strength.[37]

[37] Ibid., pp. 49–50. Party leaders themselves recognized that a more precise formulation of strategy would eventually be needed. According to a document captured by ARVN forces in 1966, the decision by the Fifteenth Plenum was described as follows: "How were these responsibilities, aims, and processes of the South Vietnam revolution to be implemented? What must the main forms and procedures of the struggle be?" At the time, the document said, party strategists lacked a clear knowledge of evolving conditions in the south and a knowledge of circumstances in neighboring Laos. Only two years later would the problem be resolved. See *Working Paper on North Viet-Nam's Role in the War in South Viet-Nam* (Washington, D.C.: U.S. Department of State, 1968), item no. 301, entitled CRIMP document.

For reasons that have never been satisfactorily explained, the decisions reached at the Fifteenth Plenum of January 1959 were not implemented until May. Some outside observers have speculated that there may have been two separate sessions of the Central Committee or that disagreements within the party leadership resulted in a delay in implementation. But a senior official in Hanoi recently insisted that the delay was caused by the fact that the decision gave rise to a number of tactical questions which needed to be resolved before final approval could be granted.[38]

In fact, during the months that followed the meeting, a series of crucial decisions were made. In March, the Politburo directed that southern commanders begin construction of a revolutionary base area in the central highlands, a region inhabited primarily by minority peoples that was strategically vital to the cause and was already becoming the focus of intensified conflict between the Saigon regime and the resistance forces in the south. Two months later, the Military Commission of the Central Committee ordered the creation of a new secret organization (called "Group 559" because of the date of creation), which was assigned the task of building a system of trails that could be utilized to transport troops, weapons, and supplies to the revolutionary fighters through the mountainous regions of lower Laos adjacent to the DMZ and into the south. A similar organization to set up a maritime route along the coast, called Group 759, was created in July. The first shipment was carried in July 1961, when a cargo ship carried 4 tons of provisions from North Vietnam to the province of Kien Hoa, in the Mekong delta.[39]

Beginning in 1959, the first organized shipment of equipment and personnel began to move south. Supplies were carried by special units called the Bo Doi Truong Son, or Central Mountains Troops. At first they carried equipment on foot or on bicycles; later the trails were expanded to handle truck traffic. At this early stage of the war, the vast majority of those sent south were apparently "regroupees," southerners who had been sent north for training and indoctrination

---

[38] For the debate over the publication date of the communiqué and the circumstances of the plenum, see Post, vol. 2, pp. 308–309, and Thayer, *War by Other Means*, pp. 183–187.

[39] *CKC*, pp. 52–53.

Transporting provisions down the Ho Chi Minh Trail.

after the Geneva conference. Most returned enthusiastically to seek the liberation of the land of their birth. As one commented:

> It was a very interesting time for us in the northern part of Vietnam. We had always been strong fighters for the Viet Minh, and we always admired Ho Chi Minh and the other Viet Minh leaders. The trip to North Vietnam was very difficult and very long, but we did not ever complain, because we knew the difficulties were for the revolution.
>
> Our training in North Vietnam was also difficult. Sometimes the food was not good. Sometimes we were very lonely and wanted to go home and see our family and friends. But we learned after a while not to be lonely, and learned to find strength in our revolutionary struggle. We learned not to think much about our families any more. We learned not to miss our families any more—like Ho Chi Minh.[40]

[40] James Walker Trullinger, Jr., *Village at War: An Account of Revolution in Vietnam* (New York: Longman, 1980), p. 71.

THE "SPONTANEOUS UPRISINGS"

Information about the decisions of the Fifteenth Plenum in Hanoi did not reach the southern insurgents until late in 1959. In the meantime, resistance leaders throughout South Vietnam had been gearing up for a more active effort to defend the cause of the revolution. In May, the Diem regime had enacted a set of stringent new directives, known as Law 10/59, which provided the security services with increased authority to apprehend and punish opposition forces in South Vietnam. Roving tribunals circulated throughout the countryside trying, convicting, and executing those suspected of subversive acts.

During the final six months of the year, the insurgent forces began to respond. The first in a series of what were later to be labeled "spontaneous uprisings" occurred in the hilly uplands of the province of Quang Ngai in central Vietnam, an area that had been sympathetic to the Vietminh cause since the August Revolution. On August 28, 1959, local demonstrators, numbered at 16,000 by sources in Hanoi, protested against upcoming elections for the RVN National Assembly. The demonstrators, beefed up by regional troops operating under party leadership, managed to seize sixteen villages in Tra Bong district, on the edge of the central highlands, and were eventually able to carve out a liberated zone consisting of about fifty villages with a population of over 1000 people. Later in the year, additional popular uprisings broke out in several other provinces in the central highlands and the Mekong River delta.[41]

After the arrival of the news of the Fifteenth Plenum decisions, the pace of activity increased. In January 1960, a second major uprising took place in the Mekong delta province of Kien Hoa, known to Vietminh supporters by its previous name of Ben Tre province. Like Quang Ngai, Ben Tre had been a key area of support for the Vietminh cause during the war against the French, and in some districts under Vietminh control, land had been confiscated from absentee landowners and distributed to the local peasants. After the cease-fire in July 1954, the landlords returned and, with the support of government troops, regained control over their lands. In some

---

[41] For an account, see Pham Thanh Bien, "The 1959 Autumn Tra Bong and Western Quang Ngai Uprisings," *NCLS* (February 1962), translated in Joint Publications Research Service (hereafter JPRS) 58,128, *Translations on North Vietnam* 1326.

cases they exacted harsh reprisals and demanded retroactive rent from the previous tenants. Taking advantage of popular resentment against the Saigon regime, in January 1960 local self-defense forces disguised as regular troops attacked government outposts, and with the aid of popular demonstrations liberated dozens of villages in the district. Unlike the case in Tra Bong district to the north, however, ARVN troops were able to restore government control over the region.[42]

The background to that outbreak has been described by Nguyen Thi Dinh, a participant in the Ben Tre uprising and later a deputy commander of the party's armed forces in the south. In her autobiographical work, *No Other Road to Take*, Madame Dinh described how the plans were made at the conference before the uprising.

> The conference discussed for a long time and in minute details how the uprising would be organized and carried out. First, we had to immediately set up action cells comprising cadres and unswervingly loyal sympathizers who would be armed with spears, to eliminate the traitors and tyrants. Youths from one village would be sent to another to operate, disguised as newly arrived Main Force units. The conference hit upon the idea of producing a large quantity of various types of rifles made out of wood and coconut trunk, and to have many covers for rifles made, small ones and large ones, to give the impression that our armed forces were large and to frighten the enemy. Village officials, security police agents and informers were divided into three categories: (a) tyrants who had blood debts toward the people, (b) those who were lukewarm in their service [to the Diem regime] and (c) those who had been forced to serve. . . . The action cells had to keep close watch over the tyrants who had incurred blood debts toward the people, so that once the masses rose up they could be nabbed immediately—otherwise if there was any delay, these fellows would get away.

Madame Dinh graphically described the assault on one of the villages held by the enemy.

---

[42] See Ta Xuan Linh, "Ben Tre: Land of Concerted Uprisings," *Vietnam Courier* 27 (August 1974): 5. According to the prominent North Vietnamese historian Tran Van Giau, over 2000 "struggles" with about half a million participants took place during the year. See "Great Strategic Effect of the Guerrilla War in South Vietnam through Ten Years of Armed Struggle," *NCLS* (July 1969), in JPRS 49,387, in *Translations on North Vietnam* 639.

Sometime after 9:00 P.M., I had just arrived in the permanent office when I heard the sounds of drums and wooden blocks echoing from one village to another and resounding everywhere, followed by the happy shouts of the people. . . . As the night advanced, the sound of drums and wooden bells intensified and became insistent as though urging everyone to rise up. This was the people's signal for combat being transmitted everywhere. . . . Suddenly there was a shout: "The post is on fire, and it's burning rapidly!"

The forces encircling the posts had been ordered to burn down any posts they captured. The people immediately tore up the flags, and burned the plaques bearing their house numbers and family registers. On the roads, the villagers cut down trees to erect barriers and block the movement of the enemy. . . . All the posts were surrounded by the people who made appeals to the soldiers through bullhorns. . . . It was a night of terrifying thunder and lightning striking the enemy on their heads. Attacked by surprise, they were scared out of their wits and stayed put in the posts.[43]

Similar outbreaks took place elsewhere during the first months of 1960, while a "Committee of Resistance Fighters" met in March and called for the creation of a united front of progressive forces to demand reforms from the Saigon regime. But the Committee for the South remained cautious, and in a directive at the end of March it criticized some party members for launching uprisings prematurely, and for an excessive reliance on terrorism against moderate elements who might be persuaded to sympathize with the revolution. Preparations for the final uprising have not yet been completed, said the directive. "For the moment, our emphasis must remain on organizing our forces, propagandizing the masses, and preparing for the future general uprising."[44]

The increase in insurgent activity now began to attract the close attention of U.S. officials in Saigon and Washington. In mid-August 1960, a Special National Intelligence Estimate drawn up by the CIA noted:

Since January, there has been a significant increase in the number and size of insurgent Viet Cong attacks in several areas, particularly in the Southwest. Civilian travel on public roads more than 15 miles outside of Saigon has become hazardous. Attacking units, estimated to number at times in the hundreds, have operated over

---

[43] Nguyen Thi Dinh, *No Other Road*, pp. 65, 69–70.
[44] The directive of the Committee for the South is available as item number 1044, in *Race Documents*. For a translated version, see Porter, ed., *Vietnam*, pp. 59–67.

wider areas than at any time since 1954 and have assaulted Vietnamese army installations.[45]

CIVIL WAR IN LAOS

Hanoi's decision to escalate the level of revolutionary violence in the south was a matter of concern to U.S. officials in Washington, but for the moment their primary attention was focused elsewhere. In Laos, the precarious peace settlement that had been established at the Geneva conference had broken down, leading to clashes between Pathet Lao forces and units of the Royal Lao Army. The Geneva accords had assigned two provinces in the mountainous northeastern portion of the country to the former, while directing representatives of the two sides to engage in discussions to create a unified government. In November 1957, negotiations between the representatives of the Royal Lao government and Pathet Lao leaders resulted in an agreement to form a national coalition government comprising representatives of all political factions. As part of that agreement, Pathet Lao military forces were to be disbanded or integrated into the Royal Lao Army, while Sam Neua and Phong Saly, the two provinces that had been assigned to the insurgent forces, were to be turned over to government authorities.

A few months later, that precarious settlement broke down when rightist forces, supported by the CIA, seized power from neutralist Prime Minister Prince Souvanna Phouma. In mid-1959, anticommunist elements in the new government thereupon arrested leftist members of the cabinet and demanded that existing Pathet Lao units in the vicinity of the capital of Vientiane lay down their arms. The Pathet Lao were able to break out of a government blockade and escape into the hills. By the winter of 1959–1960, with armed clashes taking place between government and insurgent forces, Washington grew anxious at the possibility of a full-scale Pathet Lao attack on government-held regions in the lowlands.[46]

---

[45] See "Short-Term Trends in South Vietnam," August 23, 1960, *FRUS*, 1958–1960, vol. 1, p. 539.

[46] The standard sources of information about the civil war in Laos are Bernard B. Fall, *Anatomy of a Crisis: The Laotian Crisis of 1960–1961* (New York: Doubleday, 1969), and Arthur J. Dommen, *Conflict in Laos: The Politics of Neutralization* (New York: Praeger, 1964).

THE FORMATION OF
THE NATIONAL LIBERATION FRONT

While the civil war raged in Laos, Hanoi was still sending mixed signals about its intentions in South Vietnam. In a speech delivered in April 1960, Le Duan declared that the DRV would adopt a peaceful approach to reunification. He stressed the importance of maintaining peace in the world and said that Hanoi would "guide and restrict within the South the solving of contradictions of imperialists and colonialism in Vietnam."[47]

In September, the VWP held its Third National Congress in Hanoi. It was the first such congress since 1951, when the Franco-Vietminh conflict was at its height. About 500 delegates were in attendance, representing a party membership that had grown to half a million. The congress was convened to consider not only the schedule for socialist transformation in the north, but also the party's evolving strategy and tactics in the south.

Based on the documentation published after the close of the meeting, the primary focus was on the domestic scene. Delegates approved the nation's first five-year plan, a program designed to inaugurate the process of industrialization along socialist lines. But it also dealt with the changing situation in South Vietnam and apparently formalized the decision reached at the Fifteenth Plenum the previous year to adopt a policy of armed struggle to complete the reunification of the two zones. Yet there is ample evidence that party leaders had not yet reached a firm consensus on the approach to adopt in the south. Le Duan, who was formally selected as VWP first secretary (the new title for the general secretary, in imitation of a similar change in Moscow) at the congress, was studiously vague in referring to the issue, merely remarking that it would be "a long and arduous struggle, not simple but complex, combining many forms of struggle."

Remarks by other party leaders at the meeting confirmed that there was still disagreement over the issue. Truong Chinh lectured unnamed comrades from the south who were "too impatient" to secure victory, while Defense Minister Vo Nguyen Giap countered cryptically that "a number of our comrades are not fully aware of

---

[47] Cited in Donald S. Zagoria, Vietnam Triangle: Moscow/Peking/Hanoi (New York: Pegasus, 1967), p. 105.

Ho Chi Minh presents the political report to the Third VWP Congress in 1960. Le Duan is on his right, Truong Chinh on his left.

the plots of. . . . United States imperialism and their lackeys. They do not understand that while our policy is to preserve peace and to achieve peaceful reunification, we should always be prepared to cope with any maneuver of the enemy."[48]

The reasons for continued delay in concretizing strategy in the south are not entirely clear, although they may have been related to the effort to win approval from Moscow, as well as to reconcile differing views in Hanoi. In November, a Vietnamese delegation attended the Congress of Eighty-One Communist Parties in Moscow. It was a time of growing tension in the relationship between China and the Soviet Union, and the latter was under heavy pressure to move ideologically to the left to avoid an open break with Beijing. That may help to explain the willingness of the Soviet Union to promise increased support to national liberation struggles around the world. The statement issued at the close of the congress, while stressing the importance of world peace, added that "in conditions when the exploiting classes resort to the use of force against the

---

[48] Vo Nguyen Giap's speech is printed in *Third National Congress of the Vietnam Workers' Party*, vol. 1 (Hanoi: Foreign Languages Press, 1960), p. 54. Le Duan's political report is in ibid., vol. 1, p. 62.

people, it is necessary to bear in mind another possibility—that of a nonpeaceful transition to socialism." Two months later, Nikita Khrushchev sent shock waves through Washington when he promised that the USSR would support such struggles (and he referred specifically to the case of Vietnam) "whole-heartedly and without reservation."[49]

The continuing uncertainty over policy in Hanoi undoubtedly affected morale among the resistance elements in the south. In a letter written early in 1961 to Southern Commander Nguyen Van Linh, Le Duan denied charges that party leaders were retarding the progress of the revolution by adopting a peaceful approach. Although he admitted that Hanoi was temporarily using the concept of struggle along "peaceful lines," he insisted that "we clearly understand the necessity of moving towards insurrection chiefly by political forces in coordination with armed forces on the basis of National Unity within the national united front with the worker-peasant-soldier alliance as its nucleus."[50]

Le Duan's statement may have accurately reflected Hanoi's intentions regarding a return to revolutionary war in South Vietnam, and to provide a clearer sense of direction for its supporters there. In early January 1961, just as the new Kennedy administration was preparing to enter office in Washington, the Politburo met to evaluate the situation and set forth more concrete guidelines for the southern revolution. According to an article written in *Nhan Dan* many years later, at that meeting the Politburo concluded that the period of temporary stability in South Vietnam was at an end, and conditions for a possible popular uprising were on the increase. Although conceding that the United States might decide to send troops to the RVN to prevent a total collapse of its ally, party leaders decided to raise the level of military struggle to match that of political struggle, and to make every effort to expand liberated areas as a base of operations against the enemy.[51]

---

[49] *USVN*, bk. 2, p. 68.

[50] Le Duan, *Letters to the South* (Hanoi: Foreign Languages Press, 1986), letter to Muoi Cuc (Nguyen Van Linh), pp. 9–10. This source is an English-language translation of Le Duan's *Thu Vao Nam*, cited in the previous chapter. Unfortunately, not all the letters in the original version are reproduced in the translation. Where possible I have cited the English-language version for the convenience of the reader.

[51] The full communiqué of the January Politburo meeting has not been published, but excerpts are located in *CKC*, p. 45, and in JPRS 75,579, *Translations on North Vietnam* 2185.

Available excerpts reporting the decisions reached at the meeting do not provide specifics on how party leaders intended to pursue the revolutionary war in the south. But a letter by Le Duan to Nguyen Van Linh early in 1962 suggests that what the Politburo had in mind was a strategy that relied on a combination of political or military struggle within the framework of a protracted conflict leading ultimately to a general uprising. The author criticized both advocates of a purely political struggle and of a three-stage war to surround the cities on the pattern of the Maoist model. What is needed, he insisted, is an approach that relies primarily on what he called "the political strength of the masses," supplemented when appropriate with armed strength based in liberated areas. Le Duan was clearly still thinking of a strategy similar to that used during the August Revolution.[52]

As the party began to give more serious consideration to activating the movement in the south, it turned its attention to creating a new political base for the insurgency. According to Truong Nhu Tang, an early supporter of the southern movement and later one of its leading officials, dissident elements had become convinced of the need for a new extralegal political organization as early as 1958, and after holding several secret meetings on the issue, sent a representative to Hanoi to persuade leaders of the VWP to provide support.[53]

According to Truong Nhu Tang, most of the dissident elements affiliated with his group were progressives rather than communists. If that is so, it is likely that Hanoi's first reaction was one of skepticism and caution. But party leaders must have been thinking along the same lines. The Fatherland Front, which had been formed in 1955 as the linear successor to the old Vietminh Front, had been created primarily as an instrument of political integration in the DRV and was of little use as a vehicle for organizing revolutionary activities in South Vietnam, where suspicion of communism remained relatively strong. As Hanoi became convinced of the need to adopt a strategy of revolutionary war in the south, it gradually became aware that the best way to bring the diverse elements of South Vietnamese society together was to create a single broad alliance

---

[52] Le Duan, *Letters to the South*, letter to Muoi Cuc, February 7, 1962, p. 33.
[53] Truong Nhu Tang, *Viet Cong Memoir: An Inside Account of the Vietnam War and Its Aftermath* (San Diego: Harcourt Brace Jovanovich, 1985), pp. 66–68.

similar to the Vietminh Front that had operated in the war against the French.[54]

The first formal reference to the new front took place at the Third National Congress of the VWP in September 1960, when one of the party's veteran leaders, Ton Duc Thang, described the nature of the new organization in a speech to the assembled delegates. It would be based on the Leninist concept of the four-class alliance, he explained, but as a gesture to the diversity of South Vietnamese society it would also encompass the various religious and ethnic minorities, as well as patriotic parties and individuals in South Vietnam. The aims of the organization, he noted, should be kept correspondingly general in order to appeal to the widest possible range of the population. Its objectives would be to realize national independence and social and political reform, and its ultimate goal was the creation of a peaceful, united, democratic, and prosperous Vietnam. Unification would begin with the creation of a national democratic coalition government in Saigon that would discuss peaceful reunification with the DRV.[55]

On December 20, 1960, representatives of a wide body of political, social, religious, and ethnic groups gathered at a secret location in Tay Ninh province, near the Cambodian border, to form the National Liberation Front of South Vietnam (Mat Tran Dan Toc Giai Phong Mien Nam Viet Nam), usually referred to simply as the NLF. About fifty delegates attended the conference, representing a variety of groups in the south such as Buddhist and Catholic organizations, the religious sects, the minority tribal groups in the central highlands, and representatives of women's and youth groups and the two puppet political parties (the Democratic and Socialist parties) set up in the 1940s by the ICP in Hanoi. Virtually all the delegates were natives of the south, but a few, like the veteran revolutionary Nguyen Huu Tho, were widely recognized as former members of the Vietminh Front. The similarities between the new organization and its famous predecessor were disclosed in a memorandum that

---

[54] The old Vietminh Front had been replaced by the Lien Viet Front in 1951 in order to win support from moderate elements, who viewed the Vietminh as a tool of the Indochinese Communist Party. On the Fatherland Front, see Thayer, *War by Other Means*, chap. 3.

[55] Speech by Ton Duc Thang at the *Third National Congress of the Vietnam Workers' Party*, vol. 3, pp. 24–26.

was circulated among party members in the south shortly after the formation of the NLF. In 1941, said the document,

> the Viet Minh was established to lead all our people so that the August Revolution might be crowned with success. During the Resistance period the Lien Viet Front united all our people in a successful resistance. In the present political struggle the NLFSV is in charge of leading the South Vietnam population in struggling successfully for the liberation of South Vietnam and carrying out the unification of our country.[56]

The goals of the new front organization were listed in a ten-point program issued after the founding congress and formally promulgated by Radio Hanoi a few weeks later. The program reflected the ideas presented at the VWP Third Congress in September 1960 and bore a striking resemblance to the objectives of the Vietminh Front two decades earlier. It repeated the assertion set forth at the Third Congress that the two primary enemies of the South Vietnamese people at the present time were imperialism (U.S. domination of the south) and feudalism (the Diem regime in Saigon), but it added that the most important contradiction at the present time was that between the Vietnamese people and the forces of U.S. imperialism. For that reason, the NLF would emphasize the issue of national independence over that of social revolution. In the hope of winning the support of sympathy of rich peasants and patriotic landlords, the NLF's land policy in liberated areas would be limited to reducing rents and confiscating the land of tyrannical landlords and those who collaborated with the Saigon regime. There was no effort to deny the fact that the southern branch of the VWP was a member organization of the front, but any hint that Hanoi was the controlling force behind the NLF was carefully disguised, and the number of party members placed in leading positions of front organizations was severely restricted.[57]

As the new decade began, then, the Vietnamese revolution had entered a new phase. The era of peaceful competition between the two zones, marred in any case by the rising level of armed conflict between government forces and insurgents in the south during the

---

[56] For a detailed analysis of the NLF and its composition, see Douglas Pike, *Viet Cong: The Organization and Techniques of the National Liberation Front of South Vietnam* (Cambridge, Mass.: MIT Press, 1966), chaps. 4 and 5. For the quote above, see p. 81.
[57] Ibid., p. 81.

late 1950s, was now at an end. The second Indochina war, known to most modern observers as the Vietnam War, was about to begin.

CIVIL WAR OR INVASION?

By early 1960 party leaders in Hanoi had finally reached a decision to return to a policy of revolutionary war to bring about the reunification of north and south. But it had taken several years to reach that decision. In the meantime, the revolutionary organization in the south, to the frustration and anger of many of its leading members, had been brought to the brink of destruction.

The debate within the party—and between its northern leadership and its leading representatives in the south—was vigorous and sometimes bitter and has given rise to a lively historical dispute over the origins of the Vietnam War. Some observers have pointed to Hanoi's delay in returning to the policy of revolutionary war as a clear indication that the initial decision to fight was taken by leading members of the resistance forces in the south, rather than by party leaders in Hanoi. A well-known proponent of this view was the French scholar and journalist Philippe Devillers. In an article published in 1962, Devillers argued that "responsible elements of the Communist resistance in Indo-China" decided that they had to respond to Diem's effort to suppress the movement, despite the reluctance to act in Hanoi.

> The peasants, disgusted to see Diem's men acting in this way, lent their assistance to the Communists, and even to the sects, going so far as to take up arms at their side. . . . In the course of that December [1958] and the following January armed bands sprang into being almost everywhere. . . .
>
> It was thus by its own policy that the government of the south finally destroyed the confidence of the population, which it had won during the early years, and practically drove them into revolt and desperation.[58]

This point of view was taken up a few years later by George McT. Kahin and John Wilson Lewis in their widely used textbook, *The United States in Vietnam*. The authors contended that Vietminh

---

[58] Philippe Devillers, "The Struggle for the Unification of Vietnam, *China Quarterly* 9 (January–March 1962): 14–16.

leaders in the south, driven to desperation by Diem's brutal efforts to repress dissidents, had demanded a return to the strategy of armed struggle, but that Hanoi had "persisted in its refusal to encourage its former adherents in the South to embark upon such militant action." Only in September 1960, after the southern insurgents had begun to take matters into their own hands, did the Third Congress of the VWP approve a program for the violent overthrow of the Diem regime.[59]

The implication of this point of view, of course, is that the Vietnam War was not the result of a deliberate policy decision by militant party strategists in North Vietnam, but was the consequence of Diem's own repressive measures in the south—measures which forced desperate peasants and Vietminh supporters to take up arms to defend themselves. In that interpretation, it was not Hanoi which started the war, but Saigon. And it was not, as later U.S. administrations would claim, an invasion from the north, but a civil war in the south.

By no means did all foreign observers agree with this interpretation. Some pointed instead to the crucial role played by North Vietnam in the process. Douglas Pike, who served as a foreign service officer stationed at the U.S. Information Service in Saigon in the mid-1960s, argued in his much-quoted book *Viet Cong* that although "the ground in South Vietnam was fertile for armed revolt," Diem's effort to suppress the insurgent forces was not the sole cause of insurrection in the RVN. The Saigon regime, he pointed out, had only slight control over much of the territory of South Vietnam. Moreover, he adds, although much of the support for the NLF was indigenous to South Vietnam, the organization itself had been created at the order of the party leadership in the north. The NLF, he asserts, was "premeditated, planned, organized at length and in detail and then pushed and driven into existence and operations. Such an effort," he concludes, "had to be the child of the North."[60]

In recent years, Professor Kahin has resurrected the issue in his exhaustive study of the early stages of the war entitled *Intervention: How America Became Involved in Vietnam*. To strengthen his earlier

---

[59] George McT. Kahin and John W. Lewis, *The United States in Vietnam: An Analysis in Depth of the History of America's Involvement in Vietnam* (New York: Delta, 1969), pp. 110–115.
[60] Pike, *Viet Cong*, p. 80.

argument that the origins of the Vietnam War were indigenous to South Vietnam, Kahin referred to the March 1960 meeting of southern "resistance fighters" who expressed their frustration with Hanoi's failure to approve a policy of armed struggle by calling for the formation of a broad alliance of anti-Diemist forces to bring about changes in South Vietnam. At virtually the same time, he points out, First Secretary Le Duan publicly stated in April 1960 that the policy of the DRV was to strive for the reunification of Vietnam by peaceful means.[61]

Professor Kahin makes a good case for the frustrations of southern commanders when faced with the reluctance of party leaders in the north to embark on the road to violent struggle in the south. This frustration is amply documented in North Vietnamese documents. But his picture of a clear-cut distinction between southern militants and fearful advocates of a peaceful approach in Hanoi is too simplistic. As Le Duan chronicles in his *Letters to the South*, there were advocates of a peaceful approach in the south as well as proponents of the need for armed violence in the north. Moreover, it is clear that as early as 1956 key party figures such as Ho Chi Minh and Vo Nguyen Giap were already warning of the possibility of a return to revolutionary war, while by January 1959 the decision to return to a strategy of armed struggle had already been approved in principle. It only remained to decide when and in what form the conflict should be undertaken. Whether or not they were aware of it, the southern "resistance fighters" were only trying to hasten the process.

Moreover, in explanation of the more cautious attitude adopted by the Politburo on the issue, it should be kept in mind that, unlike their representatives in South Vietnam, party leaders in Hanoi had to worry about the attitude of their allies and the likelihood of a U.S. response to an escalation of the insurgency. Le Duan's speech in April 1960 clearly did not reflect Hanoi's full views on the subject, but was probably an effort to reassure Moscow and Beijing that it would not permit the struggle in South Vietnam to spill over into a wider conflict. While those who attended the meeting of southern "resistance fighters" in March 1960 may have justifiably been agitated over the slow transition in Hanoi to a more activist policy,

---

[61] George McT. Kahin, *Intervention: How America Became Involved in Vietnam* (New York: Doubleday, 1987), pp. 113–114.

they were clearly not aware of the possible consequences that a shift of policy would entail.

Behind this historical debate, of course, is the broader question of how to assign responsibility for the Vietnam War. Was the renewed conflict in South Vietnam a civil war between two mutually hostile indigenous groups in the south or the opening stage of an armed attack from the north? It is clear from the evidence that neither extreme view is justified. Kahin and Devillers both admit that Hanoi played an active role in the escalation of the struggle in the south, while Pike concedes that what he calls the "preconditions for insurgency" were already present in the south when the Fifteenth Plenum took place. It was, in a single phrase, an insurgent movement inspired by local conditions in the south but guided and directed from Hanoi. It was precisely that ambiguity in the situation that later led to the bitter controversy within the United States over the origins of the war.

But there is a further issue which is relevant to our discussion here. The Geneva accords had created not two separate states, one in the north and one in the south, but a single Vietnam temporarily divided into two regroupment zones. The political declaration at Geneva had provided the mechanism for consultation between administrators of the two zones and eventually for national elections which would reunify the country under a single government. In Hanoi's view, the breakdown of the Geneva process—a breakdown provoked by the Saigon regime—relieved the DRV from provisions in the accords prohibiting it from taking independent action to seek reunification. To North Vietnamese leaders, Vietnam remained one country and one people, and any actions taken to achieve that end were ultimately justifiable.

CHAPTER 4

Countering the U.S. "Special War"

For years, the U.S. strategy for the defense of South Vietnam had been based on the assumption that a threat to the Saigon regime would come in the form of an outright invasion by North Vietnamese forces across the DMZ, such as had taken place in 1950 in Korea. It will be recalled that although Laos, Cambodia, and South Vietnam were not permitted to become members of regional security pacts, they had been included in SEATO's defense provisions under the "umbrella clause," according to which an armed attack on any of them would be considered equivalent to an attack on one of the signatories. For this reason, the RVN maintained only a small military establishment that was adequate to undertake local defense operations and provide temporary resistance to a foreign invader until SEATO forces could arrive on the scene.

Less attention had been given to the possibility of internal subversion. Although Ngo Dinh Diem had sought U.S. assistance to build up Saigon's capacity to handle an internal insurgency, U.S. military advisers had generally discouraged such efforts as a distraction from the primary objective of creating a small but modern conventional military force. The SEATO treaty itself was vague on how to deal with this danger and declared that in such cases, the treaty signatories would be consulted in order to reach a unanimous decision on what action to pursue.[1]

---

[1] A copy of the SEATO agreement is located in Kahin and Lewis, *The United States in Vietnam,* pp. 451–456.

COUNTERINSURGENCY

By 1960, however, the Eisenhower administration had become sufficiently concerned about the danger of internal subversion to order the drafting of a counterinsurgency program. The first draft was just in the process of completion when John F. Kennedy assumed the presidency in January 1961. Kennedy was firmly convinced that the primary threat to the security of South Vietnam came from internal subversion, and he quickly approved the plan, while authorizing funds for an increase in the size of ARVN forces. But Kennedy also believed that the problem was as much political as military, and that it could only be resolved if the Diem regime launched political and economic reforms sufficient to (in the catch phrase of the time) "win the hearts and minds of the people." He directed the creation of an interagency task force to come up with ideas on how to deal with the issue.

But although Vietnam was a source of concern to President Kennedy and his chief foreign policy advisers, it was not the major problem facing the new administration as it came into office. There were more immediate crises to be dealt with in Berlin, in Cuba, and in the realm of U.S.-Soviet relations, where Nikita Khrushchev had badly shaken official Washington with his January speech promising active support to wars of national liberation around the globe. Even within Southeast Asia, the attention of the new team in the White House was focused not on Vietnam but on Laos, where the Pathet Lao attacks appeared to be growing daily more ominous.

In a briefing for the new chief executive in December, President Eisenhower had warned his successor that it might be necessary to send U.S. combat troops to Laos in order (as he put it) to "keep the cork in the bottle." In Eisenhower's view, the fall of Laos to the Communist-led Pathet Lao could shake the confidence of Thai leaders in U.S. promises of support and lead to a collapse of the free-world position throughout the region.[2]

President Kennedy, however, was skeptical of the advisability of intervening directly in Laos. Not only did the terrain of the country present logistical difficulties because of its jungles and moun-

---

[2] Eisenhower's briefing of Kennedy is reported in Walt W. Rostow, *The Diffusion of Power: An Essay in Recent History* (New York: Macmillan, 1972), p. 265.

tains, its landlocked character, and the lack of usable roads, railroads, and airfields, but the pro-U.S. ruling clique did not inspire much confidence as the result of its lack of political sophistication. Furthermore, the royal government controlled only a fraction of the national territory. To make matters worse, there was little support in Congress for active U.S. military operations in the area. After some hesitation, Kennedy decided to seek a compromise solution in Laos through negotiations.

In March, the administration suggested to senior Soviet officials the possibility of convening a new Geneva conference to seek an ending to the fighting in Laos. At the same time, the White House privately warned China that the United States might be forced to intervene militarily unless a satisfactory negotiated solution could be realized. To back up the threat, Kennedy placed U.S. Special Forces units in Okinawa on alert and ordered the dispatch of several ships from the Seventh Fleet to the Gulf of Thailand. After some tense moments, Moscow agreed to a cease-fire in late April, and formal discussions opened in Geneva in early May.

In the meantime, the Kennedy team was trying to come up with solutions in South Vietnam. The decision to seek a compromise settlement in Laos made it all the more essential to take action to save the Saigon regime from collapse. Such concerns were undoubtedly heightened by the fiasco in the Bay of Pigs, which had raised questions about the new chief executive's toughness under fire. Sensing his vulnerability to the charge of failing to stand up to the challenge of global communism, Kennedy remarked to Walt W. Rostow, his deputy special assistant for National Security Affairs, that unlike Eisenhower, he could "not afford a defeat in Indochina."[3]

But one problem with the decision to take a stand in South Vietnam rather than in Laos was that it forced Washington to accept the dubious assumption that a settlement in Laos could be achieved while simultaneously limiting the level of infiltration from the DRV into South Vietnam. Much of the Ho Chi Minh Trail, as the infiltration routes into the south were popularly dubbed, passed through the heavily jungled hills of southern Laos, and there was reliable information that North Vietnamese advisers were serving actively with Pathet Lao units in the field. U.S. intelligence sources predicted

---

[3] Arthur M. Schlesinger Jr., *A Thousand Days: John F. Kennedy in the White House* (Boston: Houghton Mifflin, 1965), pp. 337–339.

that infiltration would probably increase in the aftermath of a peace settlement in Laos and could result in increased insurgent activity in South Vietnam. Some predicted that the Communists were preparing for a general offensive (the famous "third stage" of Maoist "people's war") sometime in 1962. To evaluate the scope of the problem, the White House sent William J. Jorden, a former *New York Times* reporter now working with the Policy Planning Staff in the State Department, to South Vietnam to study the situation and report back to Washington.

Jorden returned to the United States in September. He reported that most members of the resistance movement had been recruited locally, but that infiltration from the north was on the increase. An intelligence estimate by the State Department in November calculated that of a total "hard core" strength of 20,000 insurgents in South Vietnam, somewhere between 5 and 30 percent had infiltrated from the DRV. Military intelligence tended to confirm those figures. Walt Rostow estimated that about one-quarter of the resistance forces were regroupees who had been trained in the north, while about 5 percent were natives of the north.[4]

THE NLF IN ACTION

It was against this backdrop that Hanoi and its representatives in the south moved to implement their own new strategy. In historical perspective, the most significant fact about the Politburo meeting of January 1961 was its decision to escalate the level of military struggle in the south. A few weeks later, southern leaders took a concrete step in that direction at a meeting in War Zone D north of Saigon, when they unified the scattered forces of the insurgency, now risen from about 2000 in 1959 to an estimated 10,000 in early 1961, and placed them under an integrated command. The formal name assigned to the new organization was the Quan Doi Nhan Dan Giai Phong—the People's Liberation Armed Forces, or PLAF. To millions of people in Vietnam and around the world, they were simply known as the Viet Cong.

For the time being, command of the new PLAF was assigned to

---

[4] For estimates on infiltration, see Memorandum from Wood to Steeves, November 14, 1961, in *FRUS*, 1961, vol. 1, pp. 596–597. Jorden's report appears on pp. 310–314.

a military committee subordinated to the Committee for the South. But in September, the latter was merged with a similar committee for central Vietnam into a revived Central Office of South Vietnam (COSVN), a recreation of the centralized directorate that had guided party activities in the southern provinces during the Franco-Vietminh conflict prior to its dissolution in 1955. Placed in command of the new organization was Nguyen Van Linh, the veteran party cadre who had succeeded Le Duan as chairman of the Committee for the South after the latter's departure for Hanoi in early 1957. A number of senior military officers infiltrated the south in order to provide experienced military leadership for the PLAF. According to U.S. intelligence estimates, infiltration from the north began to rise steadily.[5]

In organizing their military forces, party strategists took a page from their experience in the war against the French. As had been the case earlier, the PLAF was to be organized at three basic levels: (1) local self-defense forces, who would serve as farmers by day and combatants at night; (2) guerrilla forces under regional command; and (3) main force units. Local self-defense forces usually received little training and few weapons and served primarily in the defense of their native villages. The regional guerrilla forces were full-time guerrillas. They were better armed and served under district command. The best elements from the regional forces were then recruited into the uniformed main force units, organized into battalions and placed under the direct command of COSVN.[6]

As the new decade began, then, the revolutionary movement had made a perceptible shift toward a greater reliance on military force. But it is clear from the decision reached at the Politburo meeting in January 1961 that party leaders were still convinced that although the road to reunification was "the path of violence," political struggle was the key to victory. Armed struggle, in the party's parlance, had been raised to the level of political struggle, but the latter would be the decisive engine that would drive the revolution to its final triumph.

The Politburo's continued preference for a strategy that relied

---

[5] William S. Turley, *The Second Indochina War: A Short Political and Military History* (New York: Mentor, 1986), p. 44. Turley prefers the term "Central Directorate for the South" as a literal translation of the new organization, but it is commonly referred to as COSVN in the literature on the war.

[6] For a description, see Pike, *Viet Cong*, chap. 13.

primarily on political struggle was probably based on a variety of factors. In the first place, a heavy reliance on armed struggle could anger Hanoi's chief allies, who had made it clear that they wished to avoid a resumption of the Indochina conflict. Worse yet, an escalation on Hanoi's part could provoke the United States into a direct role in the war. But perhaps the decisive factor was the underlying contempt of party leaders for their adversaries in Saigon. While they harbored a degree of respect for Diem's own credentials as a patriot, he was nevertheless viewed as a tool of feudal and reactionary interests in Vietnamese society, a view confirmed (in their eyes) by the growing popular frustration and anger in South Vietnam against the Saigon regime. As Le Duan's letters to his southern compatriots make clear, he and his colleagues were convinced that if the United States could be kept out of the war, the Diem regime could be toppled without a full-scale use of force.[7]

As we have seen, it was the National Liberation Front which was designed as the vehicle for mobilizing the forces of political opposition in the south. Like its famous counterpart, the Vietminh Front, the NLF would be at once the visible symbol of Vietnamese national aspirations and the vehicle for mobilizing support for the movement at the "rice-roots" level. The front was designed as a pyramid, descending from the central level through provincial, district, and local echelons. At the base of the pyramid were the mass organizations, created to attract a broad base of support for the movement from all progressive elements in society. Those individual members with talent and dedication could then be selected to take part in positions that carried greater responsibility and a higher level of ideological commitment.

The mass organizations were the most visible aspect of the NLF at the local level. Some were based on occupation, such as the liberation associations for peasants, workers, writers and artists, and students. Others were based on gender or age. Still others were aimed at reaching specific religious or ethnic groups such as Buddhists, Catholics, or members of the national minorities.

Given the character of South Vietnamese society, it is not surprising that the largest of the mass organizations was the Farmers'

---

[7] Historians in Hanoi today often refer to Ngo Dinh Diem as a "revolutionary patriot" whose ideological views were reactionary but whose nationalist credentials were demonstrated by his resistance to U.S. domination over the RVN.

Liberation Association. The first to be established, it consisted of an estimated 1.8 million members by 1963. The program of the NLF stressed that the basic goal of the front was to realize the slogan "Land to the Tiller" (that is, the transfer of land from wealthy landlords to the tenant farmers). There was no mention of future plans for collectivization, although an internal directive meant for the use of cadres noted that party policy was "to guide the peasants gradually into cooperative programs to foster . . . the idea of the collective and thus to make them collective farmers."[8]

Recruitment into the association was affected by the economic and political circumstances of the individual peasant. Farmers were classified into a variety of categories, from wealthy landlords to landless peasants. Landlords and rich peasants were not generally permitted to enroll in the association. The bulk of the membership was to consist of poor peasants, who were considered, in the words of one internal document, to be "brutally dominated, oppressed, and plundered by the imperialists and feudalists." They were therefore presumed to be "enthusiastic and firm" in their support of the revolution.

The Women's Liberation Association, formed in March 1961, was one of the largest and most widespread of the mass organizations. Women had been considered an important component in the party's front work since the foundation of the ICP in 1930; they had played a key role during the Franco-Vietminh conflict as clandestine informants, agitprop cadres, and transportation workers. Sometimes they had even been recruited into guerrilla units. They were put to similar use in South Vietnam in the struggle against the Saigon regime and the United States.

From the beginning, the platform of the party had emphasized the issue of sexual equality in a society that still predominantly reflected the Confucian concept of male superiority. While women in traditional Vietnam had possessed more legal rights than their counterparts in other Confucian societies in Asia, their political, legal, and social status was well below that enjoyed by women in most neighboring societies in Southeast Asia. The importance of redressing that inequality was frequently stressed in programmatic announcements issued by the party and the NLF. As one statement issued in 1961 declared,

[8] Pike, *Viet Cong*, p. 168.

Women are not only equal to men in society, they are also equal to their husbands. We will abolish inequality between husbands and wives . . . as we will abolish polygamy. . . . Family property is common property. . . . Women are equal to men in standing for elections. . . . Women must be free to choose their own professions. . . . Since they carry out the same work as men, women are to receive the same pay as men. . . . Female farmers will be allocated rice fields on the same basis as men. . . . In brief, we plan to liberate all women to be totally free and equal in society and in their families.[9]

By their own account, however, party leaders encountered some problems in using women effectively as a key component of their struggle against the Saigon regime. As one report noted, women "are not enlightened, especially about their class interests. Uneducated, they suffer from self-abasement, passiveness, lack of confidence." Often, the report continued, local chapters of the Women's Liberation Association were poorly organized and lacked militancy and a sense of direction, and their members lacked ideological commitment. Still, by 1965 the association had attained a membership of over 1 million members, and in a variety of respects, women had become a vital part of the revolution in South Vietnam. In a few cases, women became active in combat operations; in one documented case in the Iron Triangle, near Saigon, a squad of female guerrillas fought fiercely against enemy troops in the tunnels of Cu Chi. Most, however, were utilized in noncombat situations, as informants and guards who were posted outside the village to warn of the approach of enemy soldiers. In her autobiographical account of life with the NLF in wartime Vietnam, Le Ly Haslip remarks that as a child, her first job as a member of the movement was "to keep an eye on our neighbors and make sure the liberation leaders knew if anyone spoke to the hated Republicans [members of the RVN]."[10]

The movement also created mass organizations to represent ur-

---

[9] Cited in ibid., p. 174.
[10] Le Ly Haslip, *When Heaven and Earth*, pp. 42–43. As she describes it, the job could be dangerous in more than one respect. On one occasion, several of the women in her village were executed by Viet Cong cadres on the accusation that they had betrayed the movement to the enemy. See ibid., pp. 110–111. For a fascinating account of the war in the tunnels, see Tom Mangold and John Penycate, *The Tunnels of Cu Chi* (New York: Random House, 1985), especially chap. 19. The authors state that in general, female guerrillas were instructed not to fight against Americans.

ban workers, students, and youth. The Youth Liberation Association was particularly important to the cause, because enthusiastic young people comprised the bulk of the party's following in urban areas and often served as the prime source of recruitment for staffing the clandestine terrorist groups organized to throw fear into the ranks of the enemy. As one NLF document declared, "Youth has its own characteristics, which are not found in older people. Youth are growing physically and mentally—and so have a spiritual eagerness, . . . they are dynamic and progressive. Youth hate the old things and are fond of new things. They love their ideas and do not fear difficulty or danger."[11]

Party strategists probably did not expect to gain widespread support from the various ethnic and religious minorities in the south, but they hoped to use mass organizations representing such groups as a means of undermining support for the Saigon regime, and to persuade wavering elements to cross over to the side of the revolution. Party cadres worked especially hard among the mountain minorities, because control over the central highlands was a vital component in their strategy in the south.

Behind the NLF structure was the shadowy organization of the party. Until 1962, party members were technically members of the VWP in Hanoi. In mid-1962, however, a new party, called the People's Revolutionary Party, or PRP, was created to provide a separate structure for VWP members working in the south. While the PRP was described as an independent organization with no direct links to the VWP, in fact it was a subordinate branch of the latter, and its leading members reported directly to senior committees in Hanoi. After victory in 1975, the PRP was dissolved and merged into the VWP in the north.

AN NLF PROFILE

By late 1961, U.S. intelligence sources began to report the extraordinary growth of support for the NLF and its subsidiary organizations all over the RVN. A State Department estimate in November said that the hard-core strength of the PLAF had risen to 20,000, an

---

[11] Pike, *Viet Cong*, p. 183.

increase from 12,000 in midsummer. About half were in regular units. Saigon intelligence sources estimated that the NLF possessed about 200,000 followers throughout the RVN.

Hanoi's success in inspiring so many thousands of southerners to join the movement was partly a carryover from the popularity of the Vietminh in the earlier war against the French. This had been the case, for example, with Nguyen Thi Dinh, one of the leaders of the spontaneous uprising in Ben Tre in January 1960. Nguyen Thi Dinh was raised in a family that had been actively involved in anti-French activities since the 1930s, and her brother had been arrested and tortured by the French. Her transformation into an active member of the NLF was a natural process of growth for someone who had imbibed the message of revolution from childhood.[12]

A different path was followed by Truong Nhu Tang, whose early efforts to form a popular alliance of anti-Diem forces has been cited above. Born the son of a wealthy businessman in Saigon, Tang was raised in an atmosphere of Confucian piety, but he imbibed the heady brew of patriotism under Japanese occupation and joined Pham Ngoc Thach's Vanguard Youth organization just before the end of World War II. While studying in France, he met Ho Chi Minh during the latter's attendance at the Fontainebleau Conference and was taken with Ho's humility and personal warmth. After returning to South Vietnam, he entered the business world but continued to sympathize with progressive causes and eventually broke with his father. Increasingly alienated by the actions of the Diem regime, he eventually moved from disapproval to active resistance.[13]

In some instances, individuals may have been motivated to join the movement for personal reasons, such as a family quarrel or a desire to evade government conscription—or simply out of a sense of adventure. Others were undoubtedly provoked by the failure of the Saigon regime to satisfy their economic or social aspirations. Interviews of defectors and prisoners undertaken by U.S. researchers during the Vietnam War indicate that the bulk of the followers of the NLF were poor peasants. A few cited their belief in socialist ideals, but many declared that they had joined the movement simply because they felt that they would have no hope for land or social

---

[12] Nguyen Thi Dinh, *No Other Road*, pp. 24–26.
[13] See his *Viet Cong Memoir*, chaps. 1–4.

justice under the Saigon government. As one villager declared to an American researcher in a village near the old imperial capital of Hue,

> The Liberation had answers for all the most important problems that we all knew. They had an answer about land reform, which was that they would give land to the poor people. They had an answer about high taxes. They said that the Liberation would spend the taxes only for the people, and would collect them without corruption. They also said that they would help the poor, and this was something else that made them popular, because many people in the village were very poor.[14]

As had happened during the Franco-Vietminh conflict, the NLF won considerable support in rural areas because of its land program, which favored the poor at the expense of the rich. Once successful in establishing its administrative authority in a village, the party would set up an organization called the Civil Affairs Commission (Ban Can Su) to evaluate the political attitudes of individual residents and undertake a survey of all farmlands in the village. Village residents would be classified according to the Chinese model as landlords, rich peasants, middle peasants, poor peasants, or landless laborers. A land reform tribunal, staffed by the most politically active members of the community, would be established to confiscate the land of the wealthy and distribute it to the poor. Those who resisted might be classified as enemies of the people and perhaps might even be executed, as had happened in North Vietnam in the mid-1950s.[15]

Some members of the NLF joined for patriotic reasons, in the conviction that Ngo Dinh Diem was the puppet of the Americans, as Bao Dai had been the puppet of the French. Front propaganda attempted to exploit this assumption, labeling Saigon the My-Diem ("U.S.-Diem") regime, with Diem portrayed as a tool of U.S. imperialism. "We often heard the Communists tell us about America," said one villager. "They said America was an imperialist country. They said America was destroying our fatherland. They said every-

---

[14] Trullinger, *Village at War*, p. 99.

[15] For a discussion of how the process worked in one village, see Trullinger. Also see William Andrews, *The Village War: Vietnamese Communist Revolutionary Activities in Dinh Tuong Province, 1960–1964* (Columbia: University of Missouri Press, 1973), p. 65.

one must unite to fight the American army. Well, I'd say that almost everyone agreed with them. I did."[16]

There seems no doubt that social pressure or the fear of reprisal was a factor in inducing some people to join the movement. Terrorist acts by clandestine units against highly visible supporters of the RVN, such as village chiefs, wealthy landowners, district officials, or administrators such as school teachers, undoubtedly made many Vietnamese fearful of becoming identified with the Saigon regime. Le Ly Haslip recounts that a popular schoolteacher in her village was assassinated by the Viet Cong because he had vocally expressed his dislike of the revolution. In some cases, the entire family of a "local tyrant" would be executed in order to send a message to those Vietnamese who supported Diem or "stood on the fence" (a practice familiar to many Vietnamese patriots during the Franco-Vietminh conflict, when it was known by the French term *"attentisme,"* or "waitism"). Frances Fitzgerald, author of one widely praised study of the movement, cites what may have been a typical case.

> In 1956–7 life was pretty easy, villagers had motorcycles. Then came law 10/59. Under this law Diem was given the right [sic] to cut off heads of persons suspected of being VC sympathizers. This actutally [sic] happened in hamlets near mine. Many people were worried. In March 1960 there was a big football game between my team and another team. The two teams fought and were mad with each other. Because the families of some of the boys worked for the government, I really believed they would take revenge on me. I went home. The VC knew that I had won the game, and they came to propagandize me. They said, "look at you, you have got to hide, but you can't really hide. You have no arms. The people will catch you and hurt you." The VC dug a shelter for me to hide in.[17]

Interviews of prisoners or defectors from the NLF, however, indicate that the bulk of the followers of the movement had joined of their own free will. Their loyalty and willingness to endure the hardship of insurgency was tested and strengthened in daily indoc-

---

[16] Trullinger, *Village at War*, p. 98. Also see John C. Donnell, Guy J. Pauker, and Joseph J. Zasloff, "Viet Cong Motivation and Morale in 1964: A Preliminary Report," Rand RM-4507/3, ISA (March 1965).

[17] Frances Fitzgerald, *Fire in the Lake* (New York: Random House, 1972), pp. 208–209. For another example, see Trullinger, *Village at War*, p. 124.

trination sessions, known as *kiem thao* (loosely, "thought reform"). Each member of the movement was assigned to a cell, consisting of anywhere from three to ten members. Cell members engaged in daily indoctrination sessions with each other in order to test their loyalty and understanding of the goals of the movement. The tactic was not always effective. As time went on, some members deserted. Most cited personal reasons in explanation, such as a reluctance to undergo hardship or a desire to return to their families.[18]

Disagreement among Western observers over the reasons for the popularity of the NLF was common during the war. Defenders of the Saigon regime stressed the role of intimidation, terror, or, as in the case of Foreign Service Officer Douglas Pike, Hanoi's highly effective organizational techniques. War critics cited the political and moral appeal of the cause or the failures of Ngo Dinh Diem as a sufficient explanation for the phenomenon. In fact, these explanations are not necessarily mutually incompatible, since it is abundantly clear that both factors were often at work.

But clearly the NLF did face severe social and institutional obstacles in building up its own support base. Traditional village attitudes of suspicion to outsiders, inertia, and fear of involvement certainly prevented many from giving their support. Although the task was undoubtedly made easier in cases where government authority was weak, even there, as Frances Fitzgerald has noted, "the people often remained submissive to the local officials and reluctant to involve themselves in what they saw as a conflict between outsiders."[19] Still, it is clear, not only from the rapid growth of the NLF but also from the high degree of loyalty shown by many members in the face of severe hardship, that, overall, NLF recruiters in the south were successful in getting their message across.

DRYING UP THE SEA

The success of the insurgent leadership in enlisting supporters to the cause was a matter of profound and growing concern to U.S. and South Vietnamese officials. Within the Kennedy administration, the effort to learn how to counter such "wars of national liberation"

---

[18] Donnell et al., "Viet Cong Motivation."
[19] Fitzgerald, *Fire in the Lake,* p. 211.

A strategic hamlet in South Vietnam.

became a matter of pressing concern. The president himself was a declared believer in the domino theory, and administration strategists, convinced that the doctrine of massive retaliation espoused by his predecessor invited either a nuclear holocaust or paralyzed inactivity in the face of a threat, formulated a new concept called "flexible response," according to which the United States would tailor its response to the nature of the threat.

In the fall of 1961, a multiagency review of the situation in Indochina resulted in a decision by the White House to approve a significant escalation of the U.S. military effort in South Vietnam. The number of U.S. troops stationed in the RVN increased substantially, while U.S. military and economic aid was increased as well. In turn, Washington urged Diem to carry out political and economic reforms to build support for his government among the general population. The president was personally convinced that the problem was more a political than a military one and could not be resolved unless Saigon became more effective in dealing with the internal problems of Vietnamese society.

For the Kennedy administration, then, the key to winning the war in Vietnam was to isolate the insurgent forces from the local population or, to revise the previously cited metaphor of Mao Zedong, to dry up the sea in which the guerrilla fish swam. The centerpiece of that effort was the so-called strategic hamlet (*ap chien luoc*). By the early 1960s, Diem's experiment with the agrovilles had been widely discredited because of the antagonism that it had provoked within the rural population. The strategic hamlet was a somewhat stripped-down version of the same concept. Instead of compelling farmers to leave their home villages in order to resettle in new, large-scale self-defense communities, the strategic hamlet was built on the foundation of the existing villages and hamlets into which the rural population of South Vietnam had traditionally been divided. In theory, the village would first be pacified, and revolutionary elements located and removed. Then the perimeter of the village would be surrounded with barbed wire, stakes, and other defensive arrangements, while the residents were appropriately armed and trained in techniques of self-defense. In the meantime, the government would attempt to win their heart and minds by providing them with essential services and improving their livelihood.[20]

Early in 1962, with approval from Washington, the Saigon regime began to implement the strategic hamlet program. The Kennedy administration did not approve of all aspects of Diem's approach (for example, Diem was determined to push the program rapidly throughout all areas of the country, beginning with the most threatened provinces, while U.S. officials preferred a more gradual approach beginning in reasonably secure areas), but it gave full support to Diem's efforts. By the end of the year, nearly 3000 hamlets had been fortified in all regions of the country.

The decision in Washington to escalate the U.S. effort in South Vietnam posed problems in Hanoi, which still hoped to maintain a relatively low level of armed struggle in the south in order to avoid provoking the United States to enter the conflict. In January 1962 the Politburo met to consider its options and to take the necessary

---

[20] Most sources identify the original idea of the strategic hamlet with the British official Sir Robert K. G. Thompson, who had applied the concept with some success against Communist insurgents in Malaya. President Diem invited Thompson to Saigon to discuss the applicability of the project in South Vietnam. President Kennedy and a number of administration officials were attracted to Thompson's ideas and agreed to work with Diem on implementing the program.

steps to cope with the challenge from Washington, whose strategy of counterinsurgency Hanoi labeled "special war." According to the resolution published at the close of the meeting, party leaders remained convinced that the overall scope of the combined political and military strategy that had been adopted in January 1959 was still valid, but they now recognized that a higher level of military struggle might be necessary than had originally been anticipated. In response, the Politburo called for the further strengthening of the PLAF and more urgent efforts to build liberated areas in the mountains and plains areas.[21]

Party strategists were quick to realize that the strategic hamlets posed a serious risk to Hanoi's plans. If successful, they would, in the words of one Vietnamese historian, expose the insurgent forces to attack by RVN military units "like fish on the chopping block." To exacerbate the problem, ARVN forces were now increasingly mobile because of helicopters provided by the United States. Party leaders began to advise their representatives in the south on how to combat the strategic hamlets most effectively. One captured document listed "eight lessons" on how to undermine the strategic hamlets and bring them under the control of the NLF. If possible, it said, they should be destroyed by armed assault. If not, they should be infiltrated and undermined from within through a combination of political, military, and psychological techniques. Women and old people were especially useful because of their ability to serve the purposes of the movement without arousing the suspicion of the government authorities. Above all, southern leaders were advised to be patient and to be prepared to attack and destroy the hamlets time and time again until government control had been eliminated.[22]

The insurgent forces were assisted by the Saigon government's own miscues. Like the agroville program before it, the program to build strategic hamlets was marred by government insensitivity and arrogance. Despite pleas from the U.S. Embassy that the government pay the costs involved in resettlement and construction, Diem transferred the costs of the program to the villagers, on the assumption that it was their security that was being provided for. The Kennedy

---

[21] Politburo resolution of February 26–27, 1962, contained in *Mot So Van Kien cua Dan Chong My, Cuu Nuoc, 1954–1965* (Hanoi: Su That, 1985), vol. 1, p. 136–158. Hereafter *Mot So.*

[22] Pike Documents I, no. 35, booklet entitled "Experiences in the Anti-Strategic Hamlet Program". Also see the Politburo resolution dated February 26–27, 1962, *Mot So,* and Le Duan's letter of July 1962 to Nguyen Van Linh, *Thu Vao Nam,* pp. 51–69.

administration also appealed to Saigon to pay the costs of land transferred to needy peasants under the land reform program, and to reduce the amount of farmland authorized to remain in the hands of individual owners to 60 hectares. But such appeals were ignored. Although government statistics indicated that strategic hamlets were built rapidly throughout the country, popular animosity toward the Saigon regime in rural areas remained as high as ever. According to one captured document from the period, Hanoi estimated that one-half to three-quarters of the hamlets in rural areas had been partly or fully liberated.[23]

SETTLEMENT IN LAOS

One favorable sign for Hanoi was the signing of the peace agreement on Laos. In negotiations held at Geneva, the Kennedy administration indicated its willingness to accept a settlement involving the creation of a tripartite coalition government consisting of rightists, neutrals, and the Pathet Lao under the stewardship of neutralist Prime Minister Souvanna Phouma. To obtain such a compromise, the administration also acquiesced in a permanent Pathet Lao presence in those areas of eastern Laos, primarily heavily forested mountains, that were already under their control. Washington's primary concern was the possibility that Hanoi would exploit such an agreement to increase the infiltration of personnel and supplies down the trail network in southern Laos into the RVN. W. Averell Harriman, a prominent member of the Democratic Party and the chief U.S. representative at the conference, argued in favor of accepting the agreement, reporting that his Soviet counterpart had promised that Moscow would restrain Hanoi from taking advantage of the settlement. It was, in Harriman's words, "a good bad deal." Some U.S. officials were skeptical, but the White House decided to sign.

---

[23] Pike Documents I, no. 257, p. 20. For U.S. appeals to Saigon to ease problems for farmers, see the U.S. Embassy cables dated March 1 and March 16, 1961 in *FRUS, 1961*, vol. 1, pp. 40–42 and 47–51. One reason why the strategic hamlets engendered such hostility may have been that one of the senior officials assigned by Ngo Dinh Diem to carry out the program, Pham Ngoc Thao, was secretly working on the side of the insurgency. Thao was later executed by the Saigon regime, but he was only one of many NLF agents working inside the RVN. For an account of Thao's interesting career, see Truong Nhu Tang's *Viet Cong Memoir*, especially p. 47. Tang contends that Thao deliberately sowed confusion in the strategic hamlet program.

Party leaders in Hanoi clearly hoped that the United States could be persuaded to accept a settlement on South Vietnam similar to the just-concluded Geneva agreement on Laos. In a letter to Nguyen Van Linh shortly after the signing of the accords, Le Duan speculated that the Kennedy administration, concerned about economic conditions and fearful that it could be dragged into a conflict similar to Korea, might be brought to see the July treaty as a model for a settlement in Vietnam. The key, Le Duan explained, was to calculate carefully how much military success the insurgent forces could afford to achieve without provoking the United States into a direct intervention in the war. "How far we win, how far they lose," he remarked, "must be calculated and measured precisely." In waging the Vietnamese revolution, he pointed out, the interests of the entire socialist camp and its desire to maintain peaceful coexistence with the West must be considered. Excessive military success in the south could have some "bad consequences," since it could bring U.S. troops into the war. The Kennedy administration had been reluctant to introduce U.S. troops into Laos, he explained, because Laos shares a border with China. South Vietnam, however, borders on North Vietnam, which Washington did not view as much of a threat as China.

The key to victory, then, was to carry on a combined political and military struggle that could keep the war from spilling over beyond the borders of South Vietnam and lead eventually to a negotiated settlement and a U.S. withdrawal. Le Duan criticized unnamed "comrades" who tended to ignore the importance of political struggle and wanted to push the revolutionary movement to unreasonable limits. Pointing to the example of Laos, where Pathet Lao forces had achieved a decisive but not a total victory and therefore had been able to nudge the United States inexorably into accepting a negotiated agreement, he instructed southern commanders to keep the conflict in South Vietnam at the level of a protracted war: to make the enemy lose, but not to such an extent that he would find it intolerable; to strengthen the movement in the mountains and plains, but to refrain from attacking the cities directly, a move which could bring about a direct U.S. role in the war. The north, he promised, would do all in its power to help.

The end result of such a strategy, Le Duan hoped, would be the isolation of the United States and the Diem regime inside South Vietnam and in the world at large. In the end, Washington might decide to replace Diem or negotiate the creation of a coalition government. In preparation for that possibility, he called on NLF leaders to escalate their efforts to win the sympathy of neutral and "progressive forces" in South Vietnam so that they could be relied upon for support in the event that a negotiated settlement led to the creation of a coalition government. Southern cadres were instructed to influence intellectuals, government workers, and members of religious organizations, as well as pro-French elements who were opposed to the Diem regime, even if they were anticommunist. Hanoi had already begun to cultivate neutral elements living in France, in order to create an "under the blanket" group who would be neutral in name but pro-Hanoi in reality.[24]

Le Duan's letter was a firm indication that Hanoi still hoped to avoid a drift toward open conflict in the south. But events during the next several months rendered such expectations impossible. In part, it was Hanoi's own fault. In the summer, U.S. officials met briefly with their DRV counterparts on possible peace talks, but by then it had become clear that the DRV was ignoring the provisions of the recent Geneva settlement, which prohibited the movement of "foreign" military forces and equipment through Laotian territory. Convinced that Hanoi's word and Moscow's promises were worthless, Washington lost interest in a negotiated settlement to the conflict in South Vietnam and turned to the strategic hamlets as the magic solution to the problem. During the next several months, U.S. force levels in South Vietnam steadily increased. In turn, Hanoi concluded that the United States was not yet interested in a negotiated settlement and instructed the Pathet Lao to abandon its participation in the coalition government.[25]

BEAR BY THE TAIL

In Communist historiography, the battle of Ap Bac marked a decisive stage in the Vietnam conflict. According to an official account

---

[24] Le Duan, *Thu Vao Nam,* letter of July 1962 to Muoi Cuc. Also see Pike Documents I, no. 257, p. 24.

[25] Maneli, *War of the Vanquished,* p. 186. When Maneli asked Pham Van Dong why the Pathet Lao had withdrawn from the coalition government, he explained that Hanoi had agreed to the compromise at Geneva in order to show good will and suggest the route to a settlement in South Vietnam. "When Washington failed to respond," Pham said, "we concluded that the United States will not agree to depart until it realizes it can't win in Vietnam."

of the war published in Hanoi, it was at Ap Bac, a village in the heart of the Mekong delta about 20 miles from the provincial capital of My Tho, that the PLAF learned how to defeat the enemy's new tactics of "helicopter mobility." Insurgent units at battalion strength had moved into the area in the final days of 1962. On learning of their presence, ARVN troops attacked the village on January 2, 1963, but encountered stiff resistance from the defenders. Communist sources put ARVN losses at 450 killed and wounded, along with 19 U.S. dead and eight helicopters destroyed.[26]

Accounts by U.S. sources tend to confirm Hanoi's portrayal of the battle, although they list lower casualty figures on the allied side. Despite a numerical edge of 4 to 1, ARVN troops absorbed heavy casualties, provoking the comment of one U.S. military source that it was "one of the bloodiest and costliest battles of the South Vietnam War." Lieutenant Colonel John Paul Vann, then an adviser to the Seventh ARVN Division, was highly critical of the behavior of South Vietnamese troops, publicly describing them as "cowards" in the press. *Washington Post* reporter Neil Sheehan quoted U.S. military sources as saying that South Vietnamese infantrymen had "refused direct orders to advance during Wednesday's battle at Ap Bac" and that an American Army captain had been killed while pleading with ARVN troops to attack.[27]

The incident sparked growing complaints in the U.S. news media that the American people were not "getting the facts" about the situation in South Vietnam. Official sources in Saigon and Washington countered that the press had exaggerated the extent of the problem and unfairly portrayed the performance of the ARVN troops, who later reoccupied the town and drove out the insurgent forces. In Saigon, senior U.S. military representative General Paul Harkins informed the White House that the situation was not as bad as it had been depicted: "They got a bear by the tail," he said, "and they didn't let go of it. At least they got most of it."

The battle of Ap Bac took place at a time when official opinion in Washington about the war was quite volatile. Some remained optimistic. Army Chief of Staff General Earle C. "Bus" Wheeler

---

[26] *CKC*, p. 53.

[27] *FRUS*, 1961–1963, vol. 2, pp. 1–2. For Colonel Vann's views, see Neil Sheehan's highly acclaimed account of Vann's fascinating and controversial career, *A Bright and Shining Lie: John Paul Vann and America in Vietnam* (New York: Random House, 1988). According to Sheehan, the success of the battle helped to stimulate recruitment efforts into the NLF. See p. 311.

returned from a visit to Saigon in January and reported that the overall situation was improving. In March, British counterinsurgency expert Robert K. G. Thompson argued that the Viet Cong were losing the initiative because they were unable to prevent the Saigon regime from building more strategic hamlets. Thompson, who had won praise for his success in suppressing Communist guerrillas in Malaya, even suggested that the administration could withdraw 1000 U.S. advisers as a token gesture of its confidence in the government of Vietnam. Intelligence analyses of the situation were mixed, however, and there were growing expressions of doubt, especially within the State Department, about Diem's capacity to lead the fight against communism in South Vietnam. Some even suggested the desirability of seeking "alternate leadership" in Saigon. But Robert Thompson insisted that there was no alternative to Diem, and for the time being, Kennedy agreed to stick with him.

Communist sources confirmed the views of the doubters. One captured document, apparently written in May, claimed that although the Saigon regime still possessed the military advantage, the insurgent forces possessed clear political superiority. Agitation by students and workers in the major cities was on the rise, and discontent in rural areas was seething. According to the document, 2600 of the 3700 strategic hamlets that had been put in operation throughout the RVN had now been destroyed. The size of the liberated area was growing steadily, and the NLF controlled three-quarters of all villages and hamlets and half of the population in South Vietnam. It is time, the document concluded, to force the enemy to negotiate.[28]

CHANGING HORSES IN SAIGON

The debate in Washington over whether the situation in South Vietnam was improving or deteriorating soon became academic. In early May, a major political crisis erupted when Diem's troops suppressed a Buddhist rally in the former imperial capital of Hue. When

---

[28] Pike Documents I, no. 793. *Communist Vietnamese Publications,* a microfilm series contained in the Library of Congress, Reel 3, pamphlet by Le Quang Dao entitled *Cach Mang Mien Nam Nhat Dinh Thang Loi Nhung Phuc Tap* [The Revolution in South Vietnam Will Certainly Triumph over All Difficulties] (Hanoi: Su That, 1963).

public demonstrations occurred, government forces reacted harshly and several people were killed in the melee. In Saigon, Buddhist activists took to the streets to protest the regime's alleged favoritism toward Catholics. Diem and his brother Nhu argued that key leaders of the Buddhist movement were allied with the Communists.

During the summer of 1963, the situation in South Vietnam steadily grew worse, despite U.S. efforts to persuade Diem to alleviate the tension by adopting conciliatory measures. As the Kennedy administration became increasingly critical of Saigon's behavior toward the Buddhists, a number of senior officers within the South Vietnamese army, concerned at the impact of the Buddhist crisis on the prosecution of the war, approached U.S. Embassy officials to inquire whether the White House would support a coup to install new leadership in Saigon. The proposal led to bitter divisions among policymakers in Washington and resulted in a highly equivocal decision by the White House to pursue the matter. Faced with apparent indecision in the United States, the dissident generals backed off.

Paradoxically, as the political situation in South Vietnam deteriorated, the war in the countryside appeared to be going better. Ngo Dinh Nhu reported to U.S. contacts that enemy units were apparently retreating into southern Laos, and that the Viet Cong were about ready to give up. Some optimistic officials in Washington agreed that the battlefield situation had significantly improved. But Nhu gave the White House something else to worry about, claiming that he was pursuing secret talks with representatives of the NLF and then revealing his activities to the press. Whether or not the Diem regime was serious about pursuing a separate peace settlement with Hanoi (Nhu remarked to confidants that he hoped to demonstrate to Washington that Saigon had no intention of becoming a U.S. puppet), it was a none-too-subtle indication to Washington that Saigon did not intend to rely entirely on the United States.[29]

In fact, the reduced level of insurgent activity during the summer and early fall of 1963 may have reflected some uncertainty in Hanoi about the political situation. According to Truong Nhu Tang, then a prominent member of the NLF leadership in the south, insurgent leaders did not want Diem overthrown, since his behavior

---

[29] For one account of the alleged contacts, see Maneli, *War of the Vanquished*, p. 128. According to him, Hanoi told Nhu that the United States had to leave as part of a settlement. Everything else was subject to negotiation.

had alienated much of the population in the RVN and brought many to the side of the revolution. Encouraged perhaps by Ngo Dinh Nhu's efforts to establish contact with the north, Hanoi continued to pursue the possibility of a negotiated settlement. Although Truong Nhu Tang claimed that NLF leaders did not take Nhu's tantalizing gestures seriously and simply encouraged the contacts to muddle Saigon's relations with the United States, Hanoi thought enough of the possibility to publicize a brief statement by Ho Chi Minh suggesting the possibility of a peace settlement.[30]

By October, the dissident generals had screwed up their courage and informed Washington that they had resumed their coup plans. The White House was still willing to give a green light to the project but was concerned that the generals might botch the job. Henry Cabot Lodge, who had been appointed as the new U.S. ambassador to Saigon earlier in the summer, was instructed to learn more about the generals' plans. Nervous about the possibility of a leak, the generals refused to divulge their intentions, and carried out the coup with a minimum of U.S. involvement on November 1. Diem and his brother Nhu fled the presidential palace in Saigon by means of a secret passageway, but they were picked up the following morning in the Chinese section of the city and promptly executed under mysterious circumstances. The coup leaders set up a Military Revolutionary Council under General Duong Van "Big" Minh.

Resistance leaders reacted cautiously to the new developments. The level of PLAF operations declined slightly during the weeks following the coup, and the NLF issued a brief statement offering to hold talks with progressive elements to bring about the total defeat of U.S. policy in South Vietnam and the construction of a democratic political system representing the will of the entire population. For its part, Hanoi also appeared initially uncertain how to respond to the change of government in Saigon. In his letter to Nguyen Van Linh in July 1962, Le Duan had alluded to the possibility that Washington might replace Diem and implied that such a change could lead to negotiations for a U.S. withdrawal. But the

---

[30] For a translation of the statement into English, see *FRUS, 1961–1963*, vol. 3, p. 85. Hanoi sources would later claim that the overthrow of the Diem regime in November was a real boon to the revolutionary movement, because of the chaotic conditions that followed his overthrow. In fact, party leaders were probably as uncertain about their prospects in a post-Diem situation as were senior U.S. officials in Washington.

events that followed shortly after the November coup were not promising. Despite a brief slowdown in insurgent activities (probably designed to test the generals' response), the new military leadership in Saigon rebuffed NLF overtures, and in late November, President Lyndon B. Johnson, who had acceded to the presidency following Kennedy's assassination on November 22, announced that existing U.S. policies would continue under the new government in Saigon. Johnson had been openly critical of the backbiting against the Diem regime that had gone on in the White House, and had opposed the coup. Although he had reportedly made a vow that his administration would continue the Kennedy policies in Vietnam, he was privately skeptical of the social reforms advocated by some officials within the Kennedy White House and saw the war primarily as a security matter.[31]

In Hanoi, party leaders convened the Ninth Plenum of the Central Committee in December 1963 to discuss prospects. They were faced with a difficult decision. Washington's initial reaction to the coup suggested that a negotiated U.S. withdrawal was not likely, at least for the foreseeable future. Their gamble that a deterioration of the situation in Saigon would induce the United States to abandon its ally had misfired. The long-term picture was less clear. How would the new president react to an increase in insurgent activities in South Vietnam? The resolution approved at the close of the conference concluded that Washington could react in one of two ways.

---

[31] In the recent film entitled *JFK*, producer Oliver Stone contends that Kennedy was preparing to withdraw U.S. troops—which by now numbered about 20,000—from South Vietnam, and that his Vietnam policies were reversed by his successor. While it is undoubtedly true that Kennedy had approved a plan to withdraw U.S. forces gradually from the RVN, that plan had been drawn up on the assumption that the security situation was improving. As to Stone's contention that Johnson deliberately reversed Kennedy's policies, I have seen no evidence to support this supposition. Johnson's first decision on Vietnam was to affirm decisions with only minor changes (embodied in NSAM-273) to remain in the country that had been reached just prior to Kennedy's death. Whether Kennedy intended to remove U.S. troops and advisers from South Vietnam after the 1964 presidential election is a matter that has been widely disputed among the president's confidantes. For speculation to this effect, based on circumstantial evidence, see John M. Newman, *JFK and Vietnam: Deception, Intrigue, and the Struggle for Power* (New York: Warner Books, 1992). The statement issued by the NLF following the coup is contained in *Nhung Su Kien Lich Su Dang* [Events in the history of the Party], vol. 3 (Hanoi: Thong Tin Ly Luan, 1985), pp. 275–277.

It could either maintain the existing strategy of "special war" (that is, using U.S. troops primarily in an advisory capacity), or it could raise the war to a higher level by introducing U.S. combat units. It was the majority view that the second contingency would be the most likely if Washington became convinced that the insurgent forces were unable to resist a larger U.S. presence. Such an eventuality was unacceptable to Hanoi, since it would erode the movement's aura of success and make it significantly more difficult to maintain the morale of the PLAF and its leaders in the south.

On the other hand, a decision in Hanoi to increase the role of the DRV in the conflict in South Vietnam would certainly strain relations with Moscow, and perhaps with Beijing. Le Duan's letter to Nguyen Van Linh in July 1962 had clearly implied that Hanoi was under heavy pressure from its chief allies to avoid moves in Indochina that could threaten world peace and run the risk of spreading the war beyond the borders of South Vietnam. Whatever his private feelings on the subject, Le Duan had made it clear that the DRV must make an effort to heed the concerns of its allies, a policy that undoubtedly had the firm support of President Ho Chi Minh.[32]

By late 1963, however, the situation had changed. While details on the course of discussions at the Ninth Plenum are not available, there are indications from several sources that the debate was lively, and probably acrimonious. Some members apparently advocated the introduction of North Vietnamese main force troops into the south to help bring the Saigon regime to its knees. Others were reluctant to take actions that could exacerbate already strained relations with Hanoi's chief allies. In the end, the Central Committee approved a policy calling for the rapid strengthening of the PLAF in the hope of achieving a decisive shift in the balance of forces and realizing victory in a relatively short period of time. The plenum now declared that the role of armed struggle would be "direct and decisive," since the immediate task was to destroy ARVN forces in preparation for a general offensive to spark a popular uprising in the major population centers.

Still, the party appeared anxious to avoid a major escalation in

---

[32] According to knowledgeable Vietnamese, Ho Chi Minh throughout his career had consistently gone out of his way to avoid irritating his country's chief allies. One source claims that he never heard Ho speak critically of either the PRC or the USSR.

the war. The Central Committee rejected a proposal for the introduction of large numbers of North Vietnamese regular troops into
the south, either out of fear that it could cause problems with Moscow or that it could trigger an escalation of the U.S. role in the war.
In order to counter the larger U.S. effort, an increase in material
assistance from the north was approved, but according to the resolution, the role of the two zones would continue to be different. The
bulk of the responsibility for the struggle in the south would still be
borne by the PLAF, whose beefed-up forces would attempt to seize
control of the central highlands and the Mekong delta areas in preparation for the final general offensive and uprising.[33]

To reassure Moscow and other socialist allies that the DRV
would not let the situation get out of hand, Hanoi sent a circular to
"fraternal parties" explaining the decision to escalate the level of
armed activity in the south. The letter stated that it was unlikely
that the United States would introduce combat troops into South
Vietnam. More likely, it would accept defeat, as it had in China
during the civil war, or negotiate a compromise settlement, as it had
in Korea and Laos. Even if Washington decided to escalate, the letter
declared, the DRV would make every effort to restrain the United
States from extending the war beyond the borders of South Vietnam.
"Let us strive to deal with the first eventuality," it said, "and prepare
for the second."[34]

The decision undoubtedly caused serious divisions within the
party and provoked a growing split with Moscow. In a speech before
the Central Committee, Le Duan referred to party comrades who
held "rightist views" and were "influenced by modern revision-
ism," an oblique reference to those who supported Khrushchev's
policy of peaceful coexistence with the West. During succeeding
months, such "revisionist" elements were purged from the VWP
and the government, an action which undoubtedly further exacerbated relations with Moscow. For the next several months, Vietnamese officials studiously avoided Soviet diplomats at ceremonial occasions held in Hanoi. As a veiled warning to Soviet leaders that

---

[33] For an English-language version of the resolution issued at the close of the plenum,
see *Vietnam Documents and Research Notes*, no. 98. This series, consisting primarily of
translations of captured DRV or Viet Cong documents, was issued by the U.S. mission
in Saigon. Hereafter *VDRN*. Also see Turley, *Second Indochina War*, p. 58.

[34] *VDRN*, no. 96. The Vietnamese version is contained in *Mot So*, vol. 1, pp. 159–210.

Hanoi had other alternatives, Le Duan fulsomely praised China in his speech before the plenum, remarking pointedly that "it is the CCP headed by Comrade Mao Tse-tung which has carried out most satisfactorily the instructions of the great Lenin," an apparent reference to the fact that it was Beijing, not Moscow, which had given the most fervent support to the struggle for national liberation in South Vietnam.[35]

INCIDENT IN THE TONKIN GULF

In his remarks to President Johnson shortly after the latter's assumption of the presidency, U.S. Ambassador Henry Cabot Lodge had been cautiously optimistic about the prospects for victory under the new leadership. But it did not take long to dash the hopes of those who had urged the coup as a means of raising morale in Saigon. In December 1963, Defense Secretary Robert S. McNamara briefly visited South Vietnam and reported that the new military government under General Duong Van "Big" Minh was inexperienced, while Minh himself, although initially popular with the local population because of his local origins and affable manner, manifestly lacked the quality of leadership. Unless the current trends reversed, he warned, the country could quickly fall to the Communists or become neutral. Such thoughts occurred to others. The following January, the government of senior generals was overthrown by a group of middle-level officers under General Nguyen Khanh, commander of ARVN's I Corps in the northern provinces. Many U.S. officials in Saigon and Washington welcomed the change as a harbinger of more aggressive policies from the RVN, but Khanh was unable to halt the drift, and bickering within the regime continued. Embassy sources reported that enemy attacks were up in rural areas, and the momentum in the strategic hamlet program had been halted. A U.S. military intelligence report in March said that the Viet

---

[35] *VDRN*, no. 98, pp. 49, 57. The sudden tilt toward Beijing is an apparent indication that the influence of Ho Chi Minh on policy in the south was waning. Ho Chi Minh had consistently avoided taking a position favoring either of Hanoi's major benefactors in their growing ideological dispute and had sought vigorously to bring about a reconciliation. Le Duan apparently had fewer compunctions about antagonizing the regime's major supporters.

Cong now controlled between 40 and 45 percent of the total land area in the country, up from less than 30 percent the previous October.[36]

In Washington, the Joint Chiefs of Staff urged stronger action, but Lyndon Johnson rejected calls for direct air attacks on the north. He did approve OPLAN 34-A, which provided for a series of covert operations against the DRV. The Pentagon requested authorization to launch air strikes against the Ho Chi Minh Trail in Laos, but the White House, heeding warnings from the State Department that attacks on Laos could weaken the fragile government of the neutral Prime Minister Souvanna Phouma, rejected the proposal. For the time being, U.S. policy would focus on improving the situation inside South Vietnam.

But the situation in the RVN seemed impervious to U.S. efforts to improve it. During the spring and summer of 1964, political instability continued. Tension between Catholics and Buddhists simmered in Saigon, and demonstrations by students and workers erupted in several major cities. There was also growing unrest among mountain minority peoples in the central highlands, where traditional animosity to the ethnic Vietnamese had been exacerbated by the Diem regime's decision to settle the area with refugees, many of them Catholics, from the north.

By midsummer, senior administration officials had reached a consensus that Congress and the American people had to be prepared for stronger action to reverse the situation in the south. The pretext for such action came in early August, when North Vietnamese patrol boats attacked U.S. destroyers in the Tonkin Gulf but did not cause any serious damage. Shortly after, claiming that a second attack had taken place, the White House ordered air strikes against North Vietnamese installations in the panhandle as a reprisal, and then used the incident as a pretext to present Congress with a request to authorize the president to employ U.S. military forces as needed to protect U.S. lives and interests in Southeast Asia. With relatively little debate, the Tonkin Gulf Resolution was approved by a near unanimous vote in both houses of Congress.

The Tonkin Gulf incident became one of the most controversial

---

[36] COMUSMACV telegram, MACJ 23 2062 to JCS, March 18, 1964, in Declassified Documents Reference Service (hereafter DDRS), (R) 89D. Colby's report, dated February 16, 1964, is in ibid., (R) 39A.

issues in the Vietnam War. Doubts over the administration's claim that a second attack had taken place quickly surfaced, and some questioned the statement by Defense Secretary McNamara that the U.S. ships in question were on "routine patrol" in the area. It soon became clear that the U.S. vessels had been engaged in reconnaissance operations close to the North Vietnamese coast and may have been testing the ability of enemy radar to monitor U.S. maneuvers in the area. To muddy the waters further, a South Vietnamese guerrilla operation—probably a consequence of the recently approved OPLAN 34-A—was taking place nearby. North Vietnamese military commanders in the area were presumably convinced that the two operations were related, and reacted accordingly.

DAY OF RECKONING

It is clear from the evidence presented above that party strategists in Hanoi hoped to avoid actions that might lead the United States to escalate its role in the conflict in South Vietnam. According to the Polish representative Mieczyslaw Maneli, Ho Chi Minh and other DRV officials had persistently asked him how they should behave toward the United States. If such is the case, it hardly seems likely that the incident in the Tonkin Gulf was a deliberate provocation by Hanoi, although it might have been undertaken to warn the United States that its patience was limited.[37]

On the other hand, there seems little doubt that Hanoi's reluctance to intervene directly in the south was beginning to erode as events unfolded after the overthrow of the Diem regime, and the Tonkin Gulf incident may have had an impact on DRV strategy. According to one U.S. scholar, an extraordinary session of the Central Committee was convened a week later to evaluate the situation. Although no decision on how to respond was reached at the meeting, there was apparently some sentiment for making initial preparation to send troops to the south. The Politburo met a few weeks later to discuss the issue. Concluding that the political situation in South Vietnam was deteriorating rapidly, party leaders called for an accelerated effort to strengthen the military capabilities of the insurgent forces and "achieve a decisive victory in the next one or two years." Hanoi also called for more aggressive actions to destroy

---

[37] Maneli, *War of the Vanquished*, p. 156.

the strategic hamlets, expand liberated areas, and annihilate ARVN forces. There is no indication that the introduction of North Vietnamese troops was approved, but a training program to prepare PAVN units for operations in the south had been underway since April. According to U.S. intelligence sources, the first units departed in September and October, arriving in the south at the end of the year.

What had motivated this shift to a more aggressive approach? Historical accounts of the war published in Hanoi do not provide us with a concrete answer, but brief references to the meetings mentioned above suggest that party strategists were emboldened by the steady deterioration of the political situation in the RVN, as well as growing opposition to the war in the United States. Another favorable sign was that policy disagreements were even beginning to appear within the senior levels of the Johnson administration. If so, there was a growing possibility that if the Saigon regime reached a point of collapse, the White House might decide to pull out rather than to fight.[38]

With the shift to a more activist approach in the south, Hanoi decided to appoint a senior military commander to direct the effort. Chosen to head the entire operation was General Nguyen Chi Thanh, along with Vo Nguyen Giap one of the two military officers holding the rank of senior generals in the PAVN. Born in a poor peasant family near Hue in central Vietnam in 1914, General Thanh had entered the ICP during the late 1930s, and after imprisonment by the French in World War II he had risen rapidly to the position of director of the PAVN Political Department in 1949 and became a member of the Politburo when that body was established at the Second Party Congress in 1951.

Although General Thanh's responsibilities within the PAVN were primarily political, he was dynamic and clear-minded, and during the early 1960s he became actively involved in policy decisions dealing with the south, apparently succeeding General Giap as the leading military strategist in the Politburo. The reasons for Giap's fall from grace are not entirely clear, although there are reports that he had opposed the decision to escalate at the Ninth Plenum in December 1963, and several of his protégés were purged

---

[38] Turley, *Second Indochina War*, p.61, citing Combined Intelligence Center Vietnam, Research and Analysis Study ST 76-013, "Update: The NFA Soldier in South Vietnam," US MAG, J-2 (Saigon, October 18, 1966), p. 2.

in 1964 during a campaign to remove the influence of allegedly pro-Khrushchev elements within the party leadership. Vo Nguyen Giap had apparently been one of Ho Chi Minh's favorite lieutenants, but Ho's health deteriorated rapidly after 1964 and he was no longer active in policy decisions. According to numerous sources in Hanoi, Ho's successor Le Duan reportedly felt that General Giap lacked the spine for a tough policy in the south.

Such was certainly not the case with General Nguyen Chi Thanh. Shortly after the Tonkin Gulf incident, he visited South Vietnam in secret to evaluate the situation and present a plan of operations to the Politburo. General Thanh had now become convinced that full-scale war was inevitable, and that the PLAF could not achieve a decisive victory without more direct assistance from the north. Many of his colleagues were concerned that the PAVN did not possess the firepower to cope with an increasing U.S. role, but Thanh argued that the enthusiastic spirit of the revolutionary forces would compensate for the technological superiority of the enemy. It seems likely that Nguyen Chi Thanh was an influential force in persuading his colleagues to expand the war in the south.[39]

The first stage in General Thanh's plan was to concentrate on building up a liberated base area in the central highlands similar to the one the Vietminh had created in the Viet Bac in the war against the French. The minority population living in the area was seen as a prime source of recruitment into the PLAF, while the mountainous terrain could be advantageous for military operations against the enemy. As described by one official history of the war published in Hanoi, the new front (formally called the Central Highlands Front and established in September 1964) was

> an objective requirement resulting from the geographical, cultural, and economic conditions of the Central Highlands and its important position with regard to South Vietnam and south Indochina. It was an inevitable development of the anti-U.S. liberation war for national salvation aimed at meeting the requirement of fighting large annihilating battles or promoting the development of regular warfare.[40]

---

[39] Background information on General Nguyen Chi Thanh is available in Turley, *Second Indochina War*, pp. 71–72. For an assessment of his personality and his role in internal politics, see Georges Boudarel, *Cents fleurs ecloses dans la nuit du Vietnam* (Paris: Jacques Bertoin, 1992), *passim.*

[40] *CKC*, p. 103.

Following the creation of the liberated base in the central highlands, General Thanh intended to prepare for an eventual advance into the more densely populated areas along the central coast and in the Mekong River delta. A major focus in this process would be the flatlands surrounding the capital city of Saigon, since that was where the bulk of ARVN troop strength was located. If insurgent forces in the area could achieve major victories in their battles with the enemy, the door to Saigon would be open, and a combined general offensive and uprising in both rural and urban areas could bring a final end to the war.

On December 4, 1964, two PLAF regiments attacked the village of Binh Gia, a Catholic community about 70 kilometers northeast of Saigon. South Vietnamese units were rushed to the area, but absorbed heavy casualties in a bitter battle, leading to an estimated 200 killed and the downing of several helicopters. Lacking a strategic reserve, the attacking forces were eventually forced to withdraw. Still, to military strategists in Hanoi the battle of Binh Gia demonstrated the rising ability of the PLAF to cope successfully with the enemy's tactics of mobile warfare. The stage was set for the final confrontation.[41]

Resistance leaders also began to increase their efforts to strengthen front work in urban areas in preparation for the projected general uprising. To demonstrate their growing presence in the cities, party organizers directed a number of terrorist attacks on U.S. personnel and installations in and near Saigon. The Caravelle Hotel, a favorite haunt of foreign journalists on Thu Do Street in the heart of Saigon, was bombed in August, and a mortar attack took place at the U.S. air base at nearby Bien Hoa on November 1, on the eve of the U.S. presidential elections.[42]

The White House had pushed the Tonkin Gulf Resolution through Congress in order to free the president's hands for possible military action to protect U.S. interests in Southeast Asia. But Lyn-

[41] Le Duan; *Thu Vao Nam*, p. 141. For Hanoi's account of the battle, see *CKC*, pp. 65–66.

[42] *Nhung Su Kien*, p. 315, said 293 U.S. were killed in the attack. A later account, *CKC*, said four died. According to the Polish diplomat Mieczyslaw Maneli, previously Hanoi had solicitously avoided attacks on Americans as part of its policy of attempting to limit U.S. involvement in the war. The new policy may have been designed to warn the Johnson administration that a growing U.S. role would result in increased American casualties. See Maneli, *War of the Vanquished*, p. 156.

don Johnson had refrained from taking any major steps to escalate the U.S. role in the conflict because of the upcoming presidential elections, as well as the fragility of the situation in South Vietnam. In September, however, General Maxwell Taylor, who had just replaced Henry Cabot Lodge as U.S. ambassador to the RVN, reported that infiltration from the north was rising and warned that the United States must be prepared to adopt "new and drastic methods" to cut off the flow. The administration had announced that it would "respond as appropriate" to any Viet Cong provocation, and when the Bien Hoa attack took place in early November, Ambassador Taylor recommended a reprisal. Johnson refused, on the grounds that the provocation was not sufficient. But he did approve the formation of a new working group composed of senior officials and chaired by Assistant Secretary of State for Far Eastern Affairs William P. Bundy to advise him on possible future actions in the crisis. In the meantime, he instructed Ambassador Taylor to strengthen the situation in Saigon in preparation for the "day of reckoning."[43]

In Hanoi, party leaders were preparing for their own day of reckoning. In January 1965 the Politburo decided to expand efforts to destroy ARVN forces and prepare for the general uprising. In a letter written shortly after the meeting to the new COSVN commander, Nguyen Chi Thanh, Le Duan pointed out that the key question was whether the PLAF could defeat the enemy's armed forces before they could regain their balance and before the United States could decide whether to intervene directly in the war. If such was the case, the United States would have no alternative but to withdraw. Le Duan answered his own rhetorical question in the affirmative. The guerrilla movement, he pointed out, was strong, and the political situation presented a great opportunity. If several ARVN divisions could be disabled and others lured out of the capital area by PLAF attacks in nearby rural areas, a general uprising in the heart of Saigon might succeed. Then the political struggle could take precedence, with the collapse of the Saigon regime and the formation of a neutral government secretly under party control which would call for negotiations with the NLF. Le Duan admitted that there was no guarantee that such a strategy would succeed, but he quoted Lenin to the effect that one must not wait for guaranteed success,

---

[43] *Pentagon Papers* (Senator Gravel edition), vol. 3 (Boston: Little, Brown, 1971), document 210, pp. 35–48.

The Ho Chi Minh Trail after U.S. bombardment.

but seek out and grasp the opportunity when it arose. In such a manner, he said, the work of twenty years might be achieved in a day. Let's act, and then see. If at first we do not succeed, we can always try again.[44]

In the first weeks of the new year, the situation in South Vietnam went from bad to worse. U.S. intelligence sources reported that infiltration from the north had totaled 10,000 in 1964, with an additional 13,000 located in southern Laos. Bickering within the Saigon regime continued, while ARVN operations in the countryside had almost totally come to an end. In August, Nguyen Khanh was overthrown, but then managed to return with support from a new alliance of forces. As coup succeeded coup in Saigon, Ambassador Taylor lost his patience and lectured the generals, while in Washington Lyndon Johnson fretted about "that bitch of a war on the other side of the world."[45]

On February 7, PLAF troops attacked a U.S. Special Forces camp at Pleiku in the central highlands, killing several Americans. From Saigon, where he was staying on a brief inspection visit, Lyndon

[44] Le Duan, *Thu Vao Nam*, letter to Anh Xuan (Nguyen Chi Thanh), February 1965, p. 96.
[45] The intelligence report is in U.S. Embassy, Saigon, January 26, 1965 in DDRS, (R) 860E.

Johnson's national security adviser, McGeorge Bundy, recommended a strong response. The White House ordered reprisal strikes on DRV staging areas in the North Vietnamese panhandle, to the north of the DMZ. But on February 10, insurgent units struck again, killing twenty-one U.S. servicemen in a bombing attack on a U.S. Army billet at Qui Nhon on the central coast. Three days later, the White House announced a bombing program calling for "measured and limited air action jointly with the GVN [government of Vietnam] against selected targets in the DRV south of the 19th parallel until further notice." Eventually that step would be expanded into a program of steadily intensifying strikes over almost all of North Vietnam known as Operation Rolling Thunder.

TEST OF STRENGTH

While the White House was deciding whether to escalate, the Central Committee held its eleventh plenary session in Hanoi. The final resolution issued at the close of the meeting was brimming with optimism. The Saigon regime, it reported, was in a virtual state of paralysis, while the urban population in the south, incited by activist Buddhist monks under the leadership of the enigmatic bonze Tri Quang, was increasingly leaning toward neutrality in the war. In rural areas, the strategic hamlet program was at a standstill and the majority of the population was now living in NLF-controlled areas. Abroad, the situation was equally bright. The antiwar movement in the United States was rapidly gaining momentum, giving rise to hopes in Hanoi that the White House would be reluctant to escalate. Finally, the overthrow of Nikita Khrushchev the previous October promised a significant change in Soviet attitudes toward the conflict in Vietnam. In early February, the new Soviet premier, Alexei Kosygin, made a brief visit to Hanoi, reportedly to bring assurances that the Moscow leadership under party chief Leonid Brezhnev actively supported the Vietnamese struggle for national liberation. But Kosygin undoubtedly also cautioned his hosts against the resumption of a full-scale conflict that could erupt into a global confrontation. He apparently promised that Soviet aid would be increased, but only on condition that the latter make every effort to avoid an expansion of the war. That bargain was implicit in the resolution issued after the meeting, which announced that the current strategy in the south would be to realize a decisive victory in a relatively short period of time while trying to keep the United States from directly entering the war.[46]

But for once, Hanoi had miscalculated. The incident at Pleiku brought an end to President Johnson's reluctance to introduce U.S. ground troops into the war. In early March, U.S. Marine units landed at Da Nang, along the central coast. Although their objective was described as a "limited mission" to relieve ARVN of security duties to protect the U.S. air base at Da Nang, additional U.S. combat troops entered South Vietnam during the next few weeks. To justify the action, the White House issued a new White Paper, which documented a steady increase in the infiltration of troops and supplies from the DRV and making the case that the insurgent movement in the south was inspired, directed, and actively supported from Hanoi. Presumably, the White House hoped to make a strong case that the DRV had now engaged in what amounted to an "armed attack" on the RVN, thus enabling the United States to react "according to its constitutional processes" under the provisions of the SEATO agreement.[47]

Lyndon Johnson was gambling that once Hanoi recognized the extent of his determination to avoid defeat in South Vietnam, it would be willing to negotiate a settlement on U.S. terms. To test the waters and appease war critics, the White House launched a peace initiative to demonstrate its desire for an end to the violence. In an address at Johns Hopkins University in Baltimore, President Johnson offered a generous program of economic assistance to all the Indochinese countries following an end of the war. But the White House, too, had misread the enemy's intentions. On April 8, the day following Lyndon Johnson's Baltimore speech, DRV prime minister Pham Van Dong listed Hanoi's conditions, known as the "Four Points," for holding peace talks. The United States, he said, must unconditionally withdraw from Vietnam. A coalition government should then be formed by peace-loving peoples in the south to engage in peaceful negotiations about reunification with the north. In the

---

[46] *Mot So,* pp. 211–228.

[47] The White Paper, entitled *Aggression from the North: The Record of North Vietnam's Campaign to Conquer South Vietnam* (Washington, D.C.: U.S. Department of State, February 1965), is reprinted in Marvin E. Gettleman, *Vietnam: History, Documents, and Opinions on a Major World Crisis* (Greenwich, Conn.: Fawcett, 1965), pp. 284–315.

meantime, only the NLF was the legitimate representative of the Vietnamese people.[48]

It is possible that Pham Van Dong's peace feeler was inspired by the hope in the north that the United States might still be ready to pursue peace talks on Hanoi's terms. More likely, however, the gesture was intended to have a psychological impact on world public opinion. During the visit of Soviet premier Alexei Kosygin to Hanoi in February, North Vietnamese leaders had reportedly rejected the latter's suggestion of a negotiated settlement. The final communiqué issued at the close of Kosygin's visit merely noted that both parties supported the principle of the peaceful settlement of international disputes. The DRV also rejected Moscow's appeal for the convening of a new conference on Indochina, which was issued after Kosygin's return to Moscow.

In fact, it seems clear that Hanoi did not feel that peace talks would be useful under existing circumstances. In a letter to Nguyen Chi Thanh written a few weeks after Pham Van Dong's announcement, Le Duan underlined the Politburo's contention that negotiations were not desirable at present. "Only when the insurrection [in the south] is successful," he said, "will the problem of establishing a 'neutral central administration' be posed again." In other words, party leaders intended to await the results of the projected general offensive and uprising before sitting down at the peace table with representatives from the United States. As for the Four Points, Le Duan pointed out that they were "intended to pave the way for a U.S. withdrawal with a lesser loss of face." Undoubtedly, Hanoi also hoped to sway public attitudes toward the conflict in the United States and provide impetus to the growing antiwar movement there.[49]

During the remainder of that ominous spring, there were increasing indications that, if necessary, Lyndon Johnson was prepared to introduce additional U.S. combat troops to prevent a defeat

---

[48] Cited in Kahin, *Intervention,* p. 326.

[49] Le Duan, *Thu Vao Nam,* letter of May 1965. For information on Kosygin's trip to Hanoi, see William Smyser, *The Independent Vietnamese: Hanoi between Moscow and Beijing* (Athens: Ohio University Papers on International Studies, 1980). There were also reports that Kosygin brought a secret message from the Johnson administration to take mutual steps to deescalate the conflict, a proposal that Hanoi flatly rejected. See Melvin Gurtov, *China under Threat: The Politics of Strategy and Diplomacy* (Baltimore: Johns Hopkins Press, 1980).

in South Vietnam. Party chief Le Duan alluded to those developments in the above-cited letter to General Thanh in May, but he
reiterated his confidence that Washington feared a wider war and
would eventually accept a negotiated withdrawal. Even with over
100,000 troops in South Vietnam, he insisted, U.S. war strategy
would be essentially defensive in nature. There was thus no need to
change the existing strategy, but merely to intensify efforts to
achieve victory before the United States could make the decision to
bring thousands of additional U.S. troops into the war.

Le Duan's message indicates that Hanoi was still hoping for a
combined general offensive and uprising that would bring the Saigon regime to the point of collapse. To bring that about, he advised
that military assaults against ARVN forces in rural areas must be
combined with efforts to bring the unrest in Saigon to a peak. Party
representatives were instructed to infiltrate organizations like the
Cao Dai and Tri Quang's Buddhist movement, while preparing
youth assault teams to take the lead once the general insurrection
broke out. The ultimate objective remained the creation of a neutral
coalition government in Saigon. Le Duan defined such a government
as including a wide spectrum of political forces, including some
groups sympathetic to France and the United States. In his view, the
important thing was that such a neutral administration should be
secretly controlled by party members, who would hold the key positions in the cabinet.

Le Duan urged southern leaders not to fear the possibility of
defeat. When the opportunity arises, he remarked, don't wait for the
total certainty of success. Even if insurgent forces do not succeed,
they will still be able to pull out without having to sustain heavy
losses, while the movement's military and political nucleus will still
be essentially intact. The worst that could happen, he argued, would
be that the United States might increase its forces to engage in a
"test of strength" with the Vietnamese nation. In Hanoi, he pointed
out, party leaders "are already prepared for the worst."[50]

By midsummer, U.S. forces began to take an active part in combat operations. The first major contest took place in August, when
U.S. Marines based at Chu Lai, along the central coast south of Da
Nang, launched a concentrated assault on an insurgent base area on
the Battangan peninsula, a rocky outgrowth along the central coast.

---

[50] Le Duan, *Thu Vao Nam*, letter of May 1965, *passim*.

The area had long been known as a Viet Cong stronghold, and several thousand Marines, many of them airlifted by helicopter, attempted to surround PLAF forces in the area and annihilate them. After the fighting was over, U.S. sources reported 600 enemy dead and 122 prisoners, at the cost of 200 U.S. casualties.

General William C. Westmoreland, who had taken over from Paul Harkins as commander of the U.S. Military Assistance Command in South Vietnam (MACV) late the previous year, claimed that Operation Starlight, as the battle had been labeled, had shown that U.S. troops could defeat "any Viet Cong or North Vietnamese forces they might encounter." Predictably, Hanoi saw it differently. Official DRV sources claimed that almost 1000 U.S. troops had died in the battle. One called the battle (known in Vietnamese historiography as the battle of Van Tuong, from a hamlet at the center of the fighting) a "Stalingrad," while General Thanh pointed out that it showed that even when the United States chose the time and place, the PLAF could live to fight again. He had a point. After the battle, the insurgent forces returned unmolested to their previous locations.[51]

Before the summer was out, there were a number of other clashes between U.S. and revolutionary forces in the central highlands, where General Westmoreland had just placed units of the U.S. First Cavalry Division to forestall a predicted enemy attempt to seize Route 19 and divide the country in two. According to sources in Hanoi, the general's assumptions were correct. At the urging of Ho Chi Minh, party strategists had planned a major operation to attack an enemy post at Plei Me, in the highlands, and then advance down Route 19 to the coast. The arrival of the U.S. First Cavalry Division forced a postponement of the plan, but it was eventually approved with more modest objectives—to "lure the tiger out of the mountain" and learn how to face the highly mobile U.S. forces.

The attack on the Plei Me special forces camp took place as scheduled on October 19, 1965. Afterward, PAVN forces ambushed ARVN reinforcements rushing into the area along Route 5 and then

---

[51] For Westmoreland's interpretation of the battle, see his *Report on the War in South Vietnam* (New York: Doubleday, 1976), p. 102. Le Duan later said that U.S. losses were many times those of the PLAF. See *Thu Vao Nam*, p. 135. MACV was created by the Kennedy administration in early 1962.

VIỆT NAM DÂN CHỦ CỘNG HOÀ

ĐÁNH ĐẾN CÙNG
CỞ TÂN LONG CHÂU

Bưu Chính 12 xu

A guerrilla in action, "fighting to the end."

withdrew to prepared defensive locations in Chu Pong Mountain, a familiar Vietminh redoubt above Ia Drang Valley and adjacent to the Cambodian border. There they turned to face pursuing American troops. The battle was a bitter one and resulted in heavy casualties on both sides. Sources in MACV claimed that the battle in Ia Drang Valley was a U.S. victory, with North Vietnamese losses estimated at six times those of their American adversaries. Slightly over 300 U.S. troops died in the fighting. According to Vo Nguyen Giap, the results were worth the cost, since the battle in Ia Drang Valley showed that the PAVN could fight and win against U.S. troops.[52]

In the meantime, the political situation in Saigon continued to evolve rapidly. In June, the civilian government under Phan Huy Quat that had been in power for three months was overthrown by a military coup led by the young air force colonel Nguyen Cao Ky. Flamboyant and mercurial, Ky did not immediately inspire much confidence, either among the South Vietnamese people or among officials at the U.S. Embassy or in Washington. Still, under Ky's

[52] Lieutenant General Harold G. Moore and Joseph L. Galloway, *We Were Soldiers Once . . . and Young* (New York: Random House, 1992), pp. 42–50. Giap's comment is cited on page 339.

THE WAR IN SOUTH VIETNAM

leadership, the political situation gradually began to stabilize. The fragile but welcome signs of stability in Saigon were undoubtedly encouraging to the White House, where Lyndon Johnson had ordered a high-level review of the situation and prospects. After a wide-ranging exchange of proposals, in late July Johnson approved a program set forth by Defense Secretary McNamara to increase U.S. troop strength to over 150,000 by the end of 1965. The United States was now fully into the war.

A WARNING FROM BEIJING

The steady increase in U.S. troop strength, combined with the failure to bring about the hoped-for general offensive and uprising, was undoubtedly a bitter pill for Hanoi to swallow. In a letter written to southern commanders early the following year, Politburo member Le Duc Tho conceded that Washington's decision to intervene directly in the war had been unexpected. "Things do not always develop in strict accordance with our subjective judgment and intentions," he noted dryly. Later, a DRV source would concede in a post mortem that party leaders had not moved rapidly enough to take advantage of the situation.[53]

But Hanoi also had an additional worry. In his letter to Nguyen Chi Thanh in May, Le Duan had promised that even in the worst of circumstances, the Vietnamese people would still have the firm support of their fraternal allies. In actuality, by midsummer North Vietnamese leaders had growing doubts about the attitude of China. Since early in the year, the Johnson administration had been sending signals to Beijing indicating its desire to avoid a direct confrontation over Indochina. China's first response had been tantalizing but imprecise. In March, Mao Zedong remarked to U.S. journalist Edgar Snow that China would not take a direct part in the war unless it was directly attacked by U.S. forces. But a few days later *People's Daily*, the official CCP newspaper, declared that China regarded the struggle in South Vietnam as its own struggle and would send all necessary assistance to the Vietnamese people.[54]

[53] Pike Documents II, no. 302.

[54] For a U.S. government study of China's reaction to the escalation of the war in Vietnam, see "CIA Secret Report on Sino-Vietnamese Reaction to American Tactics in the Vietnamese War," in *Journal of Contemporary Asia*, 13(2) (1983), p. 261. Hereafter, CIA report.

The United States raised the issue at the irregularly scheduled Sino-U.S. ambassadorial talks in Warsaw in April, but Chinese ambassador Wang Bingnan merely reiterated Premier Zhou Enlai's statement that China was ready to send the necessary aid, including troops, "whenever the South Vietnamese people want them." In fact, however, Chinese leaders were now engaged in a bitter factional dispute over internal issues, and many were anxious to avoid a direct confrontation with Washington over the situation in Vietnam. Sometime during the summer, the Johnson administration received a secret message saying that China would not intervene in the struggle unless its territory were directly attacked.[55]

How and to what degree to assist the Vietnamese had become a major issue in Beijing. Since the early 1960s, Chinese leaders had consistently urged that Hanoi restrict the level of conflict in the south until international conditions favored a revolutionary advance throughout the region. Now Moscow had just proposed that China and the USSR agree on united action to support the Vietnamese against the forces of U.S. imperialism. Some Chinese leaders wanted to accept the offer, but Mao Zedong and several of his key supporters viewed the proposal as a Soviet plot, and the proposal was rejected in late summer. In September, Defense Minister Lin Biao, one of Mao Zedong's closest supporters, published an article in the journal *Peking Review* in which he elliptically advised the North Vietnamese to carry out their struggle for national reunification by means of a policy of protracted war and self-reliance. The author quoted Mao Zedong's comment during China's war of resistance against Japan: "China has to rely mainly on her own efforts in the war of resistance. . . . We hope for foreign aid but cannot be dependent on it; we depend on our own efforts, on the creative power of the whole army and the entire people."[56]

Some U.S. officials, like Defense Secretary Robert McNamara, viewed Lin Biao's article as a Chinese version of Adolf Hitler's *Mein*

[55] According to then Assistant Secretary of State for East Asia and the Pacific, William Bundy, the message arrived sometime in late June or early July. William Bundy manuscript, Chapter 28, pp. 1–2. A copy of the manuscript is held in the Lyndon Johnson Library in Austin, Texas. According to the above-cited CIA report, a message had arrived in mid-April informing Washington that Chinese combat forces would not be sent to North Vietnam so long as U.S. or ARVN troops did not cross the 17th parallel. See CIA report, p. 269.

[56] For an English-language translation of Lin's article, see Norman A. Graebner (ed.), *Nationalism and Communism in Asia: the American Response* (Lexington: D.C. Heath, 1977), pp. 149–167.

Kampf, declaring class war on the free world. But to party leaders in Hanoi, it carried a much different message: the Vietnamese should not count on their fraternal allies to wage their revolution, but should rely on their own efforts. More ominously, Beijing's behavior only served to reassure Washington that it had nothing to fear from escalating the conflict in South Vietnam, so long as it did not directly threaten Chinese interests in the region.[57]

TOWARD LIMITED WAR

By the end of the summer, it was clear that Le Duan's projected general offensive and uprising was not going to materialize, at least for the foreseeable future. With the new government in Saigon showing some signs of endurance, and U.S. troops beginning to arrive in South Vietnam at an accelerated pace, the Politburo met in September to evaluate the situation and plan for the future. Party leaders interpreted the recent decisions in Washington as a clear indication that the Johnson administration was moving from special war to limited war (that is, from waging the war through the armed forces of the Saigon regime to waging it directly with U.S. combat troops). In the view of the Politburo, that strategy presented the DRV with new, but not insurmountable, problems. Recent actions taken by the United States suggested that U.S. leaders no longer feared that escalation inside South Vietnam would lead to a wider war, but Washington remained unlikely to attack North Vietnam directly, since it would then face the possibility of a confrontation with the entire socialist camp. Moreover, even with half a million troops in the RVN, the Johnson administration would still be faced with the key disadvantages that had plagued it from the beginning—a weak puppet in Saigon and the lack of firm public support in the United States. In the end, party leaders still hoped that Washington would ultimately accept a small defeat in Vietnam in order to avoid a larger one throughout the region.

The Politburo thus concluded that its general strategy of protracted war leading to a general offensive and uprising should remain essentially unchanged. The presence of large numbers of U.S.

---

[57] For an extended exposition of Hanoi's anger, written in the shadow of the Sino-Vietnamese war of 1979, see *The Truth about Vietnamo-Chinese Relations over the Past Thirty Years* (Hanoi: Ministry of Foreign Affairs, 1979).

combat forces changed the equation, however, and necessitated the infiltration of larger numbers of North Vietnamese regular units to bolster the forces of the PLAF in the south. Southern commanders were instructed to maintain the offensive throughout the southern provinces, and to attack U.S. as well as ARVN forces (in General Nguyen Chi Thanh's words, "stick close to the Americans, and hit them where it hurts"), although direct attacks on the former should be avoided except where the balance of forces in the immediate vicinity was advantageous to the insurgents. Otherwise, contacts with U.S. units should take the form of flank attacks and harassing actions rather than frontal assaults on fortified positions. The ultimate goal was to achieve a decisive victory (rather than a complete one) in a relatively short period of time.

Above all, southern commanders were ordered to be flexible in their approach and to adopt tactics that were appropriate to the time and the place. In the central highlands, for example, military struggle should be the standard technique, since geographical conditions and the balance of forces favored the insurgency. In urban areas, political struggle was foremost, although at the moment of general uprising, troops from the outside could be brought into the cities while special urban units fanned disorder among the general population and provoked mutinies among enemy troops.[58]

The Politburo had thus decided to confront the United States directly in the south. It now remained to seek the approval of fraternal allies, since such a decision would obviously necessitate substantial amounts of military assistance from abroad. In the fall, a delegation of senior DRV officials led by Le Duan visited both Beijing and Moscow. Evidently they received a commitment from both countries for increased military aid, but they may also have received a lecture from the former on the virtues of patience and self-reliance. In a speech at an army conference held in May 1966, Le Duan remarked that "it is not fortuitous that in the history of our country, each time we rose to oppose foreign aggression, we took the offensive and not the defensive. . . . Taking the offensive is a strategy, while taking the defensive is only a stratagem. Since the day the South Vietnamese people rose up, they have continually taken the offensive."[59]

---

[58] CKC, p. 79; Le Duan, *Thu Vao Nam*, letter of November 1965.
[59] Cited in Donald Zagoria, *The Vietnam Triangle: Moscow, Peking, Hanoi* (New York: Pegasus, 1967), p. 84.

Having received at least a qualified blessing from Moscow, the Central Committee approved the Politburo decision to escalate the level of fighting at its Twelfth Plenum in December. The resolution issued at the close of the meeting called for the mobilization of the entire nation to complete the revolution in the south. The new strategic guidelines were to fight a protracted war based on the philosophy of self-reliance, while seeking sympathy from foreign countries and the selective use of military, political, and diplomatic techniques. The slogan of the day was "Protect the North, Assist the South."[60]

DESCENT INTO THE ABYSS

By the fall of 1965, the civil conflict in South Vietnam was on the verge of becoming a full-scale war. As we have seen, each side was convinced that it had no choice but to escalate the military struggle to meet the increased efforts of the other. Hanoi had concluded that Washington's decision to introduce large numbers of U.S. combat forces left it little choice but to respond in kind. The Johnson administration argued that its decision to Americanize the war had been dictated by Hanoi's prior decision to intervene in the south to have its way. As it stated in the White Paper issued in February:

> The hard core of the Communist forces attacking South Vietnam are men trained in North Vietnam. They are ordered into the South and remain under the military discipline of the Military High Command in Hanoi. Special training camps operated by the North Vietnamese army give political and military training to the infiltrators. Increasingly the forces sent into the South are native North Vietnamese who have never seen South Vietnam. A special infiltration unit, the 70th Transportation Group, is responsible for moving men from North Vietnam into the South via infiltration trails through Laos. Another special unit, the maritime infiltration group, sends weapons and supplies and agents by sea into the South.[61]

The White Paper was essentially an accurate presentation of the facts as they were available to the State Department at that time. But

---

[60] The resolution of the Twelfth Plenum is reproduced in excerpted form in *Mot So,* II, pp. 53–55. For a brief reference, see CKC, pp. 83–84.
[61] *Aggression from the North,* p. 287.

by leaving the impression that the escalation of the struggle in South Vietnam was entirely the responsibility of a small group of party leaders in North Vietnam, the report was seriously misleading. It seems clear from the documentary evidence that Vietnamese strategists in Hanoi turned to the military option with considerable reluctance, and that even in so doing, they went to considerable pains to stress the importance of political struggle in the quest for final victory and reunification.

Hanoi, in fact, had good reasons for attempting to avoid a direct military conflict. In the first place, it was in the realm of politics that the forces of revolution possessed a marked superiority over the enemy. A generation of competition with their rivals in the south had convinced them that in an open contest, they would have no difficulty in achieving total victory in South Vietnam. At the same time, the Vietnamese were under severe pressure from their allies to avoid a resumption of the conflict in Indochina, and Hanoi's actions since the mid-1950s made it clear that they would go to considerable lengths to prevent that eventuality.

Nevertheless, there is no doubt that senior party leaders were willing to turn to the military option if such a shift in approach appeared to be in their interest. Although Hanoi's policies during the late 1950s were marked by a reluctance to engage in a direct confrontation in the south, they did not hesitate to escalate the conflict into a combined military and political one once it became clear that only violent struggle could achieve satisfactory results. As Le Duan pointed out in one of his letters to Nguyen Chi Thanh, if the United States wants a protracted war, it will have it. We will fight, he said, whatever way the United States wants.

In that sense, it can be said that the conflict became a predominantly military struggle with the characteristics of a conventional war not, as some have said, because Hanoi planned it that way, but because the United States wanted it that way. Given Hanoi's political superiority over its rivals in the south, it is perhaps not surprising that U.S. officials felt that the war could only be won by transforming the major field of operations from the political to the military realm, where U.S. firepower might make a difference. Fate would decree otherwise.

CHAPTER 5

All for the Front Lines

Shortly after the decision by the White House to introduce U.S. combat troops into the RVN, General William Westmoreland mapped out a three-stage strategy to achieve victory in South Vietnam. Up through the end of 1965, he planned to secure densely populated areas along the coast, stifle the enemy's initiative, and halt the downward trend in the war. During the dry season in the first few months of 1966, he intended to use both U.S. and ARVN troops to drive insurgent forces out of strategically important areas in the mountains and plains and cut off the flow of infiltration from the north. If needed, a final stage would be applied to bring an end to the insurgency within twelve to eighteen months.[1]

General Westmoreland was responding in part to a plan of operations drawn up by the Joint Chiefs of Staff and presented to Defense Secretary Robert S. McNamara in late August. The plan set forth three major objectives of equal priority: (1) to cause the DRV to cease directing and supporting the insurgency in South Vietnam, (2) to defeat the Viet Cong and enable the RVN to extend its control over the entire territory of South Vietnam, and (3) to deter China from direct intervention in the Vietnam War, and to defeat it should it occur.

For General Westmoreland in Saigon, the most meaningful aspect of the plan was the provision that U.S. and ARVN forces should seize the initiative to disrupt and ultimately defeat the Viet Cong in South Vietnam. In that objective he encountered some initial success over the course of the year. Operations in the heavily forested Zone D, the PLAF stronghold north of Saigon, removed the immediate

---

[1] General Westmoreland described his strategy in *A Soldier Reports* (New York: Doubleday, 1976).

threat to the capital area. The stationing of U.S. Marines along the central coast in the vicinity of Da Nang reversed that area's rapid drift to the enemy, while the deployment of the U.S. First Cavalry Division in the central highlands placed U.S. forces in a position to contest that mountain region with General Thanh's forces. Behind the American military shield, the Saigon regime had begun to stabilize. By the end of 1965, Hanoi's prospects for a collapse of the RVN had clearly declined.

EATING RICE WITH CHOPSTICKS

During the first six months of 1966, General Westmoreland began to carry out phase two of his strategy. A military campaign, labeled Operation Attleboro, was launched in the Communist redoubts north and northwest of Saigon. The area was deforested, the villages were leveled, and the population resettled elsewhere. Westmoreland also ordered search-and-destroy operations in the central highlands and followed up on the battle in Ia Drang Valley by attempting to block infiltration routes into South Vietnam through Laos. Westmoreland's aggressive approach was widely criticized by U.S. journalists in South Vietnam, who described it as overkill and the wrong way to "win hearts and minds," but it undoubtedly threw the insurgent forces off balance and removed the immediate threat to Saigon.

Although the VWP Central Committee at its meeting in December 1965 had bravely asserted that the U.S. decision to escalate did not change the fundamental situation in South Vietnam, Westmoreland's aggressive moves to provide a military shield for the Saigon regime undoubtedly inspired a considerable amount of debate in Hanoi. As we have seen, some party strategists were evidently worried that insurgent forces would be unable to cope with the technological superiority of the enemy on the battlefield. It may have been in response to that concern that in the spring of 1966, PAVN General Nguyen Van Vinh argued in a letter to a colleague that although the enemy was strong, he also had a number of weak points and could not escalate forever. In Korea, General Vinh noted, the United States was able to send all of its forces to the front because the rear was secure. That would not be the case in South Vietnam, where the presence of the revolution is strong, even in the heart of the enemy's lair. By using a combination of guerrilla and conventional tactics, he said, "we will force them to eat rice with chopsticks."[2]

That vision had undoubtedly inspired the decisions reached at the Twelfth Plenum in December 1965. In his 1966 letter to southern comrades cited in the previous chapter, Politburo member Le Duc Tho (writing under the pseudonym of "Sau") insisted that party leaders remained confident of victory. The Saigon government, he pointed out, was still the Americans' chief point of vulnerability, while public support for the war in the U.S. remained fragile. Tho took issue with unnamed comrades who allegedly thought that "the revolution in the South should be allowed to develop itself," and argued that "we are capable of achieving victory with our own resources."

Tho did admit, however, that the massive U.S. presence, now surpassing 200,000, necessitated caution. For that reason, revolutionary forces should not try to win a total victory immediately, but to win "bit by bit" over an extended period of time. They should concentrate their attacks on ARVN, the most vulnerable part of the enemy's flank, while avoiding contact with U.S. units except under favorable circumstances.[3]

In COSVN headquarters near the Cambodian border, General Nguyen Chi Thanh was undoubtedly aware of the dangers of confronting the Americans. At the same time, he favored an aggressive approach involving offensive operations by large units as a means of maintaining the initiative throughout the southern provinces. To those who expressed concern at the enemy's superiority in firepower, he responded with the Maoist dictum that spirit could always overcome material weakness. Armed with such confidence, Thanh urged his troops to accelerate their efforts to contest territory with the enemy throughout the battlefield, despite high casualties.[4]

Throughout the entire year of 1966, then, Hanoi attempted to match the U.S. escalation with an aggressive strategy of its own. Infiltration down the Ho Chi Minh Trail increased during 1966,

---

[2] *Working Paper*, app. item 303, letter of Nguyen Van Vinh dated April 1966. The letter was seized during an ARVN operation.

[3] Pike Documents II, item number 302, letter from Anh Sau, March 1966.

[4] Nguyen Chi Thanh, in Patrick J. McGarvey, *Visions of Victory: Selected Vietnamese Communist Military Writings, 1964–1968* (Palo Alto, Calif.: Stanford University Press, 1969), p. 65.

bringing the number of regular force and guerrilla troops available to over 200,000. Offensive operations were launched at points of enemy vulnerability throughout South Vietnam, from the DMZ to the swampy jungles of the Ca Mau peninsula. In articles and pamphlets written to promote his approach, General Thanh returned persistently to his theme: "To attack unremittingly is the most active and the most effective method to maintain and extend our control of the battlefield." In the meantime, to maintain high morale on the home front, Hanoi propagandists churned out stories, poems, and biographical accounts of dedicated young men and women marching joyfully to the battlefield in the southern provinces to fight for the unification of their fatherland.[5]

The cost of General Thanh's offensive strategy in human terms was high. Although insurgent military commanders had learned how to launch attacks in places of their own choosing, and to fade quickly from the battlefield when the immediate objective had been achieved, the sheer volume of the attacks, combined with the aggressive search-and-destroy tactics of U.S. and ARVN forces, resulted in growing casualties for the resistance forces. U.S. commanders in the field, operating under Westmoreland's strategy of a "war of attrition" (that is, to kill as many of the enemy as possible in order to undermine his resolve and bring him to the peace table) were encouraged to inflict as much damage as possible during allied operations. Although the ensuing body count figures were often inflated, and not infrequently included civilian dead and wounded as well as combatants, there is no doubt that the casualties suffered by the resistance forces were high, forcing them to rely increasingly on forced conscription in the south or infiltration from the north.[6]

Eventually, people in Hanoi, and even his subordinates in the south, began to question General Thanh's go-for-broke strategy as too costly and too risky for the future success of the revolution. One of the doubters was General Vo Nguyen Giap himself, Thanh's equal

---

[5] The quote is from Truong Son, *Five Lessons of a Great Victory (Winter 1966–Spring 1967)* (Hanoi: Foreign Languages Publishing House, 1967), p. 35. Truong Son ["Central Mountains"] was General Thanh's pseudonym.

[6] One U.S. Army officer who served in Vietnam claims that there were at least eighteen major allied military operations during 1966 which netted in at least 500 confirmed enemy dead. See Dave Richard Palmer, *Summons of the Trumpet: A History of the Vietnam War from a Military Man's Viewpoint* (New York: Ballantine Books, 1978), p. 152.

in rank but now replaced by the latter as Hanoi's prime strategist. Giap had long been a believer in an offensive strategy, but he had learned by bitter experience during the 1951 counteroffensive in the Red River delta that spirit alone could not overcome firepower, and he now argued for a more prudent approach that did not unnecessarily squander precious human and technical resources. In an article published in 1967 entitled "Big Victory, Great Task," he emphasized that the conflict in the south was a protracted war and added that it might take fifteen or even twenty years to realize final victory.[7]

General Thanh, however, was not one to suffer in silence. In numerous articles of his own that were published in the military newspaper *Quan Doi Nhan Dan* ("People's Army"), he defended his approach as the right one in the circumstances. In an article that appeared in the party's theoretical journal *Hoc Tap* ("Study") in the summer of 1966, he argued forcefully for his own point of view while denigrating the arguments of his critics. One unnamed doubter (probably Vo Nguyen Giap himself) was criticized for advancing "empty, illogical arguments" and harboring a preference for "old customs" that led to an imitation of the experiences of foreign countries and a concern for the need for a superiority on the battlefield. This, Thanh said, is nothing but "a kind of divination."[8]

PREPARING FOR THE GENERAL UPRISING

During the 1966 campaign, then, Hanoi's forces in the south adopted an aggressive approach on the battlefield. In the meantime, party cadres in urban areas worked secretly to prepare for the general uprising. Although the government of Nguyen Cao Ky and his Young Turks had brought an end to the game of musical chairs in Saigon, the base of the Saigon regime remained fragile. Religious tensions between Buddhists and Catholics remained high, while demonstrations by workers and students became a commonplace in the streets of the capital and other major cities throughout the RVN.

---

[7] Vo Nguyen Giap, "The Big Victory, the Great Task," in McGarvey, *Visions of Victory*, doc. 9.

[8] Nguyen Chi Thanh, article in *Hoc Tap*, July 1966. Also see "Truong Son on the Lessons of the NFLSV Victories," in McGarvey, *Visions of Victory*, pp. 119–149.

In the meantime, agents secretly loyal to Hanoi rose to influential positions within the Saigon government and armed forces or, as in the case of the journalist Pham Xuan An, worked for Western news agencies in reporting the war.[9]

There were also continued signs of factionalism within the RVN armed forces. In March 1966, the problem suddenly burst into the open when Prime Minister Ky announced that General Nguyen Chanh Thi, the ambitious and dapper young commander of ARVN's I Corps in the northern provinces, had resigned for health reasons and intended to go to the United States for medical treatment. In actuality, General Thi had been dismissed for conspiring against the Saigon regime. During the next few days, much of the population in the northern cities of Da Nang and Hue flooded into the streets to voice their support for the popular former I Corps commander.

The urban unrest provoked by the dismissal of General Thi provided southern insurgent leaders with a new opportunity to undermine the precarious stability of the RVN and move toward the final general uprising. Directives were sent to local operatives in Da Nang to take advantage of the situation by promoting popular unrest, but party cadres were too slow to act and the moment passed. Party histories would later comment that an opportunity for a great leap forward in the southern revolution had thereby been missed. By midsummer, the unrest had died down, and Nguyen Cao Ky had further consolidated his control over the country. Shortly after, at the urging of the United States, Ky and his close collaborator, General Nguyen Van Thieu, had agreed to launch preparations for the writing of a new constitution to create an aura of legitimacy for the Saigon regime. The constitution was passed by a constituent assembly in March 1967, and national elections were held in September. In the elections, the quiet but ambitious Nguyen Van Thieu outmaneuvered Nguyen Cao Ky and was elected president of the RVN for a four-year term. Ky agreed to serve as his vice president.[10]

The failure of party operatives in Da Nang to take advantage of conditions in central Vietnam during the Nguyen Chanh Thi affair

---

[9] For a reference to the case of Pham Xuan An, see Stanley Karnow, "Appearances and Reality: A Vietnam Postscript," in *The Wall Street Journal*, February 10, 1982. For a discussion of the political and social unrest at the time, see Fitzgerald, *Fire in the Lake*, chap. 8.

[10] On the elections, see Fitzgerald, *Fire in the Lake*, pp. 446–448. On the Nguyen Chanh Thi affair, see ibid., p. 372. For a brief postmortem of the Da Nang incident by Hanoi, see Le Duan, *Thu Vao Nam*, pp. 186–187.

made it doubly important to Hanoi that units in other major urban centers be prepared to exploit an opportunity when it appeared. Le Duan, who apparently considered himself to be somewhat of an expert in the matter of urban struggle, wrote a lengthy letter in the summer of 1967 to Tran Bach Dang, the secretary of the Saigon-Cholon Party Municipal Committee, advising him on how to prepare for the general uprising.

Le Duan opened the letter by pointing out that although the revolution in the south had now taken on many of the characteristics of a military conflict, the urban struggle was just as important as the war in the countryside. The cities were the weakest point in the enemy's defenses, he said, but they were essential to the survival of the Saigon regime, which had its base in urban areas. If military activities in the countryside were vital in the first stage of the revolution in the south, in the final stage the capacity to strike against the enemy lair in Saigon would be decisive. For that reason it was vitally important to anticipate the precise moment of maximum advantage for launching the general uprising so that the party's urban forces would be ready at a time when revolutionary forces were achieving great victories in the countryside.

The key role in the urban struggle, Le Duan pointed out, should be played by the workers, but other classes are of importance as well. Students and other young people must be used to form the backbone of the party's assault forces, while women were essential for carrying on propaganda and agitational activities. Even the middle class was considered susceptible to persuasion, since so many had begun to oppose the war and the puppet Saigon regime. To win the hearts and minds of the broad mass of the population, many of whom were not intrinsically sympathetic to the revolution, Le Duan suggested such noncontroversial slogans as "national independence" (from U.S. domination), "democracy," and "improved people's livelihood."[11]

IN THE DIPLOMATIC ARENA

By 1967, the struggle between Hanoi and Washington to gain an advantage in the court of world public opinion had been raging for several years. Both sides were prepared to take the conflict to the

[11] Le Duan, *Thu Vao Nam*, letter of July 1, 1967, pp. 163–195.

negotiating table, but only in conditions highly favorable to themselves. Hanoi had first suggested peace talks in 1962, at a time when the situation in Indochina was favorable to the revolution, but the Kennedy administration, chastened by the failure of the DRV to live up to the terms of the Geneva agreement on Laos, had refused. In April 1965, shortly after the introduction of the first U.S. combat forces in the south, the Johnson administration broached the possibility of negotiations, but now Hanoi sidestepped the proposal, convinced that the time was not ripe. From that point on, both sides had settled in to await the outcome of the conflict on the battlefield.

That did not mean that each did not seek to use the lure of negotiations as a bargaining ploy, and as a means of affecting public attitudes toward the war. Although most senior officials in the Johnson administration were convinced that Hanoi would not really display an interest in peace talks until U.S. military superiority had had a meaningful impact on the situation on the battlefield, peace feelers from Washington were seen as an important means of reducing discontent in the United States over the course of the war. For their part, North Vietnamese leaders were convinced that, as the Central Committee noted in a conference held in January 1967, diplomacy "has an important role to play." Success at the peace table, said the resolution issued after the meeting, depends on success gained on the battlefield. In the meantime, diplomacy can be used to assist the struggle in the south by setting forth the demand that the United States unconditionally halt the bombing and other acts of war against the north. Only then will the DRV agree to hold peace talks.[12]

Hanoi thus used the lure of negotiations primarily to win friends in the international arena, as well as to undermine support for the war in the United States. Its negotiating proposals were carefully phrased in a vague manner to imply flexibility, while in practice DRV representatives maintained a rigid stance on conditions for a settlement. As one captured document written in 1967 noted, the ultimate objective of party strategy was to force the United States to withdraw and recognize the existence of a broad national democratic coalition government in Saigon. But that regime, it noted, "is not a coalition regime [that we should obtain] at any cost, but is a conditional one. It is conditional on the U.S. pirates withdrawing their

---

[12] Resolution of the Thirteenth Plenum, January 1967, in *Mot So*, vol. 2, pp. 35–43.

troops and the NLF playing the key role in the coalition regime." Only a regime based on these two conditions, it added, "can have the capacity to become a national, democratic, people's regime of the four revolutionary classes based on the worker-peasant alliance led by the workers, to guarantee independence for the nation, land for the tillers, reunification of our country, and a step forward in the task of building socialism for the whole country." That coalition government, in other words, should be composed in such a manner that a leading role by forces sympathetic to Hanoi would be guaranteed.[13]

The success of such a strategy depended not only on the ability of the revolutionary forces to maintain an offensive stature on the battlefield but also on the support of Hanoi's key allies. During the mid-1960s, neither China nor the Soviet Union desired a significant escalation of the war in Indochina, but both gave verbal and material support to the DRV as a means of winning Hanoi's favor in the Sino-Soviet dispute. Soviet aid was primarily in the form of advanced weapons, such as fighter aircraft and surface-to-air (SAM) missiles so that the North Vietnamese could defend themselves against the heavy U.S. bombing raids. Chinese aid was more substantial in quantity, although less advanced in technology. Sources in Beijing have claimed that total Chinese assistance to North Vietnam averaged over $200 million annually at the height of the war, and that over 300,000 support personnel were sent to the DRV to provide assistance in air defense, engineering, as well as railroad and road building. China had reportedly signaled to Washington, however, that combat forces would not be sent to Vietnam so long as U.S. and ARVN forces did not cross the DMZ, and in the summer of 1965 had turned down a DRV request for fighter pilots.[14]

That North Vietnamese leaders were not entirely satisfied with the attitude of either of their major allies is evident from references to the subject contained in captured documents. One such document,

---

[13] See "The New Situation and Mission," a VC training document (March 1968) in VDRN, no. 20, p. 4.

[14] See Duiker, *China and Vietnam: The Roots of Conflict* (Berkeley: Institute of East Asian Studies, 1987), pp. 48–51. According to Hoang Van Hoan, a high-level Vietnamese party member who defected to China after the War, the PRC provided a total of over $20 billion in aid to Vietnam from 1950 to 1978. See Hoang Van Hoan, *A Drop in the Ocean: Hoang Van Hoan's Revolutionary Reminiscences* (Beijing: Foreign Languages Press, 1988), p. 286.

consisting of an unnamed cadre's notes from a high-level indoctrination course, contained comments that were highly critical of the Great Proletarian Cultural Revolution, which had broken out in China in 1966, and emphasized that a similar movement would not be carried out in North Vietnam. The notebook indicated that China gave Vietnam "unconditional" support, but that Beijing disagreed with Hanoi's strategy of seeking a relatively quick victory (China, penned the author, "is determined to help us fight until the generations of our sons and grandsons"). As for the Soviet Union, the cadre noted that the new leadership that had succeeded Khrushchev was sincere in assisting the Vietnamese revolution, but still wanted the dispute to be settled at the conference table and therefore "does not provide us with modern weapons because the Soviet Union fears that the modern weapons types would be copied by China." Under the circumstances, the writer concluded, Hanoi must have a policy of its own.[15]

ON THE HOME FRONT

At its meeting in December 1965, the VWP Central Committee had announced a new slogan for the coming period: "Protect the North, Assist the South." It was clear by that time that the north needed protection as much as the south needed assistance. Since the initiation of Operation Rolling Thunder earlier in the year, the U.S. bombing of the DRV had steadily intensified. During the mid-1960s, an average of 800 tons of bombs a day was dropped on North Vietnam, a figure that later trebled during the height of the bombing. According to one U.S. historian, in peak years the bombing averaged out to about 300 pounds of explosive for every resident in the north and led to a total of over 50,000 deaths.[16]

Despite such figures, there were bitter debates among Washington officials as to whether the bombing had its desired effect. Some U.S. policymakers harbored serious doubts that it significantly slowed the movement of supplies and personnel to the south, while

---

[15] *VDRN*, no. 14, "NLF Thoughts on Peace Negotiations, World Policies, a Cadre's Notes on a High-Level 1967 Reorientation Course."

[16] See James P. Harrison, "History's Heaviest Bombing," in Jayne S. Werner and Luu Doan Huynh, eds., *The Vietnam War: Vietnamese and American Perspectives* (Armonk, N.Y.: M. E. Sharpe, 1993), pp. 130–131.

others argued that it had no effect in changing the minds of party leaders in North Vietnam. Some even suggested that it might have stiffened Hanoi's determination to succeed.[17]

Whatever the truth about the latter contention, there is no doubt that the bombing had a significant physical impact on the DRV. Although the damage in the downtown areas of the capital of Hanoi was slight, some smaller cities in the lower delta and along the central coast were literally wiped out. The U.S. journalist Harrison Salisbury, on a visit to North Vietnam in 1966, reported that the rail center of Phu Ly, on the main route from Hanoi toward the south, was virtually wiped off the map. Prime Minister Pham Van Dong was quoted by one Western observer as declaring that the bombing "is costing us terribly dear. I'm not acting when I say that I am obliged to cry—literally cry—at the suffering and losses."[18]

Although Johnson administration officials advanced several reasons for initiating the bombing, including its possible impact on morale in both the north and the south, the primary objective was to reduce the rate of infiltration of troops and supplies into the RVN. Infiltration had begun as early as 1959, but for the first few years had been limited in scope, with early arrivals essentially limited to "regroupees" trained in the north and then returned to the south to serve as cadres or military officers in the PLAF. By the mid-1960s, however, the figure began to increase. U.S. intelligence sources estimated that infiltration in 1964 totaled about 10,000 men. The following year, when Hanoi decided to commit regular forces of the PAVN into the struggle, the figure reached an estimated 35,300.[19]

In order to reduce or bring an end to infiltration, Washington adopted a number of techniques. Beginning in 1965, U.S. combat

---

[17] For a rigorous and dispassionate examination of the evidence on the bombing, see Mark Clodfelter, *The Limits of Air Power: The American Bombing of North Vietnam* (New York: Free Press, 1989).

[18] James Cameron, *Here Is Your Enemy* (New York: Holt, Rinehart & Winston, 1966), p. 115, quoted in Jon M. Van Dyke, *North Vietnam's Strategy for Survival* (Palo Alto, Calif.: Pacific Books, 1972), p. 25. Much of the material in the following section is taken from this source, which is still the only systematic study of war mobilization in the DRV during the height of the Vietnam War. The reference to Phu Ly is from Harrison Salisbury, *Behind the Lines—Hanoi* (New York: Harper & Row, 1967), pp. 76–77.

[19] The statistics for 1964 are taken from DDRS (R) 860E, Saigon telegram 15406 to Department of State, January 26, 1965. The figures for 1965 are cited in Van Dyke, *North Vietnam's Strategy*, p. 34.

aircraft launched sustained air strikes on transportation routes, military and government installations, and population centers in the North Vietnamese panhandle, which served as the main staging area for troops and material moving from the DRV into the south. Sorties were also carried out along the Ho Chi Minh Trail through southern Laos and on key industrial and military sites in the heart of the Red River delta. Eventually a sophisticated electrical monitoring system was set up along the DMZ in order to detect movement through the trails into the south.

Hanoi went to great lengths to surmount the obstacles placed by Washington and maintain the movement of personnel down the Ho Chi Minh Trail. For participants, the long journey began in training camps throughout the DRV. From there troops were transported by truck or rail down to Dong Hoi, the southernmost city in the panhandle and the staging area for movement into the RVN. From Dong Hoi, infiltrators generally proceeded on foot, while goods were carried by bicycle. Sometimes as much as 500 pounds was loaded on a single bicycle, which was then pushed rather than ridden. Once infiltrators reached the area of the DMZ, they left DRV territory and began moving south along hundreds of trails threading through the mountains of southern Laos. Because the forest cover was generally too dense for movement to be spotted from the air, most moved by day and then rested at night in special camps set up at 10- to 15-mile intervals. In a typical day, they would rise at about 3:30 A.M. and march until lunch. After a brief rest period, the journey would resume until dark. The average distance covered was about 10 to 15 miles per day, with one rest day per week.

The entire journey usually lasted anywhere from two to six months and often entailed considerable hardship. By the late 1960s, when the trail had been expanded, most supplies were carried by truck, usually driving by night along a few of the wider trails. To bypass the electronic monitors, new trails were built to the west across the Laotian border. Troops generally carried their own provisions, including a food ration of about 1 or 2 pounds of rice per day, supplemented occasionally by a few vegetables or some meat. About 10 to 20 percent of the infiltrators failed to complete the trip, either because of the bombing or, more likely, because of illness, such as malaria, which was quite prevalent in the mountains. Others fell victim to tigers, bears, snakes, or even poisonous mushrooms. Some drowned while crossing rivers, while others starved after get-

A bamboo floating bridge on the Ho Chi Minh Trail.

ting lost in the jungle. According to one Vietnamese source, there was a cemetery at each staging post, established about 20 to 30 kilometers apart throughout the length of the trail.

As the level of U.S. bombing along the trails increased, Hanoi attempted to develop an alternate route by sea. By the mid-1960s, thousands of small ships carried supplies down the coast to unload their cargo in countless small ports controlled by the insurgent forces in South Vietnam. Eventually, however, U.S. naval patrols began to limit the effectiveness of the maritime route. In 1967, U.S. ships sank an estimated 1400 enemy vessels, ranging from 50 to several hundred tons. The U.S. was less successful in stopping the shipment of goods into South Vietnam through the Cambodian port of Sihanoukville. The government of Cambodia tolerated the traffic as a means of avoiding problems with Hanoi, while the Johnson administration prohibited military operations or air attacks on Cambodian territory to prevent Phnom Penh from abandoning its precarious neutrality and voicing its open support for the revolutionary forces in South Vietnam.

Throughout the war, however, the major route into the south

A U.S. plane goes
down in flames.

was along the Ho Chi Minh Trail, and Hanoi assigned thousands of
laborers to the task of keeping the routes open and effective. Probably several hundred thousand workers were involved either part-
time or full-time in keeping the routes open—repairing potholes,
rebuilding bridges, and replacing damaged camouflage. Bridges
were often a major problem, since they were so vulnerable to attack
from the air. Eventually, repair crews began to construct the road-
way slightly below the surface of the water to provide increased
protection or build floating bridges constructed of a string of sam-
pans or boats which could be left along the banks except when
actually in use.

To defend the skies of North Vietnam against U.S. air attacks,
Hanoi used a variety of means, including surface-to-air missiles
shipped from the USSR, jet fighters, and antiaircraft guns. The DRV

did possess a few advanced jet fighters, but they were not often used until the late 1960s, when their performance level improved. The most effective means of defense was antiaircraft fire, although at first the gunners were not very well trained. To disguise their positions from U.S. pilots, antiaircraft batteries used a variety of camouflages, including placing of sticks and pieces of bamboo in other locations to distract attention from their actual positions.

Inspirational literature published in Hanoi portrayed the heroism of the North Vietnamese people facing the air war waged by the enemy. One such pamphlet described the reaction of the local population to an attack on the village of Hoxa, just north of the DMZ near the city of Dong Hoi.

> Aware of enemy designs, Hoxa took adequate measures. Mothers, children, and old people were evacuated to neighboring villages. Only the security forces and self-defense militia groups remained in the town. An elaborate defence system was built, made up of foxholes, gun nests, communication trenches and observation posts. Daily work was reorganized. Factory workers, office workers and handicraftsmen engaged in their daily occupations beside the trenches, with arms slung across their backs or near at hand. When the alert given by the lookout man was transmitted from street to street by drum beats, everyone ran to his combat position.

When the air raid commenced, bicycle repairman Hoang Phan was one of those manning a machine-gun nest. During the battle, his wife was gravely wounded, yet Phan remained at his post.

> Concealing his emotion, he grasped at the machine gun and fired at a diving plane. All around, light arms were cracking, anti-aircraft guns were rumbling. Suddenly an immense "hurrah" was heard. A plane was burning like a torch in the azure sky; it rolled over and crashed on the sportsground of the town. The other planes shot upwards and fled towards the sea.

After the battle, Phan cleaned his weapon and then went to the first-aid station. His wife was lying in a shroud. Crying bitterly, Phan closed his wife's eyes for the last time.[20]

The DRV developed a massive if somewhat primitive program

[20] Van Son, "On the Bank of the Ben Hai River," *With the Fighters of Quangbinh-Vinhlinh* (Hanoi: Xunhasaba, 1966), pp. 77–78.

to protect the urban population from the effects of U.S. bombing. Bomb shelters were constructed in both urban and frequently targetted rural areas. Hanoi claimed to have built 30,000 miles of trenches and over 20 million bomb shelters. Based on the slogan "Call the Shelter Your Second Home," the object was to build three or four shelters per person: one at home, one at the place of work, and one in between. In the countryside, the rural population often dug trenches from their houses to their farmlands, or to the sea if they were fishermen. Some bomb shelters were large enough to contain several people (in the words of one popular song of the day, "Our home protects us from wind and fog, the underground shelter preserves our blood and bone"), but most were for individuals. The standard type was about 5 feet deep and $2^1/_2$ feet in diameter, with the sides made of prestressed concrete. In the capital of Hanoi, there was an average of one shelter every 6 to 30 feet.

During his visit to North Vietnam in 1966, journalist Harrison Salisbury visited one school near Hanoi attended by children of the party and government elite. Students moved from building to building by means of a trench network dug in the schoolyard. The entrances to classrooms were buttressed by shoulder-high mud walls reinforced by bamboo. Under each school desk was a foxhole for the student, who was provided with a plaited straw helmet in case of an air attack.[21]

Despite the massive U.S. bombing campaign, Hanoi managed to keep the infiltration routes open and supplies and personnel heading southward along the trails. Estimates of the number of infiltrators for 1966 and 1967 ranged between 60,000 and 90,000 annually. They were needed, because as the level of fighting increased, party war planners faced a growing demand for North Vietnamese regulars to supplement the efforts of the PLAF. Up until the mid-1960s, the size of the PAVN was about 250,000 men, with an equal number held in reserve. Faced with a rising demand for main force troops after the U.S. entry into the war, the Hanoi regime declared partial mobilization in July 1966, and the number of PAVN troops on active service either in the DRV or in the south rose to over 400,000. In general, Hanoi preferred to rely on highly motivated volunteers, but

---

[21] Salisbury, *Behind the Lines,* p. 114. Those catchy lyrics for the song mentioned in the paragraph above are from *North Viet Nam against U.S. Air Force* (Hanoi: Foreign Languages Publishing House, 1967), p. 70.

Digging trenches in
North Vietnam against
a possible U.S. air
attack.

as demands in the south rose, the regime began to recruit virtually
all able-bodied males between the ages of 18 and 25. With nearly
200,000 males reaching adulthood annually, that produced a pool of
over 120,000 men per year. By 1967, as casualty figures increased,
draft eligibility was extended to all those from age 16 to 45.

Youths were motivated to enlist by a variety of techniques, including financial incentives such as combat pay sent directly to their
families. But undoubtedly the primary motivation was the call of
duty to the country. A heavy emphasis in patriotism suffused all
aspects of Vietnamese society, including books, films, radio programs—even theater and poetry. Heroic figures such as Nguyen
Van Troi, a South Vietnamese who had tried unsuccessfully to assassinate U.S. Defense Secretary McNamara, were given special trib-
ute in the press and even appeared on DRV postage stamps.

Upon arrival in South Vietnam, the North Vietnamese soldier

was assigned to a PLAF or PAVN unit. At first the regime attempted to mix troops of minority nationalities with ethnic Vietnamese, but that frequently led to racial tensions so they were eventually placed in separate units. In general, the *bo doi* (the Vietnamese equivalent of G.I. or "grunt") only fought about one or two days per month. The remainder of the time was devoted to rest or to growing his own food. As the number of troops in the resistance forces increased, food supplies inside South Vietnam were inadequate, so heavy efforts were devoted to importing grain from Cambodia.

Even days devoted to rest and recuperation were often a time of terror, particularly for those in areas subjected to heavy U.S. bombardment. As described by the ex-NLF official Truong Nhu Tang, air raids by the massive U.S. B-52 bombers could be an especially terrifying experience.

> From a kilometer away, the sonic roar of the B-52 explosions tore eardrums, leaving many of the jungle dwellers permanently deaf. From a kilometer, the shock waves knocked their victims senseless. Any hit within a half kilometer would collapse the walls of an unreinforced bunker, burying alive the people cowering inside. Seen up close, the bomb craters were gigantic—thirty feet across and nearly as deep. In the rainy seasons they would often fill up with water and often saw service as duck or fishponds, playing their role in the guerrillas' never-ending quest to broaden their diet. But they were treacherous then too. For as the swamps and lowland areas flooded under half a foot of standing water, the craters would become invisible. Not infrequently some surprised guerrilla, wading along what he had taken to be a familiar route, was suddenly swallowed up.[22]

As we have seen, civilians as well as soldiers were expected to contribute to the cause. With its slogan of "All for the Front Lines," the regime tried to mobilize every citizen to contribute in some way to the war effort. The elderly were put to work in repair teams, in surveillance work, or in the village militia. Teams were established to apprehend downed U.S. airmen. Women as well as men were drafted into the cause. Some were used as transportation workers or on antiaircraft teams. Others replaced men in factories and other manual jobs. The slogan of the day was that women in the DRV had "three responsibilities": (1) to replace men at work, (2) to care for

---

[22] Truong Nhu Tang, *Vietcong Memoir*, pp. 167–168.

their families, and (3) to serve in militia units. Most undoubtedly replaced their male family members in the fields. It has been estimated that over two-thirds of all farm workers in the DRV during the war were women.[23]

As the bombing increased in the late 1960s, civilians were increasingly exposed to casualties. Beginning in February 1965, the regime began to encourage those urban residents not considered vital to the war effort to resettle in refugee camps or on collective farms outside the major cities. Some evidently did so, mainly children and the elderly. But many citizens in cities like Hanoi and Haiphong were reluctant to evacuate and either often ignored directives or returned home once the immediate danger appeared over. Undoubtedly one reason was the prevalence of overcrowding and disease in the refugee camps. By general estimate, only about one-third of the population of Hanoi had left the city by late 1966.

The regime also attempted to relocate factories and government offices in anticipation of a U.S. decision to bomb the heart of Hanoi. In the summer of 1966, many government ministries, schools, and nonmechanized factories were moved into the suburbs. In fact, however, despite the overall severity of U.S. bombing attacks on the DRV, the most densely populated areas of the two major cities, Hanoi and Haiphong, were not heavily damaged, as the policy of the Johnson administration was to avoid massive attacks on the capital, with the accompanying risk of casualties for the foreign diplomatic corps living in the city. Most of the U.S. attacks took place in the suburbs or consisted of surgical efforts to bomb factories, bridges, military installations, or power plants without affecting residential areas. The port area of Haiphong was also off limits, so shipping proceeded without major interruption until the early 1970s, when President Richard Nixon launched attacks on the city to bring Hanoi back to the peace table.

U.S. planners were apparently less squeamish about attacking population centers in the smaller cities of the DRV. Industrial cities such as Nam Dinh, Thanh Hoa, and Vinh were badly damaged. The latter, which was the largest industrial city in the panhandle and served as a major staging area for infiltration into the south, was especially hard hit, with the downtown area being almost entirely destroyed.

---

[23] Van Dyke, *North Vietnam's Strategy*, p. 96.

ĐỊA ĐẠO CỦ CHI

, TRONG BÁO CÁO CỦA ĐẾT-MO-LEN

GỞI TỔNG THỐNG MỸ

The tunnels of Cu Chi, an underground Viet Cong base area in South Vietnam.

THORN IN THE EYE

After the decision by both sides to escalate in December 1965, the war in the south reached its highest level. Gambling that high casualty figures would intensify antiwar protests in the United States, General Thanh and his colleagues fought desperately to maintain their crucial liberated base area in the central highlands and their toehold in key areas in the lowlands.

In some cases, the insurgent forces were able to thwart massive U.S. efforts to dislodge them. When in January of 1966 General Westmoreland launched U.S. units into the Iron Triangle to clean out Viet Cong bases in the area and bring it under Saigon's control, the insurgents simply descended into their tunnels and waited for the departure of the Americans above them. Since the majority of the vast tunnel complexes (estimated by one source as totaling over 200 kilometers) were not discovered by the intruders, the insurgents simply went about their work and continued to use the area as a conduit for sending cadres into the capital region and maintaining communications with COSVN headquarters beyond the Cambodian border.

Early the following year, Westmoreland tried again. In Operation Cedar Falls, 30,000 U.S. forces swept through the area to clean out insurgent forces and then removed the underbrush with chemicals and sweeping operations to clear away the ground cover. Convinced that even the civilian population actively supported the enemy, the U.S. command forcibly evacuated the key villages in the area and relocated the residents elsewhere. General Westmoreland pointed out in *A Soldier Reports* his account of his own role in the war:

> So closely entwined were some populated localities with the tentacles of the VC base area, in some cases actually integrated into the defenses, and so sympathetic were some of the people to the VC that the only way to establish control short of constant combat operations among the people was to remove the people and destroy the village. . . . That it was infinitely better in some cases to move people from areas long sympathetic to the Viet Cong was amply demonstrated later by events that occurred when the discipline of an American company broke down at a place called My Lai.[24]

Because of their intense preparations and the assistance of much of the population in the Iron Triangle, the insurgent forces were often able to thwart such massive efforts by their adversaries to throw them off balance. Although the U.S. Military Command in Saigon announced that Operation Cedar Falls had killed nearly 1000 "confirmed enemy" and seized tons of weapons, munitions, and supplies, after the departure of U.S. forces the Viet Cong were once again able to resurface in the area and resume their activities. Once again, the labyrinth of tunnels had not been essentially disturbed. As one PLAF veteran later remarked, "After the operation I in-

---

[24] William D. Westmoreland, *A Soldier Reports*, cited in Mangold and Penycate, *Tunnels of Cu Chi*, p. 168. The evacuation of the residents in the area was immortalized in Jonathan Schell's highly critical account, *The Village of Ben Suc* (New York: Random House, 1967). The risk of such a strategy, of course, was that it might alienate the local population and make them more willing to support the Viet Cong. The most telling indictment of U.S. policy in Vietnam, to many war critics, was the inadvertent comment made by one U.S. military officer after the Tet offensive in 1968 that "we had to destroy the village to save it."

spected the tunnels and did not find any length more than fifty meters that had been discovered or damaged by the Americans. They had destroyed only about a hundred tunnels with explosives, and a lot of civilians' bomb shelters."[25]

From a U.S. military standpoint, Operation Cedar Falls was an example in microcosm of what went wrong with the war. Despite enormous firepower and logistical superiority, the operation was only a partial success, and the adversary was able to return after the battle to resume his activities. According to Mai Chi Tho, the brother of Le Duc Tho and at that time a leading party official in the south, the tunnels of Cu Chi continued to be used as "a springboard for attacking Saigon" (a thorn stabbing in the eye, as he put it), and it was from here that insurgent units were trained and then infiltrated into the capital area in preparation for the Tet offensive in early 1968.[26]

In fairness, it should be pointed out that the U.S. strategy, however wasteful of U.S. resources and however damaging to the civilian population, did pose enormous problems for the insurgent leadership and seriously set back the course of the revolution in the south. Aggressive search-and-destroy missions by U.S. and ARVN forces disrupted enemy operations and gradually drove them from base areas in the mountains while depriving them of provisions and recruits in the highly populated lowlands. One captured document seized in the central coastal province of Phu Yen lamented that by the winter and spring of 1966–1967, 90 percent of the population in that province had been removed from the control of the NLF. Many units had suffered grievous losses and were often short of weapons, ammunition, and food supplies. Even in the Iron Triangle, although insurgent units had managed to survive Operation Cedar Falls, a captured document dated shortly after the operation declared that local party leaders were concerned with the lack of rice and the low level of enthusiasm among the local population in the area.[27]

---

[25] Mangold and Penycate, *Tunnels of Cu Chi*, p. 175. According to the authors, although U.S. "tunnel rats" displayed enormous courage in trying to root the enemy out of the tunnels, U.S. commanders in general lacked the patience to remain in the area to destroy the entire complex and remove it from use by the enemy.

[26] Ibid., p. 33.

[27] *VDRN*, no. 4, "Within a VC Stronghold: Deliberations of the Supply Council, Chan Thanh district, Binh Duong Province." For the situation in Phu Yen, see *VDRN*, nos. 2–3, "Problems of a North Vietnamese Regiment."

Such problems inevitably led to a loss of morale within the movement as well as a perceptible decline in support from the surrounding population. According to the captured report cited above, low morale among the troops in Phu Yen led to "corrupt, easygoing, reckless and deceitful" soldiers. Many of the troops had a "bad attitude" toward the people, while "a certain number" had deserted. One document said that some soldiers "despise the people and confiscate their property" and commit "deplorable acts." The party apparatus itself was increasingly strained. One report declared that many PRP party members were no longer "living by labor with the masses" and nearly 80 percent in some areas were "acting independently or if they are still in the party cells, they do not attend meetings regularly and so do not really reinforce all Party cells at the village or hamlet level."[28]

Not surprisingly, such conditions eroded the close relationship between the party and the masses, and damaged the impression so carefully fostered by the leadership that the insurgency would ultimately be victorious. As the war escalated, it was increasingly difficult to get volunteer forces and support from the villages, and party leaders were forced to rely on the conscription of recruits and the taxation of the peasants. Taxation had replaced voluntary contributions in 1963 and 1964, and after 1965 such exactions increased to an average of between 10 to 20 percent of the farmer's gross income.[29]

The report from Phu Yen declared that the confidence of the people in the movement had been severely damaged in that province, while in the area of the Iron Triangle, "separation from the masses in a very alarming way" was viewed as the most outstanding problem. In My Thuy Phuong village, just south of Hue, a U.S. researcher estimated that with victory for the NLF no longer viewed as a probability, support for the movement had dropped from over 80 percent to only about half the population.[30]

By the early autumn of 1967, then, the vision of victory in Hanoi remained elusive. Although the political situation in South Vietnam

---

[28] *VDRN*, no. 6, "The PRP in Rural Areas," p. 4; for the earlier report, see *VDRN*, nos. 2–3, p. 6.

[29] Robert L. Sansom, *The Economics of Insurgency in South Vietnam* (Cambridge, Mass.: MIT Press, 1970), p. 66. Also see Andrews, *The Village War*, p. 101.

[30] *VDRN*, nos. 2–3; *VDRN*, no. 6; Trullinger, *Village at War*, p. 143.

continued to be fragile, the passing of the new constitution and the election of Nguyen Van Thieu as president in the elections held in September created a measure of stability that had previously been lacking. At U.S. urging, the Saigon regime initiated plans to launch a new land reform program—funded in part by the United States—in rural areas. In the United States, the antiwar movement continued to increase in intensity but had little impact in changing policy in the White House.

TET

Since the early 1960s, the concept of the general offensive and uprising had guided the strategic thinking of party leaders as they focused on the liberation of the south. It had been the standard assumption in Hanoi that the final campaign would take place at a time of steady weakening of ARVN forces and declining self-confidence on the part of Saigon's American ally. At an appropriate time, a combined military attack and popular insurrection could bring about the collapse of the Saigon regime, leading to a U.S. withdrawal from South Vietnam and the formation of a coalition government dominated by the NLF.

The steady escalation of the U.S. military presence in the RVN, which caused a general weakening of the NLF position in the south and growing morale problems among the PLAF, forced Hanoi to reexamine its assumptions, but it evidently did not lead to a scaling-back of ultimate goals. While the battlefield situation was somewhat less favorable than had been anticipated, party leaders still believed that their strategy could bring about a major shift in the balance of forces on the ground and shake the foundations of the Saigon regime.

Precisely when the decision to launch a major offensive was taken is not entirely clear. General Nguyen Chi Thanh visited Hanoi in the summer of 1967 to discuss the issue and then died under mysterious circumstances shortly afterward.[31] Thanh had reportedly

---

[31] There have been several versions of General Thanh's demise. Some allege that he was killed in a U.S. air raid, while others maintain that he died of cancer. One Vietnamese source claims that he died of a heart attack at a banquet after submitting his proposal for a new general offensive to the Politburo.

presented a plan calling for an all-out attack on the South Vietnamese cities involving North Vietnamese regular units. Although his death did not lead to the scrapping of his proposal, it did strengthen the hands of advocates of a more cautious approach which would rely primarily on the forces of the PLAF. The final decision may not have been reached until December, when the Politburo issued what Vietnamese historians have labeled a "historic resolution" to launch a general offensive and uprising aimed at achieving a decisive victory and forcing a U.S. withdrawal from the south. That decision was given final approval at the Fourteenth Plenum of the Central Committee the following month.[32]

The Tet offensive is usually identified in the United States with the sudden attacks on major cities that took place at the end of January 1968. But from Hanoi's point of view, the first stage of the campaign was launched late in 1967, with a series of sharp thrusts by insurgent units on South Vietnamese military posts in the central highlands. Then, on January 21, 1968, North Vietnamese troops overran a number of U.S. fire bases in rough scrub and mountainous country just south of the DMZ and placed the Marine base camp at Khe Sanh under siege.

American military forces had been in Khe Sanh since the summer of 1966, when U.S. intelligence sources had reported a buildup of North Vietnamese troop strength just south of the demilitarized zone. Apprised of the enemy buildup, General Westmoreland had ordered the construction of a string of U.S. fire bases along the border to reduce the level of infiltration and forestall a possible North Vietnamese attempt to seize the northern province of Quang Tri and turn it into a liberated area.

Reacting to the sudden attack south of the border in mid-January 1968, General Westmoreland concluded that North Vietnamese strategists hoped to win a significant victory in the area to achieve a psychological impact equivalent to that realized by the battle of Dien Bien Phu during the war against the French. He rushed reinforcements to the area and publicly declared that Hanoi was seeking

[32] *CKC*, pp. 100–101; *Nhung Su Kien*, p. 406; Turley, *Second Indochina War*, p. 102. General Tran Van Tra confirms these sources, claiming that southern commanders only had about three months to prepare for attack. According to him, this is one of the key reasons why it did not realize greater success. See Tran Van Tra, "Tet: The 1968 General Offensive and Uprising," in Jayne Werner and Luu Doan Huynh, *The Vietnam War*, p. 42.

to create another Dien Bien Phu at Khe Sanh, while Lyndon Johnson reportedly ordered the construction of a mock replica of the battlefield in the White House so that he could follow the course of the fighting in detail.[33]

General Westmoreland was probably correct in his assumption that North Vietnamese strategists hoped to win a significant victory in the area just south of the demilitarized zone. Histories of the war written in Hanoi have stated that as early as June 1966 party leaders had decided to open a campaign in the northern provinces with the aim of driving newly arrived U.S. forces out of the area. And it is not unlikely that in approving new offensive operations in the area in mid-January 1968, Vietnamese leaders hoped to seize Khe Sanh. A successful assault on the U.S. Marine base there would have the dual effect of opening up the border area to higher levels of infiltration, and administering a severe psychological blow to the United States.[34]

But Hanoi's goals for the dry season campaign in 1968 were far more ambitious than simply imposing a limited defeat on U.S. forces in a remote area of the RVN. Rather, they hoped to set in motion a train of events that could lead to the total withdrawal of U.S. forces and the formation of a coalition government under NLF domination. In the larger scheme of things, the primary purpose of the attack at Khe Sanh was to draw U.S. forces away from major urban centers farther south in order to open up opportunities for offensive operations throughout the country—operations that were designed to shake the Saigon regime to its very foundations. In Hanoi's estimate, a series of successful military attacks on provincial capitals, combined with attacks on military and government installations by suicide ("dare-to-die") squads could lead to a widespread popular uprising which could force the resignation of the Thieu government and open up the possibility of a negotiated settlement with the United States.

On the surface, party leaders appeared to be optimistic. Documents issued by the Politburo and the Central Committee before the opening of the offensive claimed that insurgent forces had defeated their U.S. counterparts in the field both strategically and tactically

---

[33] Westmoreland, in *A Soldier Reports*, p. 317, claimed that Johnson had a "fixation" about Khe Sanh.
[34] *Nhung Su Kien*, p. 410.

North Vietnamese troops attack Khe Sanh.

and possessed the initiative throughout the country. By contrast, the enemy was pessimistic and passive. A directive sent to lower echelons at the outset of the campaign declared that the campaign in the central highlands the previous fall had created a situation more favorable than that which existed in early 1965 and that victory was close at hand. If we act fast, the directive predicted, the enemy will be confused and "cannot avoid collapse." As for the situation in the cities, "the majority of the people have sympathy for and confidence in the Revolution."[35]

Policymakers in Hanoi, however, did not harbor the illusion that total victory was certain. As in 1965, they planned for several contingencies. In a letter to southern comrades written in mid-January, Le Duan outlined three possibilities. In the optimum situation, he pointed out, the offensive would lead to a great victory and negotiations with the enemy on Hanoi's terms. A second pos-

[35] *VDRN*, nos. 28–29. "The Decisive Hour: Two Directives for Tet."

sibility was that the revolutionary forces would win some victories, but the enemy would survive and be able to continue the war, although in a weakened condition. The third scenario was that the campaign would not surpass the level of victory achieved in recent years, although it might extend the war to new areas of the country. And there was always the chance that Washington would decide to increase the size of U.S. forces and expand the war. We must hope for the first, he concluded, but prepare for the second. There is little likelihood of the third, but we will guard against it.[36]

Beginning on January 31, at the beginning of the annual Vietnamese New Year, insurgent forces attacked towns and villages throughout the RVN. In some cases the attack was led or supported by guerrilla forces operating in the vicinity. In others, the responsibility lay on local units alone. In general, Hanoi refrained from using its regular forces. "We are not so dumb," said Le Duan in his letter cited above, "as to use our main force units." According to one directive, in many villages and hamlets the uprising was to be directed by the local party committee. Each committee was instructed to draw up a roster of "wicked tyrants" who would be assassinated by "dare-to-die" squads composed of enthusiastic local youths. After the elimination of such hostile elements, mass strikes and agitation activities should be carried out, while sympathetic elements among the local population, normally poor and landless peasants, should be mobilized to rise up and seize control of the local administration to annihilate the enemy.[37]

During the next few days, thousands of hamlets, villages, and market towns throughout the country were seized by the insurgent forces. To many people outside Vietnam, however, the most visible aspect of the Tet offensive took place in major cities like Saigon and Hue. In Saigon, Viet Cong sapper units attacked civilians and military installations and occupied radio stations. In the most publicized incident, one suicide squad attacked and briefly occupied the ground floor of the new U.S. Embassy, located only a few hundred yards from the presidential palace in downtown Saigon. In Hue, a massive attack by local forces supplemented by PAVN units in the vicinity seized the old imperial capital and rounded up thousands

---

[36] CKC, p. 100. Le Duan, *Thu Vao Nam*, letter of January 18, 1968, pp. 199–201.
[37] VDRN, no. 28, pp. 4–5.

of individuals identified as supporters of the Saigon regime. Their bodies were discovered in mass graves when ARVN forces regained control of the city a few weeks later.

Party leaders hoped that the attack in Saigon would spark an urban insurrection to bring down the regime. In the wake of military attacks, local resistance units were ordered to march through the streets, passing out leaflets and announcing the onset of the uprising to overthrow Saigon's power. Directives to local operatives expressed optimism that the people would follow their lead. Still, there was a grudging admission that not all the people in the cities supported the cause of revolution. Some people, remarked the author of one captured document, have been misled by the enemy and have "various anxieties" or "are ignorant of our line and policies." Living in "the false happiness and demagogic culture of the enemy," their mental life was therefore "complex, impractical, and luxurious." It was to bolster morale and encourage the undecided elements, as well as to defeat the enemy in his last stronghold, that 4000 guerrillas were infiltrated into the city to assist the urban apparatus. "If we do not use our military force to neutralize the enemy force," said one document, "the masses will not be able to gain victory through political action alone." Hanoi recognized the importance of creating an image of success to incite the people to embrace the cause of the revolution.[38]

The Tet offensive flashed dramatically on television screens in the United States and around the world. The sight of the Viet Cong in the U.S. Embassy shook the confidence of many Americans in the prospects for final victory in South Vietnam. Media attitudes in the United States took an increasingly critical turn, and reporters stationed in Saigon sarcastically ridiculed General Westmoreland's contention that the Tet offensive had actually been a costly setback for the Communists.

In fact, Westmoreland's judgment was not that far off the mark. While U.S. claims that the attacking forces suffered over 40,000 casualties out of their total force of 80,000 may have been a slight exaggeration, estimates of over 30,000 dead, wounded, and captured seem to be valid. To make matters worse, the bulk of those losses were among members of the local apparatus that the party had built

[38] *VDRN*, no. 29, pp. 10–12.

up painstakingly over the years in the south. In places like Saigon, the municipal apparatus surfaced for the first time during the Tet offensive and was virtually eliminated.[39]

One reason for the failure was that party strategists had miscalculated the reaction of the local populace in Saigon. While they had admitted that it would be difficult to motivate many of the townspeople, the response even among poorer sectors of the population was disappointing. As one after-action report noted, the people's spirit for uprising was still weak. This was particularly the case in the major cities, but it was also true in the villages, where the movement "could not arouse the enthusiasm required to put unrelenting pressure on the enemy."[40]

So General Westmoreland was not totally wrong. But what he did not say was that the offensive had exerted a massive effect on the political landscape of South Vietnam, particularly in rural areas, where thousands of villages and hamlets were placed back under the control of the NLF, some for the first time since the arrival of U.S. forces nearly three years earlier. According to an NLF broadcast in mid-May, a new "people's administration" had been established in 600 liberated villages between January 31 and March 15. Reflecting this optimistic turn of events, a COSVN resolution issued in March stated that the situation in the south "has shifted in our favor." To take advantage of the circumstances, a new phase of the general offensive and uprising, described by North Vietnamese sources as a "very fierce and complicated strategic offensive period," would now take place for the next three or four months throughout the country. During this period (called "mini-Tet" by the Western media), insurgent units were called upon to "launch continuous attacks" throughout South Vietnam in order "to make use of violence to overthrow the enemy state power and build the people's revolutionary state power."[41]

It is clear from such comments that Hanoi's objective was not

---

[39] Turley, *Second Indochina War*, p. 110.

[40] *VDRN*, no. 30–32, "After Tet: Three VC Assessments," pp. 3–10. At a recent conference on the war, General Tran Van Tra conceded that the general offensive had not been sufficiently successful to spark a major popular uprising, but he claimed that it was nonetheless a military success. See Tran Van Tra, "Tet" in Werner and Huynh, *The Vietnam War*, pp. 57–58.

[41] *VDRN*, no. 38, "The Sixth Resolution, Central Office of South Vietnam," p. 7. The Viet Cong radio broadcast was quoted in *VDRN*, no. 35.

just to disrupt the enemy administration but to permanently broaden the liberated areas. A COSVN resolution urged people to

> build combat villages and hamlets, set up a tight defense, defeat all enemy activities aimed at thrusting rangers into these zones for sweep operations, cut off all vital lines of communications to isolate towns, cities, and municipalities and, at the same time, connect our controlled zones with large rural areas of the rear to create a strong position in which we can permanently encircle and exert pressure on the enemy and quickly create [favorable] conditions for liberating towns and cities.[42]

Once in power, revolutionary units were instructed to establish a new people's revolutionary administration, confiscate the land of "cruel tyrants" and distribute it to the poor, and "indoctrinate the people to pay their contributions" to the revolution. Money collected was to be delivered to the district as soon as possible and not to be retained in the village.[43]

It was that image of Viet Cong success that predominated in much of the United States. Critics of the war, and even key officials within the administration, were emboldened by recent events to question the war policy, and more doubts surfaced when reporters leaked a request by William Westmoreland to the Joint Chiefs' chairman, Earle C. Wheeler, for 200,000 additional U.S. troops to place increased pressure on the enemy. (Westmoreland contends with good reason that the request had been solicited by Wheeler on a brief visit to Vietnam.) Defense Secretary Clark Clifford, who had replaced Robert S. McNamara in the position a few weeks previously, was now convinced that the war could not be won at a reasonable cost and sought to persuade the president to seek a negotiated settlement. At first Johnson was reluctant to admit failure and convened a meeting of senior advisers, popularly dubbed "the wise men," to counsel him. Earlier, they had encouraged him to continue the U.S. commitment to the RVN. Now they expressed serious reservations about any further escalation in the war. In a major address presented on March 31, a shaken Lyndon Johnson announced a halt in U.S. bombing operations above the 20th parallel as a means of promoting a move to the conference table. He closed his speech with

---

[42] Ibid., p. 8.
[43] *VDRN*, no. 52, "An Activities Plan for Village Revolutionary Administration."

a statement that he would not run for reelection. General Westmoreland's tentative request for additional troops was tacitly ignored.

Washington's announcement of a partial bombing halt and the offer of a full cessation in return for productive negotiations was much less than Hanoi had been demanding as a condition for the opening of formal peace talks. But in light of the somewhat disappointing results of the Tet offensive, party leaders were willing to accept the offer as a beginning, while hoping to extend their gains during the mini-Tet offensive that had begun in March. On April 3, Hanoi agreed to discuss with U.S. officials the unconditional end to the bombing. Clearly, however, party leaders did not harbor much hope for a satisfactory settlement until the situation on the battlefield clarified. As one document stated, "Americans are more impressed by force than by reason." The goal of the current fighting, it said, was not simply to begin negotiations but also to improve the battlefield situation in order to exploit the differences between hawks and doves in the United States and gain U.S. acceptance of the NLF four-point program of 1965. "No agreement," it concluded, "can be reached as long as we fail to win on the battlefield. . . . We will discuss peace in our own way, that is, in the position of a winner, not as a loser."[44]

On April 24, the Politburo met to evaluate the current situation and the results of the Tet offensive. By then it had become clear that mini-Tet had produced a harvest of high casualties and limited victories, leading some senior party officials to demand retrenchment. According to one history of the war written in Hanoi, party leaders now concluded that although Tet had been a great victory and a turning point in the war, further military successes might be delayed for years. If that is the case, the decision to open discussions with Washington about the end of the bombing was probably not seen by North Vietnamese leaders as an immediate prelude to productive peace talks, but simply as an opening gambit to put pressure on the U.S. to offer further concessions.[45]

Discussions between the two sides opened in Paris on May 13.

[44] *VDRN*, no. 39, "Indoctrination Notes on Peace Talks: A Call for 'Violent Revolution'' to the End."

[45] The Politburo meeting is discussed briefly in *CKC*, p. 106. For Truong Chinh's call for a more prudent approach, see Thai Quang Trung, *Collective Leadership and Factionalism* (Singapore: Institute of Southeast Asian Studies, 1985), p. 55.

At first, DRV representatives insisted that they would only negotiate about a full cessation of the U.S. bombing of the north, and for months the talks were stalled on that issue. But during the late spring and summer, U.S. and ARVN forces began to recoup the losses suffered during the Tet offensive. Many rural areas that had recently been seized by insurgent forces now reverted to the control of the RVN. On June 5, Radio Hanoi claimed that 100 villages and 600 hamlets had been placed under revolutionary administration, considerably less than an NLF broadcast had asserted three months earlier. Confidential party documents conceded that the spring offensive "did not meet the political and military requirements we had set." They encountered particular problems in areas inhabited by religious minorities, such as the Cao Dai and Catholics, where many local residents fled from the revolution to seek refuge in the cities.[46]

The failure of the revolutionary forces to consolidate their gains undoubtedly came to the attention of U.S. officials in Saigon and Washington and raised the confidence level among some officials in the Johnson administration. The president was reluctant to make concessions, but in October, just before the presidential elections, he agreed to a full bombing halt, although he refused to put it in writing. Hanoi reluctantly accepted, and peace talks formally began in Paris in early November.

A TURNING POINT?

The Tet offensive was generally viewed at the time as a turning point in the Vietnam War, and few observers today would dispute that fact. After Tet, the United States no longer sought to win a complete victory in South Vietnam and recognized that there were finite limits to the level of the U.S. commitment. In so doing, Washington tacitly signaled its willingness to accept a compromise peace that would embody a solution considerably short of complete victory. Some critics hoped that the sobering effects of Tet would lead to a quick peace, but it soon became evident that there was still a long way to go. In his last months in office, Lyndon Johnson hard-

[46] *CKC,* p. 109.

ened his position on key issues and appeared increasingly reluctant to follow through on the implications of the decisions reached the previous spring.

As for the North Vietnamese, they had clearly gained from the Tet offensive in terms of breaking the pattern of escalation that had dictated U.S. policy since the early 1960s. But it had been a costly achievement in terms of casualties, and Hanoi party leaders were still faced with the necessity of achieving further military and political victories in order to force the United States to offer more concessions at the peace table. In a recent paper presented at a conference on the war convened in the United States, General Tran Van Tra conceded that the Tet offensive had been "too ambitious," poorly planned, and marked by confused coordination.[47]

Extravagant statements on both sides about whether Tet was a victory or a defeat, then, appear to be misplaced. From Hanoi's point of view, it was clearly a little of both. In strictly military terms it was a costly operation. The PAVN would need several years to recoup its strength, while the PLAF was decimated and would never be the same. On the other hand, Hanoi did bring about a partial change in U.S. policy and a defeat of the Johnson presidency. The dynamics of the war had been changed, and the stage was set for new initiatives.[48]

---

[47] Tran Van Tra, "Tet," in Werner and Huynh, *The Vietnam War*, pp. 54–59.
[48] Cited in Turley, *The Second Indochina War*, p. 116.

CHAPTER 6

Defeating Vietnamization

As the momentous year 1968 came to an end, party leaders in Hanoi must have felt at least a twinge of frustration. Although they had registered some gains during the Tet offensive, a final victory was still tantalizingly elusive. The incoming U.S. president, Richard M. Nixon, had stated during the presidential campaign that he had a "secret plan" to bring an end to the Vietnam War, but he had declined to disclose it to the public. Moreover, his reputation as a staunch anticommunist militated against any assumption that the new administration would be willing to withdraw from Vietnam under humiliating circumstances. Hanoi had to assume that much more effort would be needed to achieve reunification with the south.

Adding to Hanoi's difficulties, the failure of the Tet offensive to achieve a "decisive victory" had undoubtedly exacerbated morale problems within the ranks. According to one local circular, some people

> have lost confidence in the higher echelon leadership and in the revolutionary capability of the people. They think that our assessment of enemy capabilities is inaccurate, our strategic determination is erroneous, and we have to lower our requirements and prolong the war. They become doubtful of victory, pessimistic, and display a shirking attitude. [Some think] that we have come to a deadlock and thus they completely rely on the Paris Conference and on outside help, plunging themselves into an illusion of peace.[1]

But party strategists had some trump cards. As contrasted with 1965, there were now nearly 100,000 North Vietnamese regulars in

[1] *VDRN*, no. 61, "Decisive Victory: Step by Step, Bit by Bit," p. 7.

the south. The bombing of the north was at least temporarily at an end. North Vietnamese units had taken little part in the fighting during the Tet offensive, except in the northern provinces, and thus were virtually intact. As for the enemy, the Nixon administration was clearly boxed in by public weariness with the war, a condition which had compelled his predecessor to begin to shift to a clear and hold strategy and seek a negotiated end to the conflict. A U.S. troop pullout was clearly in the realm of possibility. Once that occurred, Hanoi could face the future with confidence.

THE ROAD TO DISENGAGEMENT

Whether Nixon's claim that he had a secret plan was true has been a matter of debate, since he refused to divulge the plan on the grounds that disclosure would render the strategy less effective. Some have dismissed Nixon's plan as a campaign ploy, but there is evidence that he did have some ideas on bringing the war to a conclusion, although they may have existed only in general terms.

There were several sometimes contradictory pieces to his plan. At the Republican Convention he had hinted that he would adopt the approach that Eisenhower had used to bring the Korean War to a conclusion—to threaten massive retaliation. "What we've got to do," Nixon said, "is to walk softly and carry a big stick." Later in the campaign, he made a similar comment to his adviser H. R. Haldeman, remarking that because of his reputation as a hard-line anticommunist, he would be able to use the principle of excessive force to persuade Hanoi to engage in legitimate peace discussions. The key to success, as Nixon recognized, was his own reputation (according to Haldeman, Nixon himself referred to it as his "madman theory") and the assumption that he might do *anything* to stop the war.[2]

Such views, voiced in general terms, only served to reinforce the impression that Nixon was adopting the strong anticommunist line that he had held as vice president during the 1950s. In fact, however, Nixon's views on the war and on the means to contain

[2] Seymour Hersh, *The Price of Power: Kissinger in the Nixon White House* (New York: Summit Books, 1983), p. 52. H. R. Haldeman, *The Ends of Power* (New York: Times Books, 1978), pp. 82–83.

Asian communism had evolved considerably since the Eisenhower era. In the first place, he was willing to concede that in the current state of public opinion, a clear-cut military victory in Vietnam was out of the question. At best, military force could be used to bring about some form of political settlement. Second, although Nixon shared the view of his predecessor in the White House that China posed a serious threat to U.S. national security in Asia, his views about the nature of the threat and how to deal with it were strikingly different than they had been a decade earlier. As a keen observer of the global scene, Nixon had become convinced that the growing intensity of the Sino-Soviet dispute provided the United States with an opportunity to use the split to its own advantage. If the level of hostility between Washington and Beijing could be reduced, China might eventually be transformed from the primary source of radical revolution into a peaceful member of the community of nations in Asia and a trump card to play in any future confrontation with Moscow.[3]

In effect, the new president was convinced that his predecessor had overreacted to the immediate danger of communism in Vietnam while ignoring the momentous changes that were taking place elsewhere in the world, and within the socialist camp itself. Under his direction, U.S. foreign policy would shift the focus of attention from Vietnam, which was a mere symptom of the Cold War, back to the source of the problem, the hostility and suspicion between the government leaders in Moscow, Beijing, and Washington. While determined to bring the Vietnam War to a satisfactory conclusion, Nixon was convinced that the primary foreign policy objective of his administration must be to improve relations with China while reducing the likelihood of confrontation with the USSR. In his view, the Vi-

---

[3] Richard M. Nixon, *No More Vietnams* (New York: Arbor House, 1985), pp. 97–107. Nixon's revised opinion about how to deal with China had first been hinted at in an article published in the prestigious journal *Foreign Affairs* in October 1967. In that article he stated that while China remained a serious threat to the security of the region, the existing policy of isolation must be supplemented by a vigorous effort to transform the attitude of Communist leaders in Beijing and bring China back into the family of nations. In the short run, a policy of what he described as "firm restraint" and "creative counterpressure" was needed to persuade Beijing that its current policies were not succeeding. In the long run, China had to be pulled back into the global community, as "a great and progressing nation, not as the epicenter of world revolution." See Richard Nixon, "Asia After Vietnam," *Foreign Affairs*, 46(3) (October 1967): 111–125.

etnam conflict was an obstacle to the realization of both of these objectives.

In general, then, Nixon accepted the conclusion of his predecessor that the war had to be brought to an end, but without a humiliating defeat that could damage U.S. security interests throughout the region. Faced with the same limited options that had plagued Lyndon Johnson, Nixon devised what he termed a "five-point strategy" that involved turning the war gradually over to the South Vietnamese, training them to handle their own self-defense, diplomatically isolating Hanoi from its sponsors in Moscow and Beijing, continuing the peace negotiations with the DRV in Paris, and engaging in a gradual withdrawal of U.S. troops. In Nixon's view, the United States would remain in Vietnam until Hanoi agreed to negotiate a peace settlement or until Saigon could defend itself without massive external assistance—whichever came first.[4]

In the White House, then, there were two possible scenarios to bring the war to an end: a negotiated settlement or a gradual extrication of U.S. forces as Saigon's capacity for self-defense increased. Of the two, Nixon appeared convinced that the latter program had precedence, since Hanoi could not be expected to accept a compromise peace so long as the situation appeared favorable on the battlefield. The first matter of urgent priority, therefore, was to change the balance of forces on the battlefield. Here the options were limited. An increase in U.S. military troop strength was out of the question, while bombing the north was risky because of the volatile nature of U.S. public opinion. Strengthening ARVN was the best solution, but it was a long-term process. In the meantime, some means of reducing the enemy threat in the south and demonstrating to Hanoi the new administration's resolve had to be found.

While the administration searched for means to improve the

---

[4] Nixon, *No More Vietnams*, pp. 97–107. Nixon's views on Vietnam were mirrored by those of his chief foreign policy adviser, Henry Kissinger. A Europeanist by training and inclination, Kissinger was convinced that a military solution in Vietnam was not a feasible option and felt that the key to preventing a humiliating defeat was to strengthen the RVN while persuading Hanoi to accept a compromise settlement. Kissinger was thus on the same wavelength as the president, but he was privately less sanguine that the results would be fully satisfactory. At one point he had declared that the best that could be achieved in Vietnam was a "decent interval" between a U.S. military withdrawal and a Communist takeover. See Hersh, *The Price of Power*, p. 47.

battlefield situation inside South Vietnam, it also began to explore the prospects for a negotiated settlement of the war. In the weeks immediately following the presidential elections in early November, substantive talks had been delayed by a dispute over the nature of participation by the Saigon regime and the NLF (soon to be replaced in diplomatic guise by the Provisional Revolutionary Government, or PRG, established by Hanoi for the purpose of creating a formal alternative to the RVN in June 1969). After that issue was resolved in January by a compromise allowing both to participate in the peace talks, Nixon sent a letter to Hanoi suggesting serious negotiations. Hanoi replied by reiterating its existing demands for the total withdrawal of U.S. troops and the replacement of the Thieu regime by a tripartite coalition government.

For the next few weeks the two sides continued to spar for position in Paris. Sensing the futility of open negotiations, which simply provided a forum of posturing and propagandizing on both sides, U.S. representatives suggested private talks between National Security Adviser Henry Kissinger and a high-ranking official on the North Vietnamese side. Hanoi agreed, and talks between Kissinger and Politburo member Le Duc Tho began in late March. To grease the wheels, on May 14, Nixon presented his first major address on Vietnam. The centerpiece of his proposal was an offer to set a precise timetable for the mutual and simultaneous withdrawal of all foreign troops from South Vietnam. The White House also agreed to free elections under international supervision and to an active role for the NLF in the South Vietnamese political process. At the same time, the administration sent a message to Hanoi that if no settlement was reached, the United States was prepared to escalate the war.[5]

North Vietnamese representatives at Paris did not flatly turn down the U.S. proposal, but they avoided a direct reply and eventually flatly rejected the initiative. According to the writer Seymour Hersh, a Vietnamese official informed him that Hanoi was convinced that Nguyen Van Thieu had no intention of giving the NLF a genuine share of political power in Saigon. A more likely reason for the rebuff was that the PLAF had been severely weakened by the Tet offensive and its aftermath and did not feel that the time was ripe for substantive discussions. Like Washington, Hanoi was deter-

---

[5] *The Washington Post*, May 15, 1969; Henry Kissinger, *White House Years* (Boston: Little, Brown, 1979), p. 270; Hersh, *The Price of Power*, p. 78.

mined to negotiate from strength and had concluded that serious negotiations could not take place until a future general offensive had created a more favorable situation on the battlefield.[6]

With diplomatic talks essentially at a standstill, the White House now turned to the other component in its Vietnam strategy, the use of overwhelming force to coerce Hanoi into a compromise while Washington proceeded with the gradual withdrawal of U.S. forces and the strengthening of the Saigon regime. The Johnson administration had not formulated a specific plan for the withdrawal of U.S. troops, and its guiding principle had been the so-called Manila formula of October 1966, whereby U.S. forces would be withdrawn as the North Vietnamese withdrew and the level of violence subsided in the RVN. At a news conference in December 1968, Defense Secretary Clark Clifford had confirmed that there were no plans for a reduction in U.S. troop strength in South Vietnam.

The gradual removal of U.S. forces from South Vietnam was an essential component of Richard Nixon's plan to end the war. The objective of gradual withdrawal was not only to placate U.S. public opinion and buy time for the administration to strengthen ARVN but also to convince Hanoi that its strategy of protracted war would not succeed since, with enhanced political support at home, a smaller number of U.S. troops could remain indefinitely until the RVN was capable of its own self-defense. At a news conference in mid-March, President Nixon announced his decision to begin troop withdrawals and posed the U.S. conditions for their continued departure: (1) progress in the capacity of the Saigon regime to undertake its own defense, (2) progress in the peace talks, and (3) the level of enemy operations in South Vietnam. At Defense Secretary Melvin Laird's suggestion, the term "Vietnamization" was adopted to describe the program. Two weeks later, the White House issued a directive calling on appropriate agencies to draft a schedule for the removal of U.S. forces.[7]

COUNTERING VIETNAMIZATION

In April 1969, the Politburo concluded that its forces must continue to maintain an offensive position on the battlefield to prevent the

---

[6] Hersh, *The Price of Power*, pp. 80–81.
[7] Kissinger, *White House Years*, p. 272.

United States from settling in and attempting to prolong the war. It predicted that U.S. troops would withdraw "only after they have been struck hard by us and when they realize that if they carry on the war, they will suffer heavier defeat." During the spring and summer of 1969, the level of insurgent activity remained high. But the frenetic pace set by General Thanh in the mid-1960s had been replaced by a more selective approach, as southern commanders tried to build up their forces for a new "great leap forward" in the undetermined future. Official sources warned the rank and file against harboring "an illusion of peace" and predicted that victory would come "not suddenly but in a complicated and tortuous way." Presumably that was a warning that strategists had concluded that the end of the war would come not with a total military victory but through the formation of a coalition government.[8]

The 1969 campaign was clearly a disappointment. Casualty rates remained high and there were few gains on the battlefield. "Generally speaking," noted a COSVN resolution issued in October, "our campaign was not strong or continuous." South Vietnamese forces, still benefiting from the massive U.S. troop presence, aggressively pressed pacification operations in areas previously under enemy control. These efforts were supplemented by the new RVN land reform program that reduced landlessness and assigned farmlands to tenants at the expense of the U.S. taxpayer. Reflecting on these conditions, COSVN concluded that the immediate goal could no longer be "victory in a short period of time," while General Vo Nguyen Giap weighed in with an article that advocated the adoption of a cautious strategy for the time being, while preparing for a return to regular war to realize final victory.[9]

THE INVASION OF CAMBODIA

Ever since the early stages of the conflict in South Vietnam, one of the key elements in Hanoi's success had been its ability to take advantage of the neutrality of neighboring Laos and Cambodia. Both the Kennedy and Johnson administrations—despite appeals from the Pentagon and some officials in the State and Defense depart-

---

[8] *CKC*, p. 115.
[9] *VDRN*, no. 70, "The Party's Military Line is the Ever-victorious Banner of People's War in our Country."

ments—had prohibited "hot pursuit" attacks on Viet Cong sanctuaries inside Cambodian territory. North Vietnamese use of southern
Laos as an infiltration route into South Vietnam had been tolerated
in order to minimize the risk of spreading the Vietnam War into
neighboring areas of Indochina. This policy had enabled Hanoi to
extend the Ho Chi Minh Trail through southern Laos while establishing COSVN headquarters just inside the Cambodian border, less
than 50 miles from Saigon. Much of the material destined for the
use of revolutionary forces in the south now came through the Cambodian port of Sihanoukville on the Gulf of Thailand, while the
eastern provinces of the country provided a high percentage of the
food supplies consumed by insurgent units operating in neighboring
South Vietnam.

Hanoi had taken considerable pains to retain the advantages
inherent in that situation. The leaders of the people's revolutionary
parties in both Laos and Cambodia had been carefully instructed to
refrain from launching major attacks against the neutral governments in their countries on the grounds that victory must come first
in South Vietnam. In turn, both Souvanna Phouma and Norodom
Sihanouk, the neutralist leader of Cambodia, had prudently turned
a blind eye to Vietnamese occupation of much of their territory in
order to avoid being dragged into the Vietnam War. Sihanouk in
particular had been consistently critical of U.S. policy in Southeast
Asia for favoring his country's main rivals—the Thai and the South
Vietnamese—and was convinced that China and North Vietnam
would eventually become the dominant forces within the region. In
his view, only if he could maintain good relations with Beijing and
Hanoi would he be able to guarantee his small country's survival.

The tacit consensus on all sides to keep the war in Vietnam from
spilling over into Cambodia gradually began to break down in the
mid-1960s. One factor in the equation was a change of leadership
within the Cambodian revolutionary movement. Previously, the
leading elements in the Khmer People's Revolutionary Party (KPRP)
had been firmly pro-Hanoi in their orientation and had accepted
Vietnamese guidance in strategic matters. But now a new leadership,
trained in Paris and less inclined to accept advice from Hanoi, took
control of the KPRP and adopted a new political orientation. The
most influential member of the leading faction was Saloth Sar, best
known by his pseudonym Pol Pot. Born in 1928 to a prosperous
rural family, Pol Pot received a scholarship to study electrical engi-

neering in Paris and then returned to Cambodia to become a high school teacher. Unlike the existing leaders of the KPRP, Pol Pot was highly suspicious of Vietnam's ultimate intentions in Indochina, undoubtedly recalling centuries of Cambodian humiliation at the hands of its larger neighbor. An avid if unorthodox Marxist, he also resented the DRV for its decision to cultivate Prince Sihanouk at the expense of the Cambodian revolution. By 1963 he had become acting general secretary of the party and was instrumental in transforming it into a formal Kampuchean Communist Party, or KCP, an apparent statement that the Cambodian revolutionary movement would no longer defer to the needs of its patron but would chart its own course to the future.

When the Great Proletarian Cultural Revolution broke out in China in 1966, Pol Pot visited Beijing and reportedly found the radical ideas that were fashionable there to his liking. In turn, Chinese leaders must have been encouraged by his independent stance toward Hanoi. While the PRC had given fraternal assistance to the DRV since the late 1940s, policymakers in Beijing harbored their own aspirations regarding China's future relationship with the countries of mainland Southeast Asia and could not have been especially pleased at Hanoi's tendency to treat Indochina as its own backyard. At least partly as a means of keeping their options open in Cambodia, Chinese leaders cultivated an amicable relationship with Sihanouk and cultivated his efforts to maintain his country's neutral and independent status.[10]

After seizing formal control of the party in the mid-1960s, Pol Pot built up its forces (popularly known as the Khmer Rouge, or "red Khmer") to launch a guerrilla struggle against the Sihanouk government in the poverty-stricken northwestern provinces of the country. The revolt was vigorously suppressed by Phnom Penh, but the crackdown had the effect of undermining Sihanouk's careful pose of neutrality. Apparently unaware of the fact that the KCP was now under new management independent of Hanoi, Sihanouk held the latter responsible for the recent unrest and edged quietly but perceptibly toward the United States.

Sihanouk's shift coincided with a similar change in orientation

---

[10] For this brief outline of Pol Pot's emergence as an influential figure in the Cambodian communist movement, I have relied primarily on Ben Kiernan's *How Pol Pot Came to Power* (London: Verso, 1985).

in Washington. Even before coming into office, Richard Nixon had apparently considered air attacks on Viet Cong sanctuaries inside Cambodia as one means of disrupting communist activities in South Vietnam. Two weeks before the inauguration he had written a short memo to Henry Kissinger suggesting the possibility of U.S. operations to interdict Hanoi's supply lines through the Cambodian port of Sihanoukville on the Gulf of Thailand. A few weeks later, Joint Chiefs chairman Earle Wheeler suggested attacks on the sanctuaries as one means of disrupting a predicted enemy offensive against the south. After a brief period of hesitation, Nixon ordered air strikes on border areas on March 18 with the objective of destroying enemy supplies and the elusive COSVN headquarters, known by U.S. intelligence sources to be somewhere in the border region. A second round of attacks took place in April, and additional strikes occurred intermittently in succeeding months. The White House did not announce the operation because, according to Henry Kissinger, it did not wish to embarrass Prince Sihanouk and force him to take a hostile public position on the U.S. air attacks on Cambodian territory, but critics charged that the real reason for the decision was the desire to avoid a public outcry in the United States against the expansion of the war into hitherto neutral territory.

On March 18, 1970, Sihanouk was overthrown by members of his own government while he was abroad for medical treatment. A new government under General Lon Nol and Prime Minister Sirik Matak took power in Phnom Penh and immediately demanded the withdrawal of all Vietnamese troops from the eastern provinces of Cambodia. After a brief period of hesitation, Hanoi refused, leading to clashes between the Cambodian armed forces and Vietnamese units operating in the area.

Whether the Nixon administration had been aware of the impending coup d'état in Phnom Penh is a matter of dispute. Sihanouk has claimed that the CIA contrived to remove him from power, and the writer Seymour Hersh has amassed considerable evidence that U.S. civilian and military personnel had been giving active encouragement to anti-Sihanouk groups operating in South Vietnam and Cambodia. But Henry Kissinger has denied that the White House had any evidence of the coup and declared that it would have been opposed to any such action.[11]

---

[11] Kissinger, *White House Years*, p. 459. Also see Hersh, *The Price of Power*, pp. 175–177.

Whatever the truth of these charges, once presented with an accomplished fact, the Nixon administration was now faced with a painful dilemma. While the new regime in Phnom Penh was viewed as potentially pro-American, there was little indication as to its capacity to survive a concerted onslaught by resistance forces supported by Hanoi. On the other hand, to policymakers in the White House a return of Norodom Sihanouk was out of the question. On hearing the news of the coup, Sihanouk had flown directly to Beijing, where he placed himself under Chinese protection. Henry Kissinger claims that he discussed the possibility of a neutral Cambodia with the DRV representative Le Duc Tho in Paris, but the latter had brushed the idea off with the contemptuous remark that "we will get it eventually anyway."[12]

Faced with a variety of options, all of them unpleasant, President Nixon opted for aggressive action, approving a military assault by both South Vietnamese and U.S. armed forces across the Cambodian border in an effort to seize or destroy COSVN and remove the enemy threat to the capital city of Saigon. The action provoked massive protests in the United States, where many Americans viewed the invasion as a dangerous, unnecessary, and even immoral extension of the war into a neutral country.

Whether or not the invasion achieved its objectives has been a matter of dispute. White House sources claimed that considerable amounts of war supplies were seized, and furthermore that Hanoi's plans for an offensive against Saigon were set back immeasurably, thus enabling the administration to continue the withdrawal of U.S. troops on schedule. But critics charged that the elusive COSVN headquarters was not located and that the only result of the offensive was to push the conflict deeper into Cambodia, thus widening the war. One high-level source in Hanoi interpreted the invasion as a "serious mistake" on the part of the United States, since it spread the unrest into new areas of Indochina.[13]

But perhaps the most damaging consequence of the invasion was the impact that it had on public opinion in the United States. Antiwar protests had died down since Nixon's famous "silent majority" speech the previous November, when the president had appealed for support from the American people for a policy of gradual withdrawal from South Vietnam. Now unrest resurfaced on college

[12] Kissinger, *White House Years,* p. 469.
[13] Le Duan, *Thu Vao Nam,* letter of June 30, 1970, pp. 217–218.

campuses throughout the country, culminating in the killing of four students by a National Guard unit at Kent State University on May 4. Two other students died in protest demonstrations at Jackson State University a few days later. Ever sensitive to public perceptions of the war, Congress grew more reluctant to back Nixon's policies in Indochina and eventually forced the administration to agree to withdraw all U.S. forces from Cambodia by the end of June.

For its part, Hanoi reacted quickly to the invasion, sending Prime Minister Pham Van Dong to Beijing to meet with Sihanouk and Chinese leaders to map out a new strategy. All agreed that Sihanouk should take the offensive. A new alliance called the National United Front for Kampuchea (FUNK) was set up under his titular leadership, but with Pol Pot's Khmer Rouge forces providing the muscle, to seek the overthrow of the Lon Nol regime. PLAF and PAVN units began moving into the border region to blunt a possible U.S. effort to surround the area.

In June 1970, the Politburo met to evaluate the situation. According to scattered reports about the meeting, party leaders were pleased at current prospects. In Hanoi's view, Lon Nol was "the weakest of all puppets," while Cambodia was now the "weakest link" in the U.S. position in Indochina. There were now two possibilities: either the revolutionary forces would achieve a rapid victory there, or the United States, to avoid certain defeat, would decide to expand the war. Hanoi was willing to take the latter risk, and local commanders in the Cambodian border region were instructed to attack ARVN forces there and give active assistance to Cambodian guerrillas fighting against the government in Phnom Penh. But they were cautioned to remember that South Vietnam remained the main battlefield and to take advantage of the situation in Cambodia to concentrate efforts on improving the situation in South Vietnam.[14]

During the next several months, a revolutionary administration in the eastern provinces of Cambodia began to take shape, complete with combat villages and hamlets, as well as mass organizations in the growing liberated zone. To provide assistance (and perhaps to maintain a measure of influence), Hanoi sent about 1000 members

---

[14] *CKC*, p. 127. For an elaboration of the decisions taken at the meeting, see Le Duan, *Thu Vao Nam*, letter of June 30, 1970, pp. 216–219. Le Duan predicted that although Lon Nol was "the weakest of all puppets," the presence of ARVN forces meant that he would not yet collapse, so the balance of forces would have to change before the United States decided to withdraw.

Prince Sihanouk greets Pham Van Dong at the Indochinese Conference in April 1970.

of the Khmer Rouge movement who had been living in the DRV to help flesh out the organization. Vietnamese cadres working in Cambodia were carefully instructed to avoid condescension and arrogance in dealing with the local population, but there were inevitably tensions in the relationship, and there were persistent reports of clashes between Vietnamese and Cambodian troops.[15]

Ethnic tensions at the local level were reflected at the higher echelons. Ever suspicious of Vietnamese intentions, Pol Pot ordered a purge of party members trained in Hanoi, and soon few remained in positions of influence. In the meantime, the Khmer Rouge began to recruit actively throughout occupied areas of the country, building up its size to an estimated 200,000 in 1972. A high percentage of them were poor peasants from rural areas, and many were as young as 12 or 13 years old.

Nixon administration sources maintained that the Cambodian

---

[15] *VDRN*, no. 88, "VC's March-April plans for expanding control in Cambodia."

invasion set back Hanoi's plans for offensive action in South Vietnam, but evidence for that contention is inconclusive. There are no concrete indications in available captured documents that party strategists were planning a new general offensive and uprising in the immediate future, although a plenary meeting of the Central Committee in January had predicted that the decisive period would be in late 1970 or early 1971, while local commanders in the south were instructed to step up their attacks on ARVN forces and move toward a strategy of conventional war. After the Cambodian campaign, Le Duan cautioned Politburo member Pham Hung, Hanoi's senior representative in the south since the death of General Nguyen Chi Thanh, to concentrate attacks in rural areas rather than in the cities, while simultaneously strengthening and preserving his forces for a major effort to seek a decisive victory sometime between mid-1971 and 1972.[16]

In early 1971, South Vietnamese forces crossed the border to attack the Ho Chi Minh Trail in southern Laos. Washington's hope was that ARVN could strike toward Tchepone and remain in the area long enough to destroy the trail facilities and defeat the North Vietnamese in the area. But Hanoi had been forewarned, and the campaign had little success. After an early penetration into the mountainous areas of Laos, the attack bogged down rapidly despite U.S. air cover, and South Vietnamese forces eventually retreated in disarray.

The Laos campaign was undoubtedly a tonic for the North Vietnamese, since it demonstrated their ability to compete successfully with ARVN forces, even though the latter possessed U.S. air cover. But the results also showed that the North Vietnamese still had their own limitations. As the Politburo concluded at a meeting held in May 1971, there had as yet been no "strategic transformation" on the battlefield. The task remained to continue the buildup of revolutionary forces sufficient to achieve a decisive victory in 1972.

BREAKING THE STALEMATE

By early 1971, then, the situation had reached a temporary stalemate. Revolutionary forces were not strong enough to win, but with U.S.

---

[16] Le Duan, *Thu Vao Nam,* letter to Bay Cuong (Pham Hung), July 7, 1970, pp. 238–239; *CKC,* p. 124.

troops now withdrawing at an average of 50,000 every six months, it clearly made sense for Hanoi to wait out the Americans. That attitude was reflected in the peace talks. When in February 1970 the U.S. had proposed mutual withdrawal from the south, with no formal announcement of the departure of the North Vietnamese, DRV representative Le Duc Tho had been uncompromising, insisting on a unilateral U.S. withdrawal and the overthrow of the Thieu regime.

That, in fact, was the source of Henry Kissinger's fear in Washington. Since the early months of the Nixon administration, it had been White House policy to combine Vietnamization with negotiations in the hope that Hanoi would eventually conclude that it could get a better deal through a compromise settlement than to await the final stabilization of the Thieu regime in Saigon. In actuality, however, North Vietnamese leaders had concluded that the longer they waited, the more vulnerable Saigon would be. As Kissinger now pointed out to President Nixon, the two objectives had become incompatible, since the continuing departure of U.S. troops simply strengthened the enemy's will to resist. To sweeten the pot, Nixon abandoned the demand for mutual withdrawal provided that Hanoi would agree to end infiltration. But again, the latter had little interest in the proposal, since it left Thieu in power. To encourage further concessions, it asked the United States to stop supporting Thieu and let a new regime be established in Saigon. Washington refused.[17]

Hanoi's obdurate attitude was increasingly frustrating to the White House. But Nixon still had a trump card. Even while the Cambodian invasion was underway, delicate negotiations were taking place between Washington and Beijing over an end to the mutual bitterness and hostility that had ensued after the end of the Chinese civil war. The breakthrough had begun shortly after Nixon's assumption of the presidency, when the latter had signaled Beijing that he was interested in improving relations with the PRC. With his overture to China, Nixon hoped, among other things, that Beijing could be persuaded to play a moderating role in the Vietnam War.

The first substantive discussions between Chinese and U.S. officials over Indochina apparently took place in July 1971, when Henry Kissinger made his first secret visit to Beijing. According to Kissinger, the two sides said little about the issue on that occasion, but Hanoi has claimed that after Kissinger's visit, China began to

---

[17] Kissinger, *White House Years*, pp. 971–972.

pressure the North Vietnamese to accept a compromise settlement in the south, implying that the two sides had reached some form of accommodation to defuse the Vietnam issue.

Insofar as they were aware of Sino-U.S. contacts, party leaders in Hanoi were obviously uncomfortable at the possible repercussions. In November, DRV Prime Minister Pham Van Dong went to Beijing to appeal to Chinese leaders to cancel the projected Nixon visit to the PRC, scheduled to take place early the following year. Mao not only refused, but he also advised his visitor to accept a long-term U.S. presence in South Vietnam. According to Hanoi sources, Mao commented metaphorically, "as our broom is too short to sweep the Americans out of Taiwan, so yours is too short to do the same in South Vietnam."[18]

THE EASTER OFFENSIVE

In 1954, the DRV had been compelled to defer to its more powerful allies at Geneva. Having learned to their cost that Vietnamese interests were not high on priority lists in Moscow and Beijing, party leaders now resolved to press on. With the steady withdrawal of U.S. forces continuing (U.S. force levels were down to less than 200,000 at the end of 1971 and were scheduled to decline to a residual force of 50,000 by the summer of 1972) and a presidential election approaching in the fall of 1972, they were convinced that the time was ripe for a new leap forward in the situation in the south.

Since the Tet offensive in 1968, party strategists had been preparing for a major campaign in the early 1970s. In late 1971, Vo Nguyen Giap had declared that the only effective way to defeat the United States was to return to the strategy of general offensive and uprising. Only a decisive defeat on the battlefield, he argued, would convince the Nixon administration and the American people that there were only two alternatives to a negotiated withdrawal—further escalation or humiliation.[19]

The plan for a new general offensive was given final approval at a meeting of the Central Committee in February 1972. Because Washington and Saigon would undoubtedly be anticipating that any

---

[18] See Duiker, *China and Vietnam*, p. 60.
[19] See Vo Nguyen Giap's speech in *VDRN*, no. 106.

attack would take place during Tet, Hanoi chose the Easter holidays instead. The offensive was scheduled to open in Quang Tri province, just south of the DMZ, and then culminate with a series of sharp thrusts in the central highlands. On the surface, the Easter offensive was reminiscent of the Tet offensive four years before, but there were some key differences. In the first place, there was no attack on the cities, since the party's urban apparatus had been badly decimated in the earlier offensive. Hanoi strategists may also have tacitly recognized that sympathy for the revolution in the big cities was not as strong as they had earlier assumed.

A second difference from the 1968 campaign was that Hanoi now committed North Vietnamese regular troops to the battle. With the size of the U.S. troop presence now reduced to less than 100,000, party leaders had little fear that their precious main force units would be wiped out. And, of course, active involvement in the campaign by the PAVN would increase the chances of success. A successful operation could not only stimulate a revival of the lagging antiwar movement in the United States, it might also influence the 1972 presidential elections and bring about U.S. concessions at the conference table.[20]

In their opening attacks below the DMZ, crack North Vietnam troops mauled unprepared and inexperienced ARVN units in the area and drove them in disarray toward the south. Only the last-minute intervention of a veteran South Vietnamese division, supported by heavy U.S. air cover, blunted the attack and prevented further panic. Nevertheless, most of Quang Tri province had fallen to the attackers, and the provincial capital lay in smoldering ruins. In the end, it had been a near thing.

THE PARIS AGREEMENT

In early May, Hanoi's secret negotiator Le Duc Tho returned to Paris to test the Nixon administration's willingness to make concessions for peace. His confidence bolstered by the growing strength of the antiwar movement in the United States and the peace campaign of Democratic Party candidate George McGovern, Tho adopted a tough line in the talks. But Nixon reacted strongly to the Easter

---

[20] *CKC*, pp. 145–147.

A U.S. prisoner
of war in North
Vietnam.

offensive and resumed the bombing of North Vietnam, while U.S. warships placed mines in Haiphong harbor. Hanoi stalled for two months, but when it became clear in late August that the reelection of the president was probable, Le Duc Tho presented a new proposal, calling for the formation of a coalition government including representatives of both the PRG and the Thieu regime, as well as neutral elements selected by each side. For the first time, Hanoi had offered a settlement that left Thieu in power.

Sensing an advantage, the White House rejected the idea of a coalition in any form. On October 8, another breakthrough took place when Tho abandoned the North Vietnamese demand for a coalition government and agreed to a cease-fire in place, followed by the total withdrawal of U.S. forces and the exchange of prisoners of war. According to the tentative agreement, the United States would be permitted to continue providing military and economic aid to the Saigon regime. The provisions of the peace agreement would be supervised by a tripartite body to be called the National Council for Reconciliation and Concord (NCRC) and composed of representatives of the PRG, the RVN, and neutral elements. At U.S. insistence, the NCRC was not to be considered a formal government, but a subgovernmental body created specifically to deal with political issues after the signing of the cease-fire.

On his return from Paris, a euphoric Henry Kissinger announced that "peace is at hand." But as always, nothing came easily in the Vietnam conflict. When informed of the results of the secret U.S.-DRV talks, President Thieu balked. To Saigon, the proposed settlement was a poor bargain, since it said nothing about the departure of North Vietnamese troops in the south. With the patent hope of sabotaging the agreement, Thieu posed a number of conditions as a prerequisite for his signature to the treaty.

Nixon and Kissinger were exasperated at Thieu's obdurate attitude, but they agreed to present some of Saigon's conditions to Hanoi. When Hanoi rejected the bulk of Thieu's demands, and then presented some new ones of its own, the talks were adjourned in mid-December. Determined to demonstrate his toughness to Hanoi, Nixon ordered a blockade of Haiphong harbor and renewed the bombing of the DRV. During the Christmas bombing, as it was known in the United States, a total of over 20,000 tons of explosives were dropped in and around the capital of Hanoi. On January 8, Le Duc Tho agreed to most of the U.S. conditions, and when Thieu under duress reluctantly agreed to drop his objections, the final agreement was signed two weeks later.

Who won the most at Paris? The Nixon administration was quick to claim victory in the Paris agreement. In his book on Vietnam written a decade later, Richard Nixon claimed that although there were some weaknesses in the settlement (notably the continued presence of North Vietnamese troops in the south), the United States had essentially won the war. With the signing of the cease-fire, U.S. troops had been withdrawn from South Vietnam under conditions that favored the Saigon government. In his own account, Henry Kissinger contended that it was Hanoi that had conceded on the key issues that brought the long conflict to a temporary conclusion. It was Hanoi, he says, that abandoned the demand for the overthrow of the Saigon regime and agreed to a cease-fire agreement which left Nguyen Van Thieu in power.

Others drew different conclusions from the evidence. Some claimed that the Nixon administration had stretched the war out for four years in order to reach a settlement that could have been achieved much earlier. From Saigon, Nguyen Van Thieu felt that Washington had betrayed its honor and its commitment in agreeing to the removal of U.S. troops without the corresponding departure of the North Vietnamese. In his own autobiographical account of the last two years of the war, PLAF General Tran Van Tra claimed that the departure of U.S. forces from South Vietnam was a great coup for the revolutionary cause and set the stage for the final victory two years later. General Tra, however, was somewhat more dispassionate in his analysis, since he conceded that the resistance forces "had won a victory, but not a total victory," while the United States had suffered only a "partial defeat." That result, he remarked, was "the clearest manifestation of the balance of forces at that time."[21]

These wide variations in opinion make it difficult to achieve a balanced view of the Paris agreement, since any judgment of that policy is bound to be affected by the individual's view of the legitimacy of the war itself. At a minimum, one would have to say that Nixon had managed to extricate the United States from a difficult situation with its credibility and its prestige reasonably intact. Critics who charge that the Paris agreement could have been achieved four years earlier are not being entirely fair, since it was only in 1972 that Hanoi agreed to a cease-fire that left the Saigon regime intact. Moreover, as a result of four years of Vietnamization, the RVN now had, in Kissinger's words, a "decent interval" to demonstrate whether it could cope with the threat from the north without a major U.S. military presence.

But perhaps the greatest success of Nixon's Vietnam policy was his success in redefining the terms of the conflict. By improving relations with China and contributing to the emergence of the PRC

---

[21] Tran Van Tra, *Vietnam: History of the Bulwark B2 Theatre,* vol. 5, *Concluding the 30 Years War,* translated into Southeast Asia Report, no. 1247, JPRS 82783 (February 2, 1983), pp. 35–37. This is a translation of his *Nhung Chang Duong Lich Su cua B2 Thanh Dong: Ket Thuc Cuoc Chien Tranh 30 Nam* (Ho Chi Minh City: Van Nghe, 1982).

from a decade of isolation, the White House had reconstructed the balance of power in the Pacific region and transformed Indochina from a cancerous outgrowth of the Cold War into a relatively minor skirmish whose importance to the United States could no longer easily be demonstrated. In one stroke, with the signing of the Shanghai communiqué at the end of Nixon's visit to China in early 1972, the domino theory had been shelved.

But it is quite another thing to claim that the Paris agreement represented a victory for the United States, and that the latter, in Nixon's phrase, had "won the war." If Hanoi had conceded the survival of the Thieu regime, Washington had remained silent on the continued presence of over 100,000 North Vietnamese troops in the south. Under the circumstances, it is hard not to agree with Tran Van Tra that Hanoi had the best of the bargain. To be sure, the Paris agreement provided the conditions for a political solution to the dispute. But nothing could have been more obvious to U.S. policymakers than that such a solution was unlikely, if not virtually impossible. It only remained to be seen whether Saigon could defend itself from the next onslaught from the north. As Henry Kissinger well knew, the prognosis was not good.

Not all members of the revolutionary movement, however, shared the optimistic evaluation issued in Hanoi. In fact, many members of the southern movement were apparently depressed at what they viewed as a second sell-out of the revolution in the interests of peace. One directive from COSVN issued in October 1972 took pains to point out the differences between the projected agreement in Paris and Geneva accords in 1954:

> Today, in South Viet-Nam we have large liberated areas, a people's administration, and strong people's liberation armed forces, especially the main forces; we have a political force, a complete system of leadership from high to low levels and a time-tested infrastructure; we have the National Front for the Liberation of South Viet-Nam and the Provisional Revolutionary Government of the Republic of South Viet-Nam which enjoy a great prestige on the international scene; and we will occupy a position of equality in the administration of national concord. . . . Since the enemy's main support, which is the U.S. massive military strength and the war which is his key measure, will be limited, we will be in an advantageous position over the enemy. Especially our political superi-

ority, which is our basic strength, will have the conditions to develop to the highest extent, opening new prospects.[22]

THE FRAGILE PEACE

As with the earlier settlement at Geneva, the political provisions of the Paris agreement never really came into effect. Both sides predictably blamed the other. Hanoi claimed, with some justification, that the Thieu regime harassed DRV and PRG representatives assigned to the tripartite mission in Saigon, while ARVN units aggressively sought to expand the area under the authority of the Thieu government throughout the RVN after the signing of the cease-fire. On the other hand, Saigon and Washington complained that North Vietnamese troops engaged in operations of their own in the countryside, while Hanoi ignored the provisions in the Paris agreement prohibiting the infiltration of troops and materiel into the south.

There seems little doubt that Saigon did its best to undermine the accords. President Thieu was fairly blunt about his own intention to ignore the agreement, and at one point even the U.S. Embassy complained to the RVN about its aggressive efforts to expand the territory under its control. Washington's complaint that Hanoi ignored the provisions of the agreement by infiltrating personnel and supplies into the south is more difficult to document. In *No More Vietnams*, Richard Nixon claimed that by May 1973, 35,000 men and 30,000 tons of goods had been shipped to the south. Nor did North Vietnamese forces withdraw from either Laos or Cambodia, as they had promised to do at Paris. In his own account of this period, Tran Van Tra claims that the resistance forces, worn out by years of fighting and confused by the illusory effects of the peace, suffered from an acute shortage of troops and weapons. As a result, in his words, Saigon's provocative actions caused "considerable difficulties for us." Many units reacted passively to ARVN attacks or even withdrew unilaterally from areas previously under revolutionary administration.[23]

---

[22] *VDRN*, no. 108, "PRP Abandons Plans for a Revolution in Saigon," cited in Duiker, *Communist Road*, pp. 298–299.

[23] Tran Van Tra, *History of the Bulwark B2 Theatre*, pp. 31–33. Nixon, *No More Vietnams*, p. 173.

Tran Van Tra himself was firmly convinced that the revolutionary forces must respond strongly to Saigon's provocations. A few weeks after the conclusion of the Paris agreement, he was recalled to the north to take part in a meeting of the Politburo designed to formulate a new strategy. According to General Tra, the discussion at the meeting was tempestuous and sometimes acrimonious, indicating that there were wide disagreements over future options. The key issue centered on Hanoi's assessment of the current balance of forces in the south. Some party leaders were convinced that South Vietnamese forces were temporarily superior in strength to those of the revolution. They therefore recommended that the latter avoid an all-out confrontation, at least for the time being. Others, including Tran Van Tra himself, argued that even though the party's forces in the south were outnumbered by three or four to one (according to General Tra, ARVN had almost 1 million men under arms, while the revolutionary forces numbered only about one-third that amount), the latter possessed a higher level of commitment and morale than their adversaries. In the end, Tra's point of view prevailed. Resolution 21, issued at the close of the meeting, stated: "At present the position and strength of the revolution in South Vietnam are stronger than at any time since 1954. . . . The new victory of the people of Vietnam, Laos and Kampuchea [the name given by the Khmer Rouge to Cambodia] has led to a change in the comparison of forces in the Indochinese Peninsula that is more favorable than ever for the South Vietnamese revolution." It also stated that the path to victory in South Vietnam was the path of revolutionary violence. Hanoi would place no more hopes on the implementation of the Paris agreement.[24]

As clashes escalated during the next several months, the Politburo continued to monitor the situation carefully. At a COSVN conference held in the fall to plan the 1973–1974 dry season campaign (the dry season in South Vietnam corresponded roughly to wintertime in the United States), southern commanders were sufficiently optimistic about the situation to propose a strategy designed not only to maintain control over existing liberated areas but also to expand them into areas under enemy administration.

COSVN's prognosis was correct. During the next several months the overall strategic position of the revolutionary forces in South

---

[24] Tran Van Tra, *History of the Bulwark B2 Theatre*, p. 45.

Vietnam improved, while the momentum of Saigon's territorial advances was gradually reversed. In June 1974, the southern command met to review the situation and concluded that although the strength of the insurgent forces in the south was not yet adequate to achieve a decisive victory, the Thieu regime was in a state of "serious decline." If additional main force troops could be provided, there was a real possibility of a favorable end to the war in the near future. Nguyen Van Linh, now deputy secretary of COSVN under Pham Hung, noted that 1975 could be a "pivotal year," with final victory to come through a broad general offensive and uprising in 1976. It would be important, however, to keep the United States from reentering the war.[25]

The likelihood of that latter prospect was steadily diminishing. In a letter to Nguyen Van Thieu in November 1972, President Nixon had promised that the United States would take "swift and severe retaliatory action" in response to any serious transgression of the projected treaty by the DRV. The following April, he had invited President Thieu to San Clemente, California, where Nixon once again promised a "vigorous reaction" if the cease-fire were to be violated. But despite his overwhelming victory in the 1972 presidential elections, Nixon had been severely weakened by public and Congressional resistance to further involvement in Vietnam. He was also restrained from strong action by the pending release of U.S. prisoners of war (POWs), as called for by the Paris agreement.[26]

With the patience of the American people for U.S. involvement in Vietnam now virtually at an end, the administration was reduced to strengthening ARVN for the predicted North Vietnamese general offensive. Yet even here there were problems, as Congress cut the appropriations bill for military aid to the RVN from $2.27 billion in fiscal year 1973 to about $1 billion in 1974. The following year it fell further to only $700 million. With the attention of the White House and the American public as a whole now increasingly distracted by the Watergate scandal, the Vietnam issue was assigned to the back burner. Nixon's resignation from the presidency in August 1974 contributed to the paralysis in Washington. His successor, Gerald

[25] Ibid., pp. 92–93.
[26] Henry Kissinger, *Years of Upheaval* (Boston: Little, Brown, 1982), pp. 309–310; Nguyen Tien Hung and Jerrold L. Schecter, *The Palace File* (New York: Harper & Row, 1986), pp. 124–130.

Ford, less personally involved in the policy decisions on Vietnam and highly sensitive to his position as an unelected "caretaker" president, adopted a detached view of the situation from the start, as did a number of his cabinet officers.

By fall, the prospects for the revolutionary forces appeared to be steadily improving. Areas under their control were expanding in several regions of the country, including the strategically crucial central highlands and the Mekong River delta. In the meantime, ARVN casualty figures were high, while U.S. aid levels to the South Vietnamese armed forces were beginning to fall. General Van Tien Dung, the recently appointed senior military figure in charge of operations in the south, was prompted to remark that Saigon was being forced to fight "a poor man's war."[27]

At the end of October, the Politburo ordered regional commanders in the south to report to the General Staff in Hanoi. Pointing to the shortage of troops and supplies in the south, the latter expressed skepticism about COSVN's request for reinforcements and its plan for a major attack with conventional forces along the Cambodian border. Some party leaders were also nervous at the possibility of a U.S. reintervention in the war. Tran Van Tra took his case to Le Duan, who approved COSVN's plan on condition that it could be carried out with a minimum of additional main force units.[28]

In December, revolutionary forces seized the district capital of Dong Xoai, not far from the Cambodian border. When Saigon did not respond vigorously, COSVN leaders appealed to Hanoi for permission to launch a second attack on the nearby provincial capital of Phuoc Long. To evaluate the rapidly evolving situation, the Politburo met on December 18 to consider a proposal to launch a major campaign during the spring of 1975 in the central highlands. Ac-

---

[27] See Van Tien Dung, *Our Great Spring Victory* (New York: Monthly Review Press, 1977), p. 37. The discomfort in Saigon over the declining level of U.S. military assistance is chronicled in Hung and Schecter, *The Palace File*, chaps. 13–15. An analysis of Saigon's weakness in the face of the increase in Communist strength is contained in Stephen T. Hosmer, Konrad Kellen, and Brian M. Jenkins, "The Fall of South Vietnam: Statements by Vietnamese Military and Civilian Leaders," Rand R-2208-OSD (HIST) (Santa Monica, Calif.: Rand Corporation, December 1978), pp. 61–62.

[28] Tran Van Tra, *History of the Bulwark B2 Theatre*, pp. 111–113; Van Tien Dung, *Our Great Spring Victory*, p. 20. General Dung claims that the majority view within the Politburo was highly optimistic.

cording to Tran Van Tra's account, the major question at issue was the attitude of the United States. Prime Minister Pham Van Dong expressed confidence that the Nixon Administration would not intervene.

> We are in a new phase. The United States has withdrawn its troops in accordance with the Paris Agreement, which it regards as a victory after suffering many defeats with no way out. Now, there is no way that they could intervene again by sending in troops. They may provide air and naval support, but that cannot decide victory or defeat. I'm kidding, but also telling the truth, when I say that the Americans would not come back even if you offered them candy.[29]

In the end, the Politburo approved the plan for a major offensive centered on Ban Me Thuot, the largest city in the central highlands. The objective remained to achieve a major victory setting the stage for the final takeover of the south in 1976, but some party strategists, undoubtedly affected by the news that the entire region around the provincial capital of Phuoc Long had fallen to the revolutionary forces in early January, expressed optimism that the end might come sooner.

THE FINAL OFFENSIVE

They were right. The attack on Ban Me Thuot, launched early in March, not only led to the rapid seizure of the city by revolutionary forces but also to a panic-stricken flight of ARVN forces throughout the area. Faced with the impending collapse of Saigon's position in the highlands, President Nguyen Van Thieu ordered the withdrawal of remaining South Vietnamese forces from the cities of Pleiku and Kontum to the coast, in preparation for an anticipated counterattack. But the withdrawal soon became a rout, and Hanoi ordered PAVN commanders in the south to advance to the coast and cut the route between Da Nang and the old imperial capital of Hue. The latter fell to North Vietnamese units on March 25, and the former, in a scene of mass pandemonium, fell a few days later. On the same day

---

[29] Van Tien Dung, *Our Great Spring Victory*, p. 125.

Revolutionary forces seize the imperial city of Hue.

that Hue had been occupied, the Politburo revised its plans for a total victory over a two-year period.

> Our general strategic offensive began with the Tay Nguyen [central highlands] campaign. A new strategic opportunity has come, and conditions allow an early completion of our resolution to liberate the South. We resolve to rapidly concentrate our forces, technological weapons, and material *to liberate Saigon before the rainy season.* Seize the opportunity of the enemy's strategic withdrawal and the destruction and dispersal of Saigon's First Army Corps and the bulk of their Second Army Corps and do not allow them to withdraw and regroup around Saigon.[30]

During the next four weeks North Vietnamese units wiped up remnants of South Vietnamese resistance in the northern and central

---

[30] Ibid., p. 120.

provinces and advanced rapidly toward Saigon. Nguyen Van Thieu made a last-minute appeal to Washington to increase the level of U.S. military assistance. The Ford administration agreed to seek a supplementary appropriation of $722 million in emergency military aid from Congress, but key administration officials such as Henry Kissinger and Defense Secretary James Schlesinger were convinced that Saigon's cause was lost and advised against the use of U.S. air power to stem the Communist advance. Ford presented his request to Congress for the supplementary aid bill to South Vietnam in a speech to the American people on April 10, but the reaction in Congress was strongly negative, and the request failed to win approval. Remaining U.S. efforts were directed at facilitating the evacuation of Americans and those Vietnamese identified with the Saigon regime from South Vietnam.[31]

In a last-ditch effort to stave off complete collapse, ARVN forces made a determined stand at Xuan Loc, directly east of the capital. But spirits in Saigon were low, as it became clear that the Ford administration was not prepared to intervene. On April 21, Nguyen Van Thieu resigned as president in order to create conditions for a compromise settlement. But Hanoi ignored the gesture, and North Vietnamese troops entered the capital nine days later. The South Vietnamese government, now under the stewardship of General Duong Van "Big" Minh, called on the nation to lay down its arms, while the flag of the People's Revolutionary Government was placed on the flagpole at the presidential palace.

Why, after a generation of direct and sometimes tragic involvement in the Vietnam conflict, did Washington suddenly decide that further action to prevent a Communist takeover of South Vietnam was not in the U.S. national interest? One reason, surely, was that the American people, and their representatives in Congress, were no longer willing to pay the high price for supporting the Saigon regime. As Gerald Ford remarked to General Alexander Haig, the commander of NATO forces in Europe who had come to Washington to plead for a resumption of the bombing in order to counter Hanoi's offensive, "Al, I can't. The country is fed up with the war."[32]

Yet had the survival of an independent South Vietnam been as

---

[31] Hung and Schecter, *The Palace File,* pp. 302–303.
[32] Ibid., p. 251.

North Vietnamese tank enters the gate of the Presidential Palace on the fall of Saigon in April 1975.

important as several presidents had said it was, the Ford administration would surely have taken steps to bring its case for action to the American people. The fact is, leading figures in the administration had concluded that U.S. national interests were no longer involved in Vietnam. In an interview many years after the war, then Defense Secretary James Schlesinger reportedly remarked that Vietnam was not inherently important to U.S. strategic interests in Asia. The long U.S. involvement in Vietnam had created an investment in U.S. prestige, he said, that was not there inherently. Henry Kissinger clearly agreed. While blaming the failure of the United States to act on Congress and the impact of Watergate, Kissinger's reaction to the final disintegration of the RVN was surprisingly detached. In a discussion with Ford's press secretary, Ron Nessen, during the final days of the North Vietnamese offensive, Kissinger allegedly remarked, "Why don't those people die fast? The worst thing that could happen would be for them to linger on." With U.S. interests in the region increasingly tied to improving Sino-U.S. relations, in Kissinger's mind the final death throes of the Saigon regime were not a threat to U.S. national security but an embarrass-ment.[33]

A WAR THAT IS FINISHED?

The final stage of the Vietnam War was both dramatic and tragic. The panic surrounding the fall of Da Nang and the final evacuation of the Americans and South Vietnamese from Saigon, reproduced in graphic detail on television screens around the world, left an imprint on the mind that those who observed it are unlikely ever to forget. Yet ironically, in the United States the final fall of Saigon was something of an anticlimax. After the loss of thousands of lives, and dire predictions of the consequences of failure stretched out over a period of thirty years, the reaction of most Americans was probably relief that the long era of pain and internal discord was over. It was, as President Ford had summed up in a speech to the American people on April 23, a "war that is finished," as far as the American people were concerned.

Yet, as with all aspects of the war, the last phase of the conflict has been marked by controversy. Which side was most responsible for the failure to carry out the terms of the Paris agreement? In refusing to provide massive military assistance to the Saigon regime in its death throes, did the United States fail to live up to its moral obligation or to its political commitment to the Saigon government? Would the United States have acted decisively if Richard Nixon had not been forced to resign because of the Watergate incident? Finally, would the Saigon regime have survived if a larger amount of mili-tary aid had been provided?

The answers that have been given to the first question have often been based not so much on factual evidence as on ideological con-viction. It seems clearly established, for example, that both Saigon and Hanoi ignored the terms of the agreement. Evidence to such effect aside, however, supporters of the Saigon regime will defend its actions as a justifiable reaction to Hanoi's determination to seize power in the south by whatever means were available. Supporters of the DRV, on the other hand, will defend Hanoi's decision to replenish the strength of its forces in the south on the grounds that

[33] Ibid., p. 305.

Nguyen Van Thieu had no intention of living up to the terms of the Paris agreement.

In fact, it would be naive to assume that either party intended to live up to the agreement and carry out its terms to the letter. Official documents and statements by leaders in Hanoi, Saigon, and Washington show clearly that all sides expected the agreement to be generally ignored, and that the conflict would continue in one form or another. Richard Nixon has stated that he himself fully expected both sides to circumvent the agreement, and that Hanoi would probably return to the use of military force to realize its objectives in the south.[34]

Under these circumstances, debate over whether one side or the other lived up to the agreement is somewhat academic, and certainly less rewarding than the more vexing question of whether the United States lived up to its political and moral obligations to the Saigon regime. Strictly speaking, there seems no doubt that the Nixon administration and its successor did not live up to Nixon's promise to Nguyen Van Thieu to defend the RVN against renewed military attacks from the north. As the former president painstakingly points out in his own retrospective analysis of the Vietnam conflict, he was severely hampered by Congressional resistance to his efforts to help the South Vietnamese. Still, Nixon was well aware of the high level of public disillusionment with the war in the United States even before the 1972 presidential elections and had no business in undertaking private commitments that, given domestic realities, he must have known he could not keep. It can only be concluded that he made such commitments primarily in the effort to secure Thieu's agreement to accept the terms of the accords.

In refusing to provide Saigon with vital military assistance, did the United States fail to live up to its moral obligation to a client of long standing, however weak? Some argue that the only decent thing to do was to provide the RVN with the means of looking to its own survival after two decades of a sometimes suffocating American presence. Others counter that the ultimate collapse of the Saigon regime was a foregone conclusion, and it was the higher morality to stand aside and watch it come quickly to its tragic end. Perhaps the only logical way to answer this question is to evaluate whether the south had a reasonable chance to survive without the active

---

[34] Nixon, *No More Vietnams*, pp. 167–170.

presence and military support of the United States. After all, that had been the stated objective of several American presidents stretching back to the Eisenhower administration and culminating in the Vietnamization program carried out under Richard Nixon. The answer that is overwhelmingly suggested by the evidence is that after two decades of nation building behind the shield of the United States, the RVN was still no match for its bitter rival in the north. While some ARVN troops and their commanders fought courageously to defend their homeland, at the moment of truth the Saigon regime still looked to Washington as the guarantor of its survival. To the end, South Vietnamese leaders had still not grasped the essential point that in order to compete effectively against the dedicated forces of revolution in Hanoi, they had to be masters of their own destiny.

CHAPTER 7

Why the Communists Won

This book has concentrated on the Vietnamese side of the war on the premise that the most significant fact about that conflict is not that the United States lost but that the Communists won. Since the end of the war in 1975, one of the main issues raised in the long debate over the "lessons of Vietnam" has been whether that war could have been won at an acceptable risk and cost. Although few would deny that U.S. policymakers made a number of mistakes in the course of the country's long involvement in Vietnam, the view presented here has been that it was not those errors but the actions taken by Washington's adversaries in Hanoi that were decisive in determining the outcome.

Over the years, a variety of factors have been advanced to explain the Communist victory in the Vietnam War. It has been popular to search for single causes. Some have ascribed it primarily to the party's superior organizational ability or to its selective use of terror to intimidate or eliminate opponents. Others have referred to the aura of legitimacy that the Communist Party acquired among the Vietnamese people by virtue of its generation of struggle against the French. Others still point to the extraordinary personality and capability of Ho Chi Minh and contend that, had France or the United States responded to his appeal for support in 1945, the outcome of the revolution might have been far different.[1]

An analysis of the record shows that all of these factors played a role in the final outcome. The emphasis here, however, has been

[1] For the above interpretations, see Douglas Pike, *Viet Cong* (Cambridge: MIT Press, 1967), Paul Mus and John T. McAlister, *The Vietnamese and Their Revolution* (Boston: Harper & Row, 1971), and Archimedes Patti, *Why Vietnam? Prelude to America's Albatross* (Berkeley: University of California Press, 1980).

placed primarily on the Communist Party's program and strategy. The genius of that program was that it was able to combine patriotic and economic themes in an artful way to win the allegiance of a broad spectrum of the Vietnamese population in the party's struggle against its adversaries. The political program of the Vietminh Front in 1941 linked the ICP with the most dynamic forces in Vietnamese society under French colonial rule, the desire for economic and social justice as well as the drive for the restoration of national independence. The alliance between those two forces enabled the Vietminh to mobilize a solid popular base for their struggle against the French. That alliance was revived during the war against the United States, when the NLF won widespread support from the rural and urban poor by its promises of social reform and national self-determination while at the same time allaying the fears of urban moderates and foreign observers alike that it would embark on a program of radical social change after the seizure of power in Saigon.

By contrast, rival nationalist parties were consistently unable to formulate a program that could appeal widely to the mass of the Vietnamese population. The ineffectiveness of the nationalist movement forced its political leaders from Bao Dai to Ngo Dinh Diem and Nguyen Van Thieu to rely on outside support for their survival. From the beginning, such individuals and their organizations were compromised in the minds of many Vietnamese by their lack of a coherent program for nation building and by their willingness to collaborate with the French or, later, with the United States. It is not too much to say that the ICP had won the political battle with its rivals by the mid-1940s and, despite massive efforts by the French and the Americans, was able to retain that advantage for the next generation.

A second major factor in Communist success lay in the domain of revolutionary strategy. Here the genius of the party's approach lay in its ability to make optimum use of a combination of political and military struggle. Those who claim that Hanoi's victory was primarily a military one miss the mark. The evidence shows that in the absence of foreign intervention, the party would have easily bested its nationalist rivals in the political arena. That had been the lesson of the August Revolution, and it was reaffirmed during the later struggles against the French and the United States. It was the political superiority of the Communists over their nationalist rivals that forced Paris, and then Washington, to turn to the military option and thus transform a civil conflict into a revolutionary war.[2]

It was the introduction of outside armed force that compelled the Communists themselves to adopt a strategy of revolutionary violence. At first they seized on the Maoist model of people's war, which had worked so well in China. But they soon discovered that moving to the Maoist third stage of general offensive was not as easy against a powerful Western adversary as it had been for the CCP against Chiang Kai-shek. The result was the gradual adoption of a more flexible strategy that relied on a combination of political and military techniques in both urban and rural areas with a diplomatic and psychological offensive that undermined public support for the party's rivals, in France and the United States as well as in Vietnam itself. Once the conflict had escalated into a military conflict, Hanoi's ultimate strategic objective was not to win a total victory on the battlefield, but to bring about a psychological triumph over its adversaries, leading to a negotiated settlement under terms favorable to the revolution. Although, as many have pointed out, the final 1975 campaign was a conventional military assault by regular units of the North Vietnamese army, it was the strategy of combined political and military struggle, supplemented by diplomatic and psychological tactics to undermine the strength of the enemy, that had brought the war to that point and enabled the offensive to realize total success.

Because of his ability to grasp the underlying nature of the dynamic forces at work in modern Vietnam and to formulate a program and strategy appropriate to the circumstances, Ho Chi Minh is the central figure in the Vietnamese revolution. Although his compelling personality and his talent for reconciliation were trump cards in his contest with his adversaries, the ace in the hole lay in his ability to conceptualize the fundamental issues at stake in the Vietnamese revolution, and thus to give his movement an aura of legitimacy that was the underlying factor in its victory.

---

[2] For the argument that the Vietnam War was above all a conventional military contest, see Harry G. Summers Jr., *On Strategy: A Critical Analysis of the Vietnam War* (Novato, Calif.: Presidio Press, 1982). To be fair, Summers concedes that political factors were dominant before 1963, but he appears to believe that once the war had escalated in the mid-1960s, the solution was primarily military in nature.

THE HEART OF THE MATTER

All of the above theories help to explain the Communist victory in Vietnam, but none of them gets to the heart of the matter. Why were the nationalist parties not as well organized, motivated, and effectively directed as their rivals? Why was it the Communist Party which most effectively donned the mantle of legitimacy in the Vietnamese struggle for national independence, and why did Ho Chi Minh, who was clearly the most talented political figure of his generation in Vietnam, choose Leninism for his model instead of the U.S. Declaration of Independence or the French Declaration of the Rights of Man?

The answer, of course, might simply be a historical accident. But some observers have ascribed the Communist victory to deep-seated historical factors at work in Vietnamese society. It has been argued, for example, that French efforts to eliminate all forms of nationalist opposition in colonial Vietnam discredited the moderate approach to national liberation and inadvertently provided an advantage to clandestine organizations like the ICP. Others have pointed to alleged similarities between Confucianism and Marxist doctrine, characteristics which made it easier for talented and dedicated Vietnamese intellectuals like Ho Chi Minh, Vo Nguyen Giap, and Truong Chinh to embrace the Leninist vision of social revolution than the individualist doctrines of Western capitalism.[3]

One of the more interesting recent hypotheses has been presented by the historian Gabriel Kolko. In a provocative study entitled *Anatomy of a War*, Kolko explains the Communist victory as a consequence of the weakness of the Vietnamese bourgeoisie under the domination of the French colonial system. In his analysis, that weakness prevented the Vietnamese middle class from taking the lead in waging a capitalist revolution, thus leaving a historical vacuum that was ultimately filled by the small but articulate working class led by its vanguard organization, the Communist Party.[4]

Kolko's argument is persuasive in pointing out that the weak-

[3] Two proponents of these respective points of view are Joseph Buttinger, *Vietnam: A Dragon Embattled*, 2 vols. (New York: Praeger, 1967), and Nguyen Khac Vien, "Confucianism and Marxism in Vietnam," in Nguyen Khac Vien, ed., *Tradition and Revolution in Vietnam* (Berkeley, Calif.: Indochina Resource Center, 1974), pp. 15–74.

[4] Gabriel Kolko, *Anatomy of a War: Vietnam, the U.S., and the Modern Historical Experience* (New York: Random House, 1985).

ness of the Saigon regime had deep historical roots that transcended the personalities and actions of individual leaders. As he has noted, one of the factors responsible for that weakness lay in the failure of the French to encourage the emergence of a strong and vibrant middle class capable of providing leadership and purpose after the realization of national independence. That fact was never totally grasped by U.S. policymakers, who, while recognizing the endemic weakness of the nationalist forces in Vietnamese society, constantly deluded themselves into believing that the key to a stable South Vietnam was just around the corner.

But Kolko does not adequately explain why similar results did not then occur in other colonial societies in Southeast Asia, where the local middle class faced comparable obstacles from colonial regimes. As Indian and Indonesian nationalist leaders would be quick to point out, the performance of the British and the Dutch was little better than the French in that regard. Nor does he explain why the Vietnamese Communist movement was able not only to fill the consequent vacuum but then to surmount enormous challenges to triumph over the concentrated power first of France and later of the United States.

Perhaps a more persuasive answer for the weakness of the middle class in modern Vietnam was the historic weakness of the commercial sector during the traditional period. Like China, Vietnam had been a predominantly agricultural society, and trade and manufacturing had never realized the influential position that they acquired in Europe or in several other countries of Asia. Confucian official doctrine displayed a distaste for the crass pursuit of wealth allegedly represented by the merchant class and expressed a clear preference for the honest labor of the rice farmer, whose fields produced the food necessary for sustenance of the entire population. Such prejudices undoubtedly affected attitudes and behavioral patterns in colonial Indochina and contributed to the distaste for Western capitalism on the part of many Vietnamese intellectuals.

Historical factors may also help to explain the surprising strength of the Communist movement in Vietnam. As the contemporary Marxist intellectual Nguyen Khac Vien has pointed out, some of the key characteristics of Confucian doctrine predisposed Vietnamese intellectuals to the Marxist, rather than the capitalist, vision of the contemporary world. While in many respects Marxism and Confucianism are strikingly different, key similarities between the two doctrines may have facilitated the appeal of Marxist ideology to traditional elites in Vietnam: a common emphasis on collective responsibility versus individual rights; the concept of an educated elite with unique access to a single truth as embodied in classical doctrine; and the stress in both ideologies on personal ethics and service to society. As Nguyen Khac Vien has noted, for centuries Vietnamese Confucianism was closely identified with the concept of selfless devotion to the cause of the fatherland, a tradition that Ho Chi Minh and his colleagues never tired of pointing out. The great Confucian statesman and strategist Nguyen Trai, who assisted Le Loi in driving out Chinese invaders in the fifteenth century, was cited as one of the nation's historic leaders in DRV literature during the Vietnam War. It was probably no accident that a high percentage of the founding members of the Indochinese Communist Party came from families connected with the Confucian ruling elite.[5]

The ideological preferences of intellectuals in colonial Indochina were hardly the decisive factor in the outcome of the Vietnam War, of course. Certainly few U.S. policymakers would have accepted the assumption that such factors decreed the defeat of capitalist forces in Vietnam. Still, the appeal of Marxist ideas among intellectuals and the historical weakness of the entrepreneurial tradition were undoubtedly significant explanations for the unusual popularity and effectiveness of communism in modern Vietnam. While they were probably not conscious of such factors, U.S. officials were well aware of that popularity, but they nonetheless resolved to press on. To some, the stakes were too high to accept a defeat. For others, the prospects of victory were uncertain, but a failed effort was considered better than no effort at all.

If these judgments are valid, it must be asked whether and how the United States could have won the Vietnam War. To some, the answer is obvious. With a massive application of firepower, it could have destroyed the war-making capacity of the DRV and reduced, if not entirely eliminated, the insurgent movement in the south. Such, at any rate, are the views of some recent critics, who maintain

[5] Nguyen Khac Vien, "Confucianism and Marxism," pp. 34–41. To distinguish the patriotic component of Vietnamese Confucianism from its more feudal nature, Vien made a clear distinction between the Confucianism of the mandarins and the Confucianism of the people.

that the U.S. defeat in Vietnam was above all the result of a failure of will or strategic thinking in Washington.[6]

Few would deny that the United States had the capacity to bring about the massive, if not total, destruction of the North Vietnamese regime. But there were serious risks in undertaking such an approach. In the first place, any U.S. military action that threatened the survival of the DRV raised the very real possibility of direct Chinese, if not Soviet, intervention. While Chinese leaders were obviously anxious to avoid a direct military confrontation with the United States, debate over how to deal with the growing U.S. role in the war was intense in Beijing, and a massive intervention by Chinese forces along the lines of the "volunteers" in the Korean War could not be ruled out.

Even if China had not intervened, it seems clear that, short of the total destruction of North Vietnam, any direct U.S. attack on the north would have been a lengthy and exceedingly costly operation. Communist leaders had undoubtedly anticipated the possibility of a massive U.S. invasion of the north and prepared accordingly. While such a strategy might have relieved the immediate threat of a Communist takeover of the south, it would have embarked U.S. forces on a much more difficult conflict with few prospects of quick success. From the evidence presented here, it is clear that North Vietnamese resistance would have been stubborn and protracted in nature. It is hard to imagine the American people according their firm public support for such an enterprise unless the danger to U.S. national security was a clear and present one.

The question then arises: Was the avoidance of a Communist victory in Indochina sufficiently important to justify such risks? For all the rhetoric about falling dominoes in Washington, several U.S. presidents from Truman to Kennedy had tacitly answered that question by refusing to embark on the road to a direct military role in the conflict. Eisenhower and Kennedy had come perilously close, but both had ultimately concluded that it was a Vietnamese war to win or lose. Even Lyndon Johnson, who transformed the Vietnamese

---

[6] Summers, *On Strategy,* is the best-known example. Also see General Bruce Palmer Jr., *The 25-Year War: America's Military Role in Vietnam* (Lexington: University of Kentucky Press, 1984), and Norman B. Hannah, *The Key to Failure: Laos and the Vietnam War* (Lanham, Md.: Madison Books, 1987).

civil conflict into an American war, tacitly conceded in his final months in office that there were limits to how far the United States could go in guaranteeing the survival of an independent South Vietnam. Presidents Nixon and Ford put on the final touches by first accepting a compromise settlement and then refusing to take military action to prevent a Communist victory in the spring of 1975. In extremis, a generation of U.S. presidents, by their actions if not by their words, had recognized that Vietnam was not vital to U.S. national security. Whether the consequences of the war have validated that judgment must be dealt with in the final section of this book, as we take a brief look at the events that have taken place in the region since the end of the war.

Epilog

History teaches that the most difficult stage of a revolution often takes place after the seizure of power, when new leaders must seek to harvest the fruits of the revolution. Such was certainly the case in Vietnam. In a comment to journalist Stanley Karnow, Pham Van Dong more or less conceded the point. "Waging a war is simple," he noted, "but running a country is very difficult."[1] Today, nearly two decades after the fall of Saigon, Pham Van Dong's comment remains apt. Vietnam is one of the poorest countries in Asia. Until recently, it has been a virtual pariah in foreign affairs and its leaders still feel surrounded by enemies. By its own actions, the ruling Communist Party has lost the support of a large proportion of the Vietnamese people and seems uncertain about the future of the revolution.

Why were leaders who were so adept at making war so unsuccessful at winning the peace? Part of the answer undoubtedly stems from the difficulties encountered in recovering from the physical damage and psychological bitterness caused by the war and making the transition to a peaceful society. Ironically, however, an additional answer to the question may be that in the case of the North Vietnamese, their very success in the war deluded them into underestimating the challenges they faced in the postwar era. Seduced by their own propaganda, which had portrayed the final victory over Saigon as confirmation of their self-image as the legitimate representatives of the Vietnamese people and the vanguard of the Vietnamese revolution, they embarked on an overly ambitious course of action which has led their nation into severe difficulties, both at home and abroad.

[1] Cited in Stanley Karnow, *Vietnam: A History* (New York: Viking, 1983), p. 9.

Perhaps the primary source of their problem was the assumption by party leaders that at war's end, the vast majority of the Vietnamese people, from north to south, were ready to advance rapidly toward the creation of a unified and fully socialist society throughout the entire country. That, of course, had not been the original plan. The program of the NLF had indicated that after the victory of the revolution in the south, the political and economic reunification of the two zones would take place gradually and by peaceful means. That policy had been based on the assumption that the initial victory in the south would be a partial one and would be followed by a negotiated withdrawal of U.S. forces and the formation of a coalition government dominated by the Communists. At some unspecified date, that government would hold negotiations with the DRV on the final reunification of the entire country.

Hanoi's primary reason for adopting such a gradual approach was undoubtedly to keep the United States from reentering the war. But a second factor was probably the assumption that it would take time to reassure southerners and induce them to support the policies to be adopted by the new revolutionary government. One way to provide that reassurance was to adopt a moderate program that delayed reunification and postponed the transition of the south from a capitalist to a fully socialist society.

As it turned out, the war ended in quite a different manner from what party leaders had expected. There were no negotiations, no deals with Washington, and no coalition government. Over 100,000 supporters of the Saigon regime fled from the country in the final weeks of the war, and Hanoi was able to put in place a provisional revolutionary regime with virtually no open resistance from the local populace.

Faced with such unanticipated circumstances, Hanoi abandoned its original plan and decided instead to embark on a program of rapid unification and socialist transformation. In July 1976, a unified Socialist Republic of Vietnam (SRV) was formally inaugurated. The capital remained at Hanoi and the wartime government, seeded with a few additions selected from leading figures in the southern movement, remained in charge of the country. The NLF itself was merged into the Fatherland Front, while the Vietnam Workers' Party, now merged with its southern subsidiary, the People's Revolutionary Party, was renamed the Vietnamese Communist Party, or VCP. At least on paper, Vietnam was now one government, one party, one people.

The decision to dismantle the capitalist system in the south was made almost as quickly. After the occupation of Saigon at the end of April 1975, the regime had assured the local population that their property and their profits were secure. But in March 1978, Hanoi suddenly announced the nationalization of all industry and commerce above the family level, while in the countryside, farmers were herded into hastily constructed low-level cooperative organizations.[2]

Whatever the rationale for the decision, it was a disaster. Although there had been little open resistance in the south to the unification of the country in 1976, under the surface, resentment among southerners at the arrogance of soldiers and bureaucrats from the north was growing, even among former members of the NLF. Although no open bloodbath of supporters of the Saigon regime had taken place, several hundred thousand southerners were sent for varying periods of time to so-called reeducation camps, while countless others were under constant surveillance and prohibited from taking meaningful employment because of their background. In some cases following the takeover of Saigon, local youths were dragged off buses by puritanical northern cadres who clipped off their long hair and stripped them of their Western-style clothes. Many southerners felt betrayed by the revolution and saw themselves as strangers in their own country.[3]

The sudden and brutal decision to eliminate the private economy in early 1978 added fuel to that resentment. A surge of refugees, an estimated two-thirds of them ethnic Chinese, fled the country on foot or by boat during the next few months, and widespread unhappiness and alienation prevailed among many of those who re-

[2] The reasons for that decision have never been satisfactorily explained. One possible factor may have been growing official fears that the southern capitalist economy, dominated by overseas Chinese interests, could ultimately undermine the socialist system in the north and delay the transition to socialism throughout the country. The official press frequently referred to "poisonous weeds of bourgeois capitalism" in the south that could allegedly have a corrupting effect on the population of the socialist north. Party leaders may have also feared that Chinese economic interests in Saigon could deliberately sabotage the national economy at a time of growing tension in Sino-Vietnamese relations.

[3] For the view that a bloodbath did indeed take place, see Jacqueline Desbarats and Karl D. Jackson, "South Vietnam Was a Bloodbath After All," in the *Asian Wall Street Journal*, April 18, 1985. One autobiographical account of a southerner's sense of disillusionment is Nguyen Long, with Harry H. Kendall, *After Saigon Fell: Daily Life under the Vietnamese Communists* (Berkeley: Institute of East Asian Studies, 1981).

mained. There were widespread reports of revolts among mountain minority groups, and the arrest and trial of dissident elements among Catholics and Buddhist religious associations. Industrial production dropped and a severe grain shortage forced the government to introduce food rationing amidst fears of widespread starvation. Even official sources began to concede that many Vietnamese now doubted the party's ability to lead the country effectively, while the noted Marxist intellectual Nguyen Khac Vien called on the party to listen to the needs of the people. Clearly, the regime had tried to accomplish too much, too soon.

To compound its problems, Hanoi had also badly misjudged the situation in foreign affairs. Its victory over the powerful forces of the United States had undoubtedly been a heady experience and may have lulled senior party figures into the conviction that imperialism was on the decline, not only in Southeast Asia but all around the world. In a major policy address before the new SRV National Assembly in the summer of 1976, party First Secretary Le Duan declared that the regime's postwar foreign policy objectives could be summed up in three general propositions: to guarantee national security, to play an active and independent role in regional and global affairs, and to maintain good relations with other countries in the socialist camp. The "foundation stones" of Vietnamese foreign policy would be a close relationship with the USSR and the establishment of intimate ties with neighboring Laos and Cambodia, which had just come under the rule of the Pathet Lao and the Khmer Rouge, respectively. The latter arrangement was to be labeled a "special relationship," a somewhat less precise version of the old Indochinese Federation, which had been discarded in the early 1950s.

There was nothing inherently unreasonable in the regime's desire to maintain a close relationship with Moscow and carry out an independent policy in world affairs. But the "special relationship" with Cambodia and Laos presented problems because it clashed with the intentions of the highly xenophobic Pol Pot government (formally called Democratic Kampuchea), which had just come to power in Phnom Penh. Also such an assertion of Hanoi's hegemony in mainland Southeast Asia surely aroused discomfort not only in other Southeast Asian capitals but also in Beijing.

The most violent response came from Phnom Penh, where the new Khmer Rouge regime interpreted Hanoi's call for a "special relationship" as a disguised effort to reassert Vietnamese domination over the Khmer people, a domination that dated back to the Vietnamese conquest of the Mekong River delta in the seventeenth century. The new Cambodian government punctuated its refusal to discuss the issue by launching military attacks along the common border with the aim of regaining control over territories lost to the Vietnamese in past centuries. The reaction from China was more subdued, but it was clear that Beijing had no desire to see Hanoi establish a dominant position over all the states of the old French Indochina.

At first the Vietnamese had tried to use a carrot-and-stick approach with the Pol Pot regime, but when Phnom Penh continued to refuse Hanoi's offer of alliance and brutally purged party members suspected of collaboration with the enemy, Vietnamese leaders gradually lost patience. Their concern was heightened when it became clear that Beijing was backing Pol Pot in his rejection of Hanoi's overtures. In December 1978, having attempted to protect itself by signing a defense treaty with Moscow, Hanoi ordered Vietnamese troops into Cambodia to overthrow the Pol Pot regime and install a new government in Phnom Penh sympathetic to the idea of a special relationship. Declaring that the "Moscow's puppet" must be punished, Beijing reacted by launching a brief but bloody punitive attack across the Sino-Vietnamese border.

The Vietnamese invasion of Democratic Kampuchea was undoubtedly welcomed by many Cambodians. With a ferocity unparalleled since the days of Adolf Hitler, in his first days in power Pol Pot had attempted to eliminate all elements in the country considered unsympathetic to the goals of the new order. The city of Phnom Penh was emptied of all its residents, and thousands were put to work in slave-labor camps in the countryside. Thousands more were tortured and killed, and their remains dumped in mass graves around the country. Pol Pot's new order was the sign of a revolution gone mad. To the relief of many Cambodians, the new pro-Hanoi government installed in Phnom Penh adopted moderate policies to win the trust of the people.

But Hanoi's invasion of its neighbor also provoked suspicion of Vietnamese intentions in the capitals of nearby countries in Southeast Asia, as well as in the West, reviving fears of the domino theory reminiscent of the height of the Cold War. During the 1980s, an unlikely alliance of China, the noncommunist states of Southeast

Victims of the Pol Pot revolution in Cambodia.

Asia (recently united in a multilateral alliance known as the Association of the Southeast Asian Nations, or ASEAN), and a number of Western nations including the United States, patched together a coalition of anti-Hanoi Cambodian groups to wage a guerrilla resistance struggle against the new government in Phnom Penh. To the discomfort of many outside observers, the dominant military force in that coalition was the Khmer Rouge, whose brutal behavior while in power had aroused demands that Pol Pot and other key leaders be tried in an international court on charges of genocide.

The dual crisis in domestic and foreign affairs created cruel dilemmas in Hanoi. Should economic or national security concerns be considered paramount? Should the regime adopt a firm approach on Laos and Cambodia at the expense of economic dislocation and improving relations with its neighbors? Should it maintain a rapid pace of socialist transformation at the risk of further antagonizing the already restive population in the south?

These dilemmas badly split the Politburo. Although some party leaders reportedly argued against policies that might create tensions at home while simultaneously antagonizing foreign powers, advocates of a tough position against China were able to assert the primacy of national security concerns and bring about the ejection of a number of reputedly "Maoist" elements from within the ranks of the party leadership. But as the internal crisis deepened, pragmatic elements argued persuasively for reforms in domestic policy, and during the early 1980s the government adopted a number of policies to reduce the pace of socialist transition and stimulate productive efforts in the economy. Conservative elements, however, reportedly resisted such measures and were able to limit their effectiveness. By the middle of the decade, the economic situation remained stagnant, and the popular mood was sour. Complaints appeared ever more frequently that the party's veteran leadership had known how to wage the war, but not how to win the peace. Surely Ho Chi Minh would not have ignored the material needs of the Vietnamese people![4]

The tension finally began to ease in 1986. In June, Le Duan died of illness at the age of 78. At a national congress of the VCP held six months later, a new leadership was elected which promised to introduce reforms to improve the national economy and hearken to the voice of the people. Veteran party leaders such as Truong Chinh, Pham Van Dong, and Le Duc Tho were dropped from the Politburo, although they retained a measure of influence as the sole members of a newly created Council of Elders.

The new general secretary was the one-time chief of party operations in the south, Nguyen Van Linh. On the face of it, the new lineup in Hanoi appeared to be a signal that the party was ready to move, however cautiously, in the direction of reform. Although Linh was somewhat of an unknown quantity, even to many of his countrymen, he soon displayed a willingness to experiment, calling for renovation (*doi moi*) and glasnost (*cong khai*) in the domestic arena, and even hinting at the need for "new thinking" in foreign affairs. He publicly conceded that the regime had attempted to move too quickly toward socialism during the 1970s and called on the Viet-

---

[4] In fact, in his testament, written shortly before his death in 1969, Ho Chi Minh had appealed to party leaders to cut agricultural taxes in order to reduce the financial burden of the war on the Vietnamese people. Ho's appeal was ignored, and the published version of Ho's testament did not mention the request. For a recent discussion of the issue, see *The Testament of President Ho Chi Minh* (Hanoi: Central Committee of the Vietnamese Communist Party, 1989).

namese people to speak frankly about past errors committed by their leaders. Foreign observers began to describe Linh as Hanoi's "little Gorbachev."

But like many of his veteran colleagues, Nguyen Van Linh was cautious by nature, and the regime soon indicated its reluctance to launch major economic changes such as those that had been recently adopted by the Deng Xiaoping leadership that had recently come to power after Mao Zedong's death in China. The all-pervasive bureaucracy stifled efforts by enterprising elements to broaden their activities in the private sector, while members of Catholic and Buddhist organizations were convicted of antiregime activities for demanding greater religious freedoms. Writers such as Duong Thu Huong and Nguyen Huy Thiep were muzzled and sometimes arrested for being too outspoken in their demands for more radical change.[5]

Hanoi's reluctance to initiate major reforms was undoubtedly strengthened when the massive popular demonstrations in downtown Beijing in the spring of 1989 underlined the risks to a totalitarian regime when it engaged in political liberalization. The Tiananmen incident, followed shortly thereafter by the collapse of Communist systems in Eastern Europe and the USSR, confirmed to suspicious minds in Hanoi that too much openness was dangerous to the survival of Marxist-Leninist parties.

Henceforth, the regime pursued a delicate line of cautious economic liberalization combined with continued party dominance over political affairs. To this date, the results have been mixed. Sparked by the rise of a small but vibrant private sector, economic conditions in the SRV have improved slightly, but serious structural problems continue to hinder the economy, and the contrast between the bureaucratic north and the more entrepreneurial south is as sharp as ever. It remains to be seen whether the regime's uneasy balance between socialism and capitalism can work.

At the heart of the problem has been Vietnam's continuing isolation in the world. As a result of the bitter dispute with China and

---

[5] Shortly after his election as VCP general secretary, Nguyen Van Linh wrote articles in the party newspaper under the pseudonym NVL, which, he explained to questioners, meant "speak and act" (*noi va lam*). As the regime backed away from its promise to encourage the freedom of speech, bitter Vietnamese reinterpreted the letters as "speak and cheat" (*noi va lua*). For a brief reference to the official persecution of critics, see F. W. Warner, "Writers' Woes," in *Far Eastern Economic Review*, May 7, 1992.

the recent collapse of the USSR, Hanoi has lost its two most powerful friends and economic benefactors from the Vietnam War. In the meantime, the Western trade boycott, established to pressure Hanoi to withdraw its forces from Cambodia, continued to cut the SRV off from commercial relations with the capitalist world. Although the defense of the pro-Vietnamese regime in Phnom Penh had cost Vietnam an estimated 50,000 dead and a quarter of a million wounded, in the late 1980s Hanoi finally agreed to abandon its special position in Cambodia and seek a compromise settlement in the country in a patent effort to bring an end to the economic embargo.

At a recent international conference, all sides finally reached a consensus on a peace process calling for UN-supervised free elections to choose a new Cambodian government. Those elections, held early in 1993, were won by a faction loyal to Prince Norodom Sihanouk, but the unwillingness of the Khmer Rouge to cooperate in the settlement casts serious doubt on its potential for success. For the Vietnamese, however, the agreement achieved at least part of its purpose, as restrictions on trade with the SRV have been relaxed by a number of capitalist countries, and international agencies are now actively considering assisting the Vietnamese in putting their economic house in order.

For Hanoi, however, the problem of Cambodia is only a part of its larger dispute with China. After the bitter interlude of the early 1980s, when Beijing and Hanoi argued over territorial issues as well as the latter's ties with Moscow and the "special relationship" in Indochina, in recent years China and Vietnam have moved closer, as conservative elements in both parties share a sense of being among the sole survivors of the now disintegrating socialist community. But Chinese arrogance—manifested today by Beijing's stubborn refusal to compromise on a dispute over the ownership of disputed islands in the South China Sea—arouses old fears of Chinese domination in Hanoi. Although Sino-Vietnamese relations have improved, the fraternal comradeship that marked the early years of the Vietnam War is not likely soon to be renewed.

THE LOGIC OF NORMALIZATION

The American people have observed these events in Indochina with a curious mixture of fascination and indifference. Some have wanted to call an end to the bitterness of the war and establish normal relations between the two countries. Others have pointed to the Vietnamese occupation of Cambodia as an indication that Hanoi's expansionist desires have not yet been slaked; they argue that diplomatic recognition should not be granted until the SRV demonstrates its willingness to live in peace with its neighbors. Still others have contended that the regime has still not met its treaty obligation to release all American prisoners of war and provide information on U.S. soldiers missing in action during the conflict; they want to use diplomatic recognition as a bargaining chip to force Hanoi to become more forthcoming about the issue.

At first, the Carter administration sought to achieve a reconciliation between Washington and Hanoi, but negotiations were hindered, first by Hanoi's demands for reconstruction assistance (in accordance with a promise by the Nixon administration as part of the Paris agreement) and then in the fall of 1978 by the Vietnamese alliance with Moscow and its subsequent invasion of Cambodia. During the 1980s, the United States played an active role in the anti-Hanoi coalition, partly as a means of compelling the Vietnamese to withdraw from Cambodia and partly to compel Hanoi to fulfill its promise to provide a full accounting of Americans killed or captured during the Vietnam War.

In retrospect, a good case can be made that the economic embargo on the SRV had some success. In recent years, Hanoi made a number of concessions on Cambodia and displayed an increasingly cooperative attitude on the MIA issue, developments that in early 1994 led the Clinton administration to drop restrictions on U.S. commercial and cultural contacts with the SRV. But many Americans remain convinced that American prisoners of war are still being held in captivity in Vietnam and argue that an improvement in relations should not take place until Hanoi has told all that it knows about the issue. Doubts over Hanoi's sincerity have been intensified by the release of documents from the Soviet archives indicating that the DRV may have held more U.S. POWs than it had indicated during the peace negotiations in Paris. Vietnamese sources deny the veracity of such documents, but the doubts remain.

Until such questions are cleared up, the issue of normalizing U.S.-Vietnamese relations will not be an easy one to resolve. Yet while the desire of American families for the fullest possible accounting of the fate of their loved ones who were killed or declared missing in the Vietnam conflict surely deserves serious consideration, it is clearly in the long-term interest of the United States to bring about better relations with the SRV. As recent events have demonstrated, Vietnam—once seen as a surrogate for Chinese expansion in Southeast Asia—today serves as the most effective bulwark against any possible future effort by China to establish its own dominance over the region. The SRV has even expressed a tentative interest in joining the regional ASEAN alliance. While Vietnamese membership in ASEAN seems unlikely in the near future, the establishment of a cooperative relationship among all the states of Southeast Asia would go a long way toward eliminating the region's history as a perennial cockpit for great power conflicts.

An additional rationale for improved relations between the United States and Vietnam is the impact that it could have on internal conditions in the SRV. A continued effort to isolate the SRV simply strengthens the case made by hard-liners in Hanoi that the country is surrounded by enemies, while it simultaneously weakens the influence of reformist elements within the party and the country as a whole. By freezing Vietnam in a time capsule, Washington is only holding back the pace of change and depriving the Vietnamese people of a greater understanding of events taking place in the outside world.

In sum, there are persuasive reasons for the United States to bury the past and establish normal relations with the SRV. If the Vietnam War had any purpose in the minds of most Americans, it was to deter Chinese Communist expansion into Southeast Asia and to enable the Vietnamese people to control their own destiny. Whether U.S. policies during the war contributed to those ends is a matter of debate. There can be little doubt, however, that it is in the common interest today to help bring the Vietnamese people out of their isolation and bring about the creation of a prosperous and secure Vietnam, able to cooperate fully in the affairs of the region.

THE LESSONS OF THE WAR: THE VIEW FROM HANOI

While Americans try to deal with the legacy of the Vietnam War, the Vietnamese people have had their own problems in coming to terms with its consequences on their own society. For Vietnam, of course, the cost of the war in human terms was far greater than it was for the United States. While somewhat over 50,000 Americans were killed in the war, nearly 2 million Vietnamese lost their lives in the conflict, in addition to 800,000 who had died during the previous struggle against the French. There are an estimated 300,000 Vietnamese missing in action.[6]

Yet Americans visiting the country today are often struck by the degree to which the Vietnamese people have put the war behind them and are anxious to get on with their lives. Undoubtedly one reason for this is the severity of the challenge that the nation faces in recovering from the war, and in the importance of better relations with the outside world as a means of achieving that purpose. But it seems equally true that surprisingly few Vietnamese express any hostility to visiting Americans, and most are openly friendly. For whatever reason, it sometimes appears as if the emotional legacy of the war is less intense in Vietnam than it appears to be in the United States.

This does not mean that the Vietnamese people have not raised their own questions and doubts about the war. Although the regime has tirelessly portrayed the conflict as a struggle for national liberation and a most glorious period in the history of the Vietnamese nation, increasing numbers of Vietnamese have begun to question whether the war was justified, or at least whether it was waged in the proper way. Novelists, filmmakers, and short story writers are beginning to employ fiction and historical biography to present a new, unofficial version of recent Vietnamese history. Soldiers at the front are no longer portrayed as automatons fighting joyfully, selflessly, and heroically for the liberation of their fatherland, but as human beings who fear death, feel pain, and sometimes even question the decisions of their superiors. Some even express doubts about the strategy employed by their leaders to achieve national independence and reunification. In a recent survey of faculty members at a Vietnamese university, interviewees were reportedly asked whom they admired most, Phan Boi Chau or Phan Chu Trinh. The majority voted for the latter, and one remarked that Vietnam would have done better to follow Trinh's reformist road to national independence than the violent course that was eventually adopted.

In part this is a natural consequence of the sense of disillusionment experienced by many Vietnamese after two decades of political

---

[6] Harrison, "History's Heaviest Bombing," pp. 133–134.

The Ho Chi Minh Mausoleum in Hanoi.

and economic malaise. But it also represents the beginning of an effort to reevaluate the trajectory of the Vietnamese revolution and to judge it in terms of its real accomplishments and failures rather than in the heroic terms ascribed to it by the ruling Communist Party. Even the beloved Ho Chi Minh is no longer admired as much as he used to be, especially by the younger generation, for whom he is not even a distant memory. Others express admiration for his steadfast patriotism but question his commitment to democracy and the right of the Vietnamese people to control their own destiny.

Whether Ho Chi Minh's revolutionary path was indeed the proper road to follow is surely a question for the Vietnamese people to decide. It may well be that, in Vietnam as in the United States, the debate over the Vietnam War will never be satisfactorily resolved, since it involves questions of emotion and intellect over which human beings often violently disagree. What is clear is that it is in the interests of neither country to perpetuate the war and poison the relations of two peoples who have been so inextricably linked by the course of modern history.

Suggested Readings

Although the Vietnam War is one of the most written about conflicts in American history, material on the Vietnamese side of the war is relatively scarce in the English language. I have therefore included a number of works in Vietnamese in this bibliography, although I am aware that they will not be accessible to the majority of readers.

General

There is no one-volume general history of the modern era in Vietnam. The closest to such a comprehensive treatment is the massive multivolume history by Ken Post entitled *Revolution, Socialism and Nationalism in Viet Nam* (Aldershot: Dartmouth, 1989). Post devotes equal attention to the issue of national independence and the struggle to build a socialist society. A one-volume interpretation of the Vietnam War from a Marxist perspective is Gabriel Kolko's *Anatomy of a War: Vietnam, the United States, and the Modern Historical Experience* (New York: Pantheon, 1985). Another general history of modern Vietnam, now dated but still useful, is Joseph Buttinger, *The Dragon Embattled*, 2 vols. (New York: Praeger, 1967). For a shorter single-volume version, see his *Vietnam: A Political History* (New York: Praeger, 1968). Another fine study, which concentrates somewhat more on the American side of the war, is journalist Stanley Karnow's *Vietnam: A History* (New York: Viking, 1983). Also see James Pinckney Harrison's sympathetic treatment of the national liberation movement entitled *The Endless War: Fifty Years of Struggle in Vietnam* (New York: Free Press, 1982).

One way to gain a better understanding of the rise of the Communist movement is through the life of Ho Chi Minh. Unfortunately there is as yet no definitive biography of the Vietnamese revolutionary leader, although a number of shorter treatments exist. Perhaps the best of the lot is Jean Lacouture's *Ho Chi Minh: A Political Biography*, translated by Peter Wiles (New York: Viking, 1968). Also see David Halberstam's shorter *Ho* (New York: Knopf, 1987). For an official sanitized version, see *Our President Ho Chi Minh* (Hanoi: Foreign Languages Press, 1970). There are innumerable accounts of Ho Chi Minh's life and political activities in the Vietnamese language.

Documentary Sources

Unfortunately, there are few documentary histories of the rise of the Communist movement in Vietnam, and most of those that do exist are in the Vietnamese language. The most comprehensive collection of documents is the multivolume *Van Kien Dang* [Party Documents] (Hanoi: Institute of History on the Party, 1977–). The series is now complete up to the 1960s, but is not widely available in the United States. A somewhat abridged version is *Nhung Su Kien Lich Su Dang* [Events in the History of the Party] (Hanoi: Su That, 1976–). For a chronological breakdown of the war period from the Communist point of view, see *Cuoc Khang Chien Chong My Cuu Nuoc, 1954–1975* [The Anti-U.S. Resistance War for National Salvation, 1954–1975] (Hanoi: Quan Doi Nhan Dan, 1980). An English-language version has been published by JPRS.

Ho Chi Minh's collected works have now been published in Vietnam under the title *Ho Chi Minh Toan Tap* [Complete Works of Ho Chi Minh], 10 vols. (Hanoi: Su That, 1980–1989). Unfortunately, many of Ho's writings are not included. A shorter version, with some materials not included in *Toan Tap*, is *Ho Chi Minh Tuyen Tap* [Selected Works of Ho Chi Minh] (Hanoi: Su That, 1960). For English-language translations, see *Ho Chi Minh: Selected Writings* (Hanoi: Foreign Language Publishing House, 1977) and Bernard B. Fall, ed., *Ho Chi Minh on Revolution: Selected Writings, 1920–1966* (New York: Signet, 1966).

Among Ho Chi Minh's colleagues, the most widely published is Vo Nguyen Giap, and several collections of his writings are available in the English language. For the most famous, see his *People's War, People's Army* (New York: Bantam, 1962), which concentrates on the French period. For his later writings, see *The Military Art of People's War: Selected Writings of General Vo Nguyen Giap* (New York: Monthly Review Press, 1970), with an introduction by Russell Stetler. On Le Duan, see *The Vietnamese Revolution: Fundamental Problems, Essential Tasks* (New York: International Publishers, 1971), as well as his *Letters from the South* (Hanoi: Foreign Languages Press, 1986). The most famous of Truong Chinh's works are contained in Bernard B. Fall, ed., *Primer for Revolt* (New York: Praeger, 1963). Also see *Truong Chinh: Selected Writings* (Hanoi: Foreign Languages Publishing House, 1977).

The Rise of Nationalism and Communism

There are a number of recent studies of the rise of the nationalist movement in Vietnam. For an excellent two-volume analysis, see David G. Marr's *Vietnamese Anticolonialism, 1885–1925* (Berkeley: University of California, 1971) and *Vietnamese Tradition on Trial* (Berkeley: University of California, 1985). A more recent provocative study is Hue-Tam Ho Tai's *Radicalism and the Origins of the Vietnamese Revolution* (Cambridge, Mass.: Harvard University Press, 1992). Also see William J. Duiker, *The Rise of Nationalism in Vietnam, 1900–1941* (Ithaca, N.Y.: Cornell University Press, 1976). A longer version, which gives considerable treatment to the traditional period of history, is Thomas Hodgkin's *Vietnam: The Revolutionary Path* (New York: St. Martin's, 1981).

On the Communist Party, see Huynh Kim Khanh's *Vietnamese Communism, 1925–1945* (Ithaca, N.Y.: Cornell University Press, 1981), and Douglas Pike's *A History of Vietnamese Communism, 1925–1978* (Stanford, Calif: Hoover Institute Press, 1978), which concentrates on the later period. For the development of Hanoi's strategy of revolutionary war over two generations, see William J. Duiker, *The Communist Road to Power in Vietnam* (Boulder, Colo.: Westview, 1981). For a critical treatment of the party, see Robert F. Turner, *Vietnamese Communism: Its Origins and Development* (Stanford, Calif.: Hoover Institute Press, 1975).

The Franco-Vietminh Conflict

There are a number of good books on the war between the Vietminh and the French. Dated but still useful for general coverage are Ellen J. Hammer, *The Struggle for Indochina, 1940–1955* (Stanford, Calif.: Stanford University Press, 1955), and Philippe Devillers, *Histoire du Vietnam de 1940 à 1952* (Paris: Editions du Seuil, 1952). On the August Revolution and the events surrounding it, see Stein Tonnesson's penetrating *The Vietnamese Revolution of 1945: Roosevelt, Ho*

Chi Minh and de Gaulle in a World at War (Oslo: Sage, 1991). For an official version, see *Histoire de la Révolution d'Août* (Hanoi: Foreign Languages Press, 1977). For an account of his own role in the events of the day, see Archimedes Patti, *Why Vietnam? Prelude to America's Albatross* (Berkeley: University of California Press, 1980). Vo Nguyen Giap gives his own perspective in *Unforgettable Days* (Hanoi: Foreign Languages Press, 1975). The beginning of the war is discussed in Stein Tonnesson's *1946: Déclenchement de la guerre d'Indochine* (Paris: L'Harmattan, 1987).

On the war itself, see Bernard B. Fall's gripping *Street without Joy: Indochina at War, 1946–54* (Harrisburg, Pa: Stackpole Press, 1961), and Edgar O'Ballance, *The Indo-China War, 1945–1954* (London: Faber & Faber, 1964). China's role is analyzed in King C. Chen, *Vietnam and China, 1938–1954* (Princeton, N.J.: Princeton University Press, 1969). For his role on the political side, see Bao Dai, *Dragon d'Annam* (Paris: Plon, 1980). The final years of the conflict are analyzed in Jean Lacouture and Philippe Devillers, *La Fin d'une guerre: Indochine 1954* (Paris: Editions du Seuil, 1960). Also see John T. McAlister Jr. and Paul Mus, *The Vietnamese and Their Revolution* (New York: Harper & Row, 1970).

The Republic of Vietnam

The two classic studies of Ngo Dinh Diem are Denis Warner's *The Last Mandarin* (New York: Macmillan, 1963), and Robert Scigliano, *South Vietnam: Nation under Stress* (Boston: Houghton Mifflin, 1963). For an inside look, see Bui Diem's (with David Chanoff), *In the Jaws of History* (Boston: Houghton Mifflin, 1987). The Communist side is investigated in Douglas Pike's oft-cited *The Viet Cong* (Cambridge, Mass.: MIT Press, 1966) and his less well known companion study, *War, Peace, and the Viet Cong* (Cambridge, Mass.: MIT Press, 1969). For a recent treatment of the evolution of Communist strategy in the 1950s, see Carlyle Thayer, *War by Other Means: National Liberation and Revolution in Vietnam, 1954–60* (Sydney: Allen & Unwin, 1989). Also see Bernard B. Fall, *Vietnam Witness, 1953–1966* (New York: Praeger, 1966), and Wesley R. Fishel, ed., *Problems of Freedom: South Vietnam since Independence* (New York: Free Press, 1961).

On the village war, see William Andrews, *The Village War: Vietnamese Communist Revolutionary Activities in Dinh Tuong Province, 1960–1964* (Columbia: University of Missouri Press, 1973), and James W. Trullinger, *Village at War: An Account of Revolution in Vietnam*

(New York: Longman, 1981). One of the most respected interpreta-
tions of this period is Jeffrey Race, *War Comes to Long An* (Berkeley:
University of California Press, 1972). For a moving account of the
war's impact on one Vietnamese, see Le Ly Hayslip, with Jay Wurtz,
When Heaven and Earth Changed Places (New York: Penguin, 1990).
Another account by a leading member of the revolutionary move-
ment is Nguyen Thi Dinh, *No Other Road to Take* (Ithaca, N.Y.: Cornell
University Southeast Asia Project, 1976).

The Vietnam War, 1964–1975

The best-known study of the war period with an insight into the
Communist side is Frances Fitzgerald's *Fire in the Lake* (New York:
Vintage, 1972). From a non-Communist perspective, see Tran Van
Don, *Our Endless War* (San Rafael, Calif.: Presidio, 1978), and
Nguyen Tien Hung, with Jerrold Schecter, *The Palace File* (New York:
Harper & Row, 1986). Life in the NLF is chronicled in Truong Nhu
Tang, *A Vietcong Memoir: An Inside Account of the War and Its After-
math* (San Diego: Harcourt Brace Jovanovich, 1985). For an interest-
ing collection of essays on both sides of the war, see Jayne S. Werner
and Luu Doan Huynh, *The Vietnam War: Vietnamese and American
Perspectives* (Armonk, N.Y.: M. E. Sharpe, 1993).

Two general histories that give useful accounts of the war era
are William S. Turley, *The Second Indochina War: A Short Political and
Military History, 1954–1975* (New York: Mentor, 1986), and Marilyn
B. Young, *The Vietnam Wars, 1945–1990* (New York: HarperCollins,
1991). Patrick J. McGarvey, ed., *Visions of Victory, Selected Vietnamese
Communist Military Writings, 1964–1968* (Stanford, Calif.: Hoover Institute Press, 1969), provides useful documentary material on the
development of a Communist military strategy in the south.

On the peace negotiations, the two most useful studies are Allan
Goodman's *The Lost Peace* (Stanford, Calif.: Hoover Institute Press,
1978), and Gareth Porter, *A Peace Denied* (Bloomington: Indiana Uni-
versity Press, 1975). Also see George C. Herring, ed., *The Secret
Diplomacy of the Vietnam War: The Negotiating Volumes of the Pentagon
Papers* (Austin: University of Texas Press, 1983). For penetrating
analyses of Vietnamese foreign policy during the war, see William
R. Smyser, *The Independent Vietnamese* (Athens: Ohio University Cen-
ter for International Studies, 1980), and Donald Zagoria, *Vietnam
Triangle: Moscow/Peking/Hanoi* (New York: Pegasus, 1972).

The end of the war is chronicled in Tiziano Terzani, *Giai Phong:*

The Fall and Liberation of Saigon (New York: St. Martin's, 1976), and Cao Van Vien, *The Final Collapse* (Washington, D.C.: GPO, 1983). For a somewhat self-serving account by one of Hanoi's leading generals, see Van Tien Dung, *Our Great Spring Victory* (New York: Monthly Review Press, 1977). For another point of view, see Tran Van Tra's *Vietnam: History of the Bulwark B2 Theatre,* translated in JPRS 82783.

The War in the North

Not much material exists in English on the DRV. Two older studies marked by considerable anticommunist bias are P. J. Honey's *Communism in North Vietnam: Its Role in the Sino-Soviet Dispute* (Cambridge, Mass.: MIT Press, 1963), and P. J. Honey, ed., *North Vietnam Today* (New York: Praeger, 1962). From the ideological left comes Wilfred G. Burchett's *Vietnam North: A First-Hand Report* (New York: International Publishers, 1967). More balanced in his treatment is Bernard B. Fall's *The Two Vietnams* (New York: Praeger, 1967). Also see William S. Turley, ed., *Vietnamese Communism in Comparative Perspective* (Boulder, Colo.: Westview, 1980). On the land reform issue, see Hoang Van Chi, *From Colonialism to Communism* (New York: Praeger, 1964), and Edwin Moise, *Land Reform in China and Vietnam* (Chapel Hill: University of North Carolina Press, 1983). For the effects of the air war in North Vietnam, see Jon M. Van Dyke, *North Vietnam's Strategy for Survival* (Palo Alto, Calif.: Pacific Books, 1972).

The Postwar Era

There have been a number of books on the situation in Vietnam since the end of the war. For a general survey, see William J. Duiker, *Vietnam since the Fall of Saigon* (Athens: Ohio University Monographs in Southeast Asian Studies, rev. ed., 1989). For an interesting account by a veteran journalist, see Robert Shaplen's *Bitter Victory* (New York: Harper & Row, 1986). Nguyen Van Canh, *Vietnam under Communism, 1975–1982* (Stanford, Calif.: Hoover Institute Press, 1983), and Nguyen Long, with Harry Kendall, *After Saigon Fell: Daily Life Under the Vietnamese Communists* (Berkeley: University of California Institute of East Asian Studies, 1981), give personal accounts of life under Communist rule. For a highly critical view, consult Doan Van Toai and David Chanoff, *The Vietnamese Gulag* (New York: Simon & Schuster, 1985).

The postwar imbroglio between Vietnam, China, and Cambodia

has brought forth a number of useful studies. The most dramatic account is undoubtedly Nayan Chanda's *Brother Enemy: The War after the War* (New York: Harcourt Brace Jovanovich, 1986). Also of interest are Robert S. Ross, *The Indochina Tangle: China's Vietnam Policy, 1975–1979* (New York: Columbia University Press, 1988), King C. Chen's *China's War with Vietnam, 1979: Issues, Decisions, and Implications* (Stanford, Calif.: Hoover Institute Press, 1987), and William J. Duiker, *China and Vietnam: The Roots of Conflict* (Berkeley, Calif.: University of California Institute of East Asian Studies, 1987).

Index